Grandson of Essie

The Oswald Harding Story

OSWALD GASKELL HARDING

LMH PUBLISHING LIMITED

© 2018 Oswald Gaskell Harding
First Edition
10 9 8 7 6 5 4 3 2 1

All rights reserved. No part of this book may be reproduced, stored in a retrieval system, or transmitted, in any form or by any means, electronic, mechanical, photocopying, recording, or otherwise, without the expressed written permission of the publisher or author.

All LMH titles, imprints and distributed lines are available at special quantity discounts for bulk purchases for sales promotion, premiums, fund-raising, educational or institutional use.

Cover design: Peta-Kaye Chin and Sanya Dockery
Book design & formatting: Sanya Dockery

Published by: LMH Publishing Limited
Suite 10 -11, Sagicor Industrial Park
7 Norman Road, Kingston C.S.O., Jamaica
Tel.: (876) 938-0005; Fax: (876) 759-8752
Email: lmhbookpublishing@cwjamaica.com
Website: www.lmhpublishing.com

Printed in the U.S.A.   ISBN: 978-976-8245-64-9 (paperback)
                                  ISBN: 978-976-8245-73-1 (hardcover)

NATIONAL LIBRARY OF JAMAICA CATALOGUING-IN-PUBLICATION DATA

Harding, Oswald Gaskell
    Grandson of Essie : the Ossie Harding story / Oswald Gaskell Harding.

    p.; cm
ISBN 978-976-8245-64-9 (pbk)
ISBN 978-976-8245-73-1 (hbk)

1. Harding, Oswald Gaskell, 1935-
2. Jamaica – Biography
3. Jamaica – Politics and government , 1962-
I. Title

920   dc 23

PREFACE

When I was approached by a publisher to have my biography written, I was more than reluctant. It seemed self-serving, somewhat egotistical; it lacked the natural modesty that has always highlighted my character.

I was eventually persuaded that some of my story might disclose some historical facts, the narrative of another age that might otherwise have been lost to subsequent generations.

An interpretation of some of the stories could yield information that might otherwise have been hidden. For example, the story of my birth suggests that mastectomy might have been practised at that time.

If my life story proves interesting then it might be better told by me, as I see it: and if I leave any "footprints on the sands of time . . . that perhaps a forlorn and shipwrecked brother, seeing, shall take heart again", and if the paths I have travelled could be followed by others to their success, then it may be worth the while telling my story. After all, I have led an interesting life, and I say so with all modesty. Further, if my story could inspire others to achieve, then this biography would have been worth the effort.

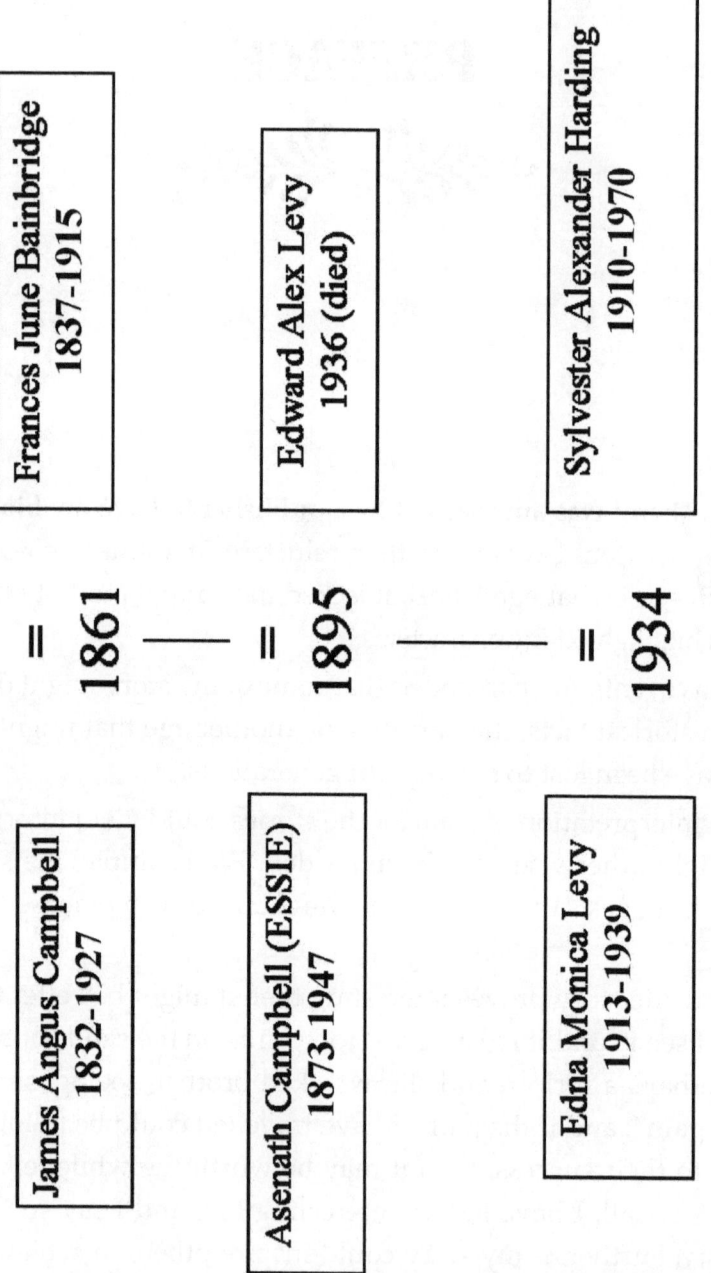

TABLE OF CONTENTS

Preface iii
Acknowledgements vii
Foreword ix
Introduction xiii
Chapter 1: The Early Years 1
Chapter 2: On to Canada 31
Chapter 3: A Foggy Day in London Town 57
Chapter 4: Homeward Journey 79
Chapter 5: To Mexico and Back 97
Chapter 6: My Art and Ceramic World 111
Chapter 7: Political Life 129
Chapter 8: Public Life 149
Chapter 9: Cameos 173
Chapter 10: Jamaican Eagle Does "Floy Hoy" 185
Chapter 11: Academia 193
Chapter 12: At Home 205
Appendices 221
Bibliography 231

ACKNOWLEDGEMENTS

This biography would not have been written without the assistance and encouragement of many persons. The idea of the project originated with Dr. Henry Lowe, scientist and entrepreneur who is the owner of a publishing company. Dr. Lowe wanted to publish biographies of well-known Jamaican personalities. He sent one of his employees, Vaughn Davis, to interview and record our conversations. This approach was not workable, as I felt that I could write the script myself. Vaughn Davis left his employment at the publishers but continued to encourage me to pursue the autobiography and spent many Saturdays with myself and my then secretary, Miss Kerry-Ann Morris, who did the typing. I am indebted to him for his encouragement and continued support; also to my friend, "Tommy" Stimpson, whose remembrances about our time in Mexico were very useful in helping me finish chapter 2; to Professor Edward Baugh, who read the script and made some useful suggestions; finally, to Mrs. Elaine Codner, my executive assistant in the Faculty of Law, who volunteered and gave the final touches.

FOREWORD

As this is the first foreword for a non-technical book that I have ever attempted, I expected that the exercise would be very challenging. To my pleasure and pleasant surprise, reading the manuscript was not only easy and informative, but also compelling. I have known the author for approximately twenty-five years, not only as a friend but also as a former boss at the Drug Abuse Secretariat. During that time, I have always admired him for his fortitude, sense of purpose, honesty and goodwill.

It was after reading his manuscript that the real Ossie Harding emerged. What do I mean by this? His complete persona has been revealed; as a lawyer, entrepreneur, lover and supporter of the arts, politician, statesman, public servant, academic and family man, all blended in an interesting set of related stories.

The four-paragraph preface almost tells it all. It outlines the nature of the man. Certainly everyone will agree that this biography is loaded with interesting and informative anecdotes and stories. These anecdotes and stories not only inform but identify, in their author, a rich resource of culture and history.

What is also interesting is the number of very useful tips about a variety of things particularly given to the analytical mind. It has always been my view that everyone has a story to tell about his or her life's journey – this is indeed exemplary.

Some of these stories might border on excellent literature, while others might be a good mix of information and mirth. The author can be described as a successful and accomplished individual, one who always made the most of the present moment and built a platform for the future, one day at a time.

Each chapter of the book is complete as an entity loaded with vital information which needs to be absorbed like a good wine, slowly and methodically. There are also several gems of principles and actions which present themselves very definitively for reflection and even adoption. The book is also about self-discipline, ambition, adversity and vision, which is based on experience and determination despite several difficulties and challenges. The author has definitively demonstrated that one can manage complex issues and challenges if critical thinking and bold actions are taken on a timely basis.

There are many questions about his life that may require answers, and there are also many answers in search of questions; but then no biography is ever complete. Although he did not have a formal acknowledgement of all the persons who impacted upon his life, one would note that the individuals vary from the humblest of persons, to prime ministers and even royalty. In my view, this book is not only educational and entertaining, and will find its place in the annals of history.

This is the autobiography of an outstanding Jamaican who has a great story to tell, and, hopefully, it will delight and inform those who have the good fortune to read it.

Henry I.C. Lowe, OJ, CD, JP, PhD, FRSH

GRANDSON OF ESSIE

INTRODUCTION

I had just received my LLB degree from the internationally acclaimed London School of Economics (LSE), University of London. The year was 1961 and I was waiting to be called to the Bar from the Honourable Society of the Inner Temple. My sponsors were Sir Hughes Parry, the head of my department at LSE, and Professor J.A.G. Griffiths; both were members of the Inner Temple. Although I was successful in my examinations, I had not completed my dinners. It was a requirement of the Inns of Court that students attend fifteen dinners over a period of three years. Attendance at these dinners was part of an ancient tradition intended to instil in students a sense of pride in the legal profession. It also enabled them to mingle with prominent members of the legal fraternity.

While I was waiting to complete the requirements of the Inn, I received a call from Chester J. Burgess, a Kingston College old boy, whom I had met in Montreal while I was at McGill, and who then was the Federal Government's West Indies Student Liaison Officer. I had been accepted to join the Foreign Service of the newly formed West Indies Federation along with Probyn Marsh, another KC old boy, who as a young graduate had taught me briefly in the Prep School at KC.

GRANDSON OF ESSIE: A JAMAICAN AUTOBIOGRAPHY

Chester (Chas) Burgess thought I should consider taking up an immediate appointment in Port of Spain, Trinidad. However, when I declared that I wanted to complete the Bar requirements, he asked me if I wanted to be super-qualified as he knew of my degree from McGill University. It is fortunate that I stood my ground, for the West Indies Federation was soon to collapse.

Destiny would call again. Shortly after being called to the Bar, I was recruited into the Jamaican Foreign Service and was appointed an administrative officer in the Jamaican High Commission in London. This office was established on the occasion of Jamaica's Independence in August 1962. With my subsequent promotion to Third Secretary diplomatic, my administrative duties placed me on the first rung of the ladder of a diplomatic career. As things were, I suppose that many of my compatriots would have envied my position, for to them the Foreign Service reflected glamour and adventure. Many saw this as a dream job – having high tea with crumpets and scones, brushing elbows with diplomats, international figures and dignitaries. Furthermore, there was a Foreign Service allowance to which home-based civil servants were not entitled. But there were few positions available in the Foreign Service.

There I was seen as a young, handsome, consummate diplomat, in a three-piece suit with a fresh carnation in my lapel each day. Europe, the cornerstone of modern history as we were taught, was at my fingertips. I was a twenty-six-year-old bachelor and had been exposed to some of the most beautiful women: English, European, Caribbean, Australian and New Zealanders. But I had a yearning to return to the land of my birth. A land I hardly knew, a land I had left on the eve of my twelfth birthday. But something was calling me. Was it the smell of the green gungo peas soup of my father's mother, Miss Alice, in the hills of Clarendon where I had spent many summers? Was it the memory of playing cricket with a coconut bough for a bat and a young breadfruit for a ball? Did I miss ring games and marbles? Was it that I was aching for a fantasy world?

INTRODUCTION

As an academic philosopher in later years, in the language of determinists, I would become keen to examine and ferret out what was behind this yearning to return. Was this return predestined? This was perhaps why I had not accepted admission to Dalhousie Law School in Canada, and opted to go to England instead. As a Dalhousie graduate I would not have been able to practise law in Jamaica and my future would have been in Canada. But this is only a reflection. I never articulated it nor even had it in my contemplation.

I am still unable to fathom my longing to return to Jamaica. I now had no compelling family ties – my father was in Canada, and so was my half-sister. I had lost my mother at the tender age of three and my grandmother Essie had died before I left Jamaica. Oh yes, I had aunts and cousins with whom I held special relationships while growing up, but these relationships could easily have been maintained by the occasional visit or certainly by letters. I was also sure that the island had changed dramatically since my departure, and my old homes and haunts had probably given way to the ravages of time. I had no idea what the professional landscape was like either, whether it would accept me or ignore me. I was a lawyer, but I did not delude myself that I would be an instant success.

Nonetheless, I yearned for Jamaica. It was a deep feeling stirring within me. I did not even know our national anthem. It was an English girl, Sue, who later married one of my flatmates, Jamaican attorney Enos Grant, who taught me the national anthem which had been composed before the island's Independence celebrations of 1962. After that, "God Save the Queen" evaporated from my consciousness and dissipated like mist. I hardly remember it.

Some people express from childhood the desire to pursue a particular career path – whether it be music, teaching, engineering… whatever. It had never been that way with me. I never had any specific goals other than a general desire to be a lawyer. I had a general direction of where I wanted to go, but I never strove for any particular goal. I just did what came next.

In London, my career path seemed clearly laid out in front of me. I was in a respected field, a lawyer, considered an eligible bachelor; I was reasonably well compensated with more than enough material things. All in all, it seemed that I simply had to play my cards right. I was promoted to Second Secretary diplomatic in charge of consular affairs.

But Jamaica kept beckoning, and it was not without some apprehension that I answered the call. I approached the leader of the visiting Jamaican Foreign Service inspectorate, the Honourable Hector Wynter, and told him that I wanted to come home. He was surprised, but receptive. I then advised Deputy High Commissioner Allan Morais of my wish. After that, it was only a matter of time.

CHAPTER 1

The Early Years

Asenath Isabel Campbell, the sixth child of James Angus Campbell and Frances Jane Campbell née Bainbridge, was born in March 1873 in the parish of St. Ann, and died at age seventy-four in 1947 at Albert Street in Denham Town, St. Andrew. Asenath, fondly called Essie, married Edward Alexander Levy in 1895 and bore nine children, the last of whom was Edna Monica, born 1915. Edna married Sylvester Alexander Harding, son of Alice Harding née Barnes, on September 30, 1934 at age nineteen, and died on September 4, 1939. Edna was the mother of Oswald Gaskell Harding, born November 3, 1935 at 57 Oxford Street in Kingston.

Not many people have the distinction of knowing details about their birth, but I do. These intimate details came courtesy of my aunt Vera, my mother's eldest sister who was there and who narrated the event to me:

> *It was the 3rd of November 1935 on a Sunday night when we were at North Street Seventh Day Adventist Church. Me and my mother was at church, and my sister Beryl and your father was at home and Edna tek in to have*

you round at East Street. And when we catch nearly to our fence it was a bright moonlight night and Beryl run and tell us that Edna tek in to have a baby and she is gone round to the nursing home and we must make haste come. I said, "Well, alright. Take these books," and I pass the books we have to her, and we went round.

When we went round we saw your father into another room close by reading a book and your mother was in pain with you. So I went in with the nurse and the nurse say she don't want my mother in there because she know that my mother heart is very weak and mama was too faint-hearted; she must go and sit down with Mr. Harding, and there are books out there to go and read.

But she say she want me in there because she know that I know a lot about that business. And a little after I went in and stand up over your mother, she was groaning then, she was in labour, and she deliver the baby. And I stretch over and you born on your left side, you were laying down on your left side and I take this hand and turn you over on your back because I wanted to know whether you was a boy or a girl baby.

And nurse now, nurse have one breast [because of] cancer. She operated on one long ago and take off one of the breast through cancer. So she take her elbow now, I was passing, she take her elbow and jook me on this breast here and I feel it. And I say to her, "Look here, Nurse Bradshaw, don't do them things you know, because you lose one of your breast you want me to lose one of my own."

I'm looking to see now whether it is a boy or a girl, and she say, "Well, you must pay a little attention to your sister too." I say, "I am looking at her face, she is alright." We stay round there with my sister until she get through, tidy her, tidy the baby, put the baby in his crib. And then about two hours after that we leave and came home, and your father went to his home in East Street and we stopped at Upper Rose Lane at our home.

CHAPTER 1: THE EARLY YEARS

The following excerpts from *The Memoirs of Lady Bustamante* present a broad picture of the economic and social conditions prevailing in Jamaica in the 1930s at the time of my birth and beyond. It is significant that the structure of the society had changed very little since the abolition of slavery in 1838, one hundred years before.

In 1935 only seven per cent of the people had the registered right to vote; a constituency was an entire parish and candidates had to rely heavily on their personal popularity to win a seat. This meant getting their names into the newspapers, because there was no local radio station to carry information. Electronic loudspeakers were non-existent, roads were rough, town centres few and far between and transportation slow and unreliable. (p. 33)

Nineteen thirty-eight marked one hundred years since the abolition of slavery in Jamaica. But the mass of Jamaica's population had little to celebrate. Indeed, the conditions prevailing in the island were not far removed from the conditions of 1838.

As had been the case a century before, the mainstay of Jamaica's economy, the sugar industry, was undergoing great difficulties. During World War 1, the overseas price of Jamaica's sugar had risen considerably. However, with the coming of peace in 1919, prices began to fall rapidly due to an over-supply of sugar on the world market. The banana trade was also experiencing hard times. Although the industry had begun to recover at the end of the war when shipping had again become possible, it was dealt a fatal blow by Leaf Spot Disease.

The effects of the low sugar price and the slump in the banana trade were felt throughout the society, but the labouring sector suffered most. Low wages, unemployment and poor working conditions were widespread...

Thousands of unemployed drifted to the city of Kingston, lured by the belief that there was work and high wages to be found on the docks. Every announcement that the Colonial Government had voted sums for public works attracted the rural unemployed. They poured into the city on cane wagons, drays, coal carts and on foot... The cost of living was high... A small room cost between three and six shillings per week and, to save expenses, five or six persons would 'cotch' in a room... Throughout the island, health conditions were poor – tuberculosis, yaws, venereal disease, hookworm and malnutrition were rife...

In short, there was total neglect of the masses. The Colonial Government was more interested in balancing the colony's budget. The Legislative Council reflected the structure of the society. Most of the elected members were too far removed from the masses of the people to have any real understanding of the social and economic conditions under which they existed. In fact, the bulk of the population was unrepresented, in that the views of the people's representatives were not the views of the people... The right to vote was based on economic position.

The social structure of the island had changed little since 1838. The white minority had grown less in numbers, and much poorer, but the more important institutions and positions in the society were still under its control. The middle class had become larger, and now included a sprinkling of dark-skinned businessmen and professionals. Both sectors were equally cut off from the working class; and it was upon this latter group that the hardships of the time fell most severely. (pp. 46–47)

My father was born to Alice Harding (née Barnes), domestic servant, on September 8, 1910 – though some later records list July 28. On his marriage to my mother Edna Monica Levy, his occupation was listed as "waiter". I believe he once worked at the Constant Spring Golf Club as a waiter. At various times he was a salesman, a clerk, and a coppersmith. He had been employed at the Jamaica Railway Corporation as a coppersmith to work on steam engines. Whatever his true designation or occupation, he was of the working class on which the hardship of the times fell most severely – born

CHAPTER 1: THE EARLY YEARS

less than seventy years after the abolition of slavery. This was my inheritance. This was the world in which I was born. This was a world of discontent, a time of struggle to throw off the yoke of slavery. This was the world in which my father struggled. Often he joined the ranks of the unemployed – when he worked at the Railway Corporation he literally had to run to work from Blount Street, Hannah Town in Kingston to get to work on time, for if he was ever late he would lose his job.

Circumstances made him seek to go away; that was his motivation to join the Canadian Forces and go to war. On one occasion when he returned to Jamaica briefly, he had to borrow money from my Aunt Vie's husband Uncle Tex (Mallett) to get back to Canada. But he made sure that he repaid the loan. So destitute was he that he sold the bicycle he had given me to ride to school. Poverty drove him to eventually take me out of the land of our birth, the land of suffering and turmoil, the land of oppression of the working class, the land of discontent, the land we had come to love despite all the difficulties; the land to which we would return.

My earliest memory of my childhood is of a two-storey, two-bedroom house at 47 Asquith Street in Jones Town, where I spent most of my infancy. We lived there with my grandmother Essie, my aunt Vera and later my cousin Curly. Curly was a truly beautiful girl, olive-skinned, slim and built like a model. She came to live with us when she was seventeen and stayed with us for a few years before she got married. My schooling started when I lived at Asquith Street. Every weekday morning some of my cousins, who lived at Ferry in the parish of St. Catherine with my aunt Vie and her husband, would come by our house before going a few chains down the road to a school run by a lady called Madam Bailey. She was a kind of Aunt Jemima figure: dark-skinned, grey-haired, fat and cuddly and a very loving person.

Madam Bailey held classes on the verandah of her little cottage. According to Grandma Essie, after my cousins came by and were leaving for classes I would always cry and chase after them, begging to go to school too. Eventually my grandmother relented and decided to let me go with them. I was three and a half years old at the time.

I got my books and my slate. Madam Bailey taught me how to write. I had not been there for more than three months when she sent for my grandmother and told her I needed new books. Grandmother was annoyed because she couldn't believe I had exhausted the material in the books she had bought me a few months earlier, especially since we didn't have much money. Madam Bailey quietly asked her, "Sister Levy, if the boy was hungry, wouldn't you give him food?"

That annoyed her even more, for that was a stupid question. "Of course I would," replied my grandmother. Madam Bailey said the books I needed were like food. Grandma Essie bought the books.

Often calling to me next door through the wire fence was my father's Aunt Rose and his 'sister of the half-blood' (half-sister) Gladys (Wright). At the time I did not know who they were and only learnt much later that they were relatives.

My mother died at age twenty-four of pneumonia, on September 4, 1939. Not surprisingly, I do not have a strong memory of her, in terms of how she looked or what she was like. They tell me she had straight hair that ran all the way down to her waist and often quarrelled with her sisters when they did not help her to comb it. I do remember a tall, slender figure standing on the balcony, against the backdrop of rain showers. It was the September rains. Orange peels put out to dry (to make spice for bun), as was the practice then, lined the banisters leading downstairs.

My family was always complaining about the man who lived across the street. He had a series of red light bulbs across the facade of his house which reflected into ours. The lights were strung up because he kept dances there every Saturday night. The noise was a nuisance and disturbed my ailing mother. She could not rest when it was party time. I clearly recall one playful incident with her. We were upstairs at the house on Asquith Street. One afternoon she was lying in her bedroom and I ran in the adjoining corridor, past her

CHAPTER 1: THE EARLY YEARS

bed. As I was passing her room, she playfully grabbed at me. I continued running, laughing to myself that I had been too fast for her to catch. She was on her deathbed then, and wasn't with us for much longer afterwards. I remember that my Uncle Allan (Levy) came and passed a hand mirror across my mother's face. At the time I did not understand what he was doing, but later learnt it was to see whether the mirror would be smeared by her breath. It was not, for she was dead.

I know that my mother was buried in the May Pen Cemetery, not very far from where we were living, and I tried unsuccessfully in later years to find the grave site. It was in the Seventh Day Adventist lot. On the day of the funeral I recall my father giving me a rough bath in the shower downstairs. He was scrubbing my ears hard, and it hurt badly, but apparently wrapped up in his grief, he didn't realize it. My cousin Harold (Mallett) and I played on the grave after the funeral. The significance of the loss didn't register on me then, but it eventually did.

For a long time afterwards I found myself sitting and thinking hard about what it meant for me, for anyone, to lose their mother so early in life. I had strong female role models in my family, of course, in my grandmother and my aunts, but I had lost out on that raw, unconditional love a mother has for her child – that emotional safety net that prepares you to cope with things like hurt and loss. My mother's death meant that she would never be there to kiss my cuts and bruises, or to hold me to her bosom and say, "Everything will be all right." I do not discount my father's influence; in fact he and I were very close and he always supported me. But for me, not having a mother made all the difference. I think to some extent that it made me more independent, more willing to be a loner sometimes, since the person who was most likely to make me cultivate feelings of deep attachment to others was gone, before she had a chance.

After Asquith Street we lived for short spells on Penso Street in the vicinity of Price Street in Jones Town. The milkman would pass with milk in large aluminium containers and you could buy a half pint or big gill or less in your own container. My grandmother would always sacrifice to make sure I got some milk to drink. There were other vendors noted for their street calls: "Buy yu green banana, see you roun' di cana, buy yu sweet pitata, see you lickle lata." We had the front part of the house and a small verandah. The other tenants, Mr. Panton and his family, occupied the back of the house, and an outhouse was located in the backyard. I was to meet some of those tenants later in life.

Located at 84 Spanish Town Road was the home of the Malletts, my Aunt Vie and Uncle Tex, sometimes called "Massa" but his name was Melvin. Uncle Tex was a white Jamaican, though local people would refer to him as a brown man. He was the superintendent of the local sewage farm operated by the National Water Commission. His house was provided by his employer. The house was built on an extensive acreage of land. In front of the house were two lawns; on the right was a rose garden as well as some shrubbery with a grape arbour which produced the occasional bunch of grapes. On the left was a large breadfruit tree with a rope swing, and sufficient land space where ring games could be played.

The cottage had a wide verandah in front. The sitting room was furnished with rocking chairs, some straight-backed chairs with plaited cane seats and a china cabinet; two modest bedrooms, a smaller bedroom at the back, and a long dining room towards the end of the house. The kitchen and appurtenances were located immediately behind in an adjoining building. The stoves were large wood- or coal-burning stoves with a small chimney to expel the smoke. There was a large chicken coop at Aunt Vie's house, and I would spend time looking at the baby chicks, the roosters and hens. I always liken my family to the chickens in that coop. When they are newborns, chickens are all alike, yellow, downy little chicks; you don't know what fate will have in store for them. Some will end up in the pot, some will get yaws, and a mongoose may devour others. Some, however, will survive to have more chicks.

CHAPTER 1: THE EARLY YEARS

I viewed all of my family like that: Aunt Vie's four children, Aunt Millie's two, Aunt Beryl's four and Uncle Allan's daughter. We were all like a bunch of chicks – indistinguishable. But as they grew, one could distinguish the roosters from the hens and so on. It's the same way with children; you don't know what they will grow up to be. I had no mother, no brothers or sisters; I was basically the odd one out, the "runt of the litter". But it was interesting to see where we all ended up in life. My cousins, all respectable, decent, working-class folk, found reasonable occupations; two of them entered the nursing profession, but none of them ever achieved as much as I have academically or professionally. I find that significant, as I always considered myself the least likely to succeed because I had no backing. I had no mother; my father had gone away after my mother's death and was now living in Canada, and I was mostly by myself growing up in an untraditional household. But destiny had a significant role in store for me.

On one side of Aunt Vie's house at the back there was a wide open space where we rode bicycles or played cricket, and then there was an exit opening up into a dirt road leading to the bottom of the property. At that spot there was a well-watered field of guinea grass growing to a height of some three or four feet. The other side of the property which housed the chicken coop bordered on the Examination Depot where drivers and vehicles were tested. This part of the property continued past the Greenwich Farm Elementary School and into some woodland where many small birds could be found. I spent a lot of time at Aunt Vie's house with my four Mallett cousins. I often had meals there, but Aunt Vera, who shared custody of me with my grandmother, was incensed that her sister would always feed me after she had fed her children.

My cousin Harry and I used to play cricket in the backyard. After I left Jamaica I was told that he used to call out in his sleep, "I was not out! I was not out!" It was in this backyard that I learnt to ride a bicycle. I remember someone holding the saddle seat while I circled around, then he would let go of the seat, and before I realized it I was riding on my own. On one occasion a man was caught stealing a goat in the grass fields. He was brought up to the yard and given a thorough thrashing with the rope that had tethered the animal, and then he was set free. No police were called.

We sometimes congregated in the front of the premises looking out at the passing traffic. On one occasion we saw Alexander Bustamante driving by. My uncle said he was in a Buick motor car. It had a musical horn which blew the tune of "God Bless America". As he drove by with his mane of hair blowing in the wind, my family who supported the PNP shouted, "Tief, tief!" Busta waved to us. I am sure he thought we were shouting "Chief, chief", which was his nickname.

One day while we were playing at 84 Spanish Town Road, the news came that my grandmother Alice Harding (Barnes) had died. My father's half-siblings, Colonel Johnson and Aunt Gladys (Wright), came to take me to the funeral. My shoes were not suitable and I had to wear my cousin Greta's shoes – luckily these shoes could also be worn by boys. En route to May Pen where my grandmother had relocated from the hills in Clarendon, Colonel Johnson sat beside me in the vehicle; his tears kept making spots on my khaki shirt.

We arrived in May Pen and went along the railway tracks past the little railway station up a hill. There was Miss Alice lying in her bed in a one-room dwelling with a thatched roof. Aunt Gladys tearfully remarked, "We come, Miss Alice." It had started to drizzle. I repeated what had often been said at times like those, "Blessed are the brides that the sun shines upon, blessed are the dead that the rain falls upon." They all nodded, feeling that I had said something really profound. Miss Alice was buried near to her little house. I felt my father's grief because he had always wanted her to live in Kingston – nearer to family and some medical facility. She must have died alone, no one knew of what ailment. When I returned to Jamaica years later, I tried to locate the burial place, but that area was now developed with many modern houses.

In my adult life I was to meet Mr. Panton of Jones Town and some of his family. One of his daughters was Millie, another Sylvia Whittingham,

CHAPTER 1: THE EARLY YEARS

the wife of a land surveyor and founder of the Land Surveyors' Wives Association. Mr. Panton was an early member of the PNP and he would tell me about the street-corner political meetings he used to attend, illuminated by street lamps. I had long returned to Jamaica and was in practice at Melmac Avenue across from Nuttall Hospital. One day I got a call that Mr. Panton was in hospital and wanted to see me. I would think he was then in his eighties. When I went to see him, he asked me to draft a will. After taking instructions I went across to my office, hurriedly prepared the will and returned. I was fearful that he might die at any moment. He signed the will in the presence of two nurses and Dr. Don Christian who was also present. I took the original back to my office and left the copy with him. He apparently left the copy in his pyjama pocket and the family found it when his pyjamas were taken to be washed. All hell broke loose.

While we were living in Jones Town, my grandmother sent me to collect something from a church sister a couple of streets away. As I entered the yard, by levering a large latch that opened a kind of barnyard door in a wooden fence, I was rushed by a pack of dogs. I froze where I was. Five or six yelping dogs surrounded me. There was no escape. The church sister emerged, clapped her hands, and they retreated under the cellar. Those houses were always built with concrete foundations like sturdy stilts. I now have dogs of my own and in general I love animals, but I am wary of strange dogs and certainly not comfortable if they are behind me. This may be the residual fear from that incident.

After Jones Town we lived for a short while in Denham Town at Albert Street and also at King Street, where we stayed for a few years. On Albert Street we lived in a two-bedroom house which was on a compound with two other houses. There was basically no income except what my father sent from Canada for my upkeep. We always managed, but some days were a lot worse than others. Although my grandmother had several children, we couldn't expect too much financial help from them because they had their own families to look after, and were people of modest means. But they did help us when they could. When it got really bad, my grandmother would put her fingers to her lips and say, "Not a pip to eat." Then she would go out, I don't know where; I think it was to visit some clergyman, and she would maybe get a shilling or two. And with that shilling she would buy some essentials, like a tin of condensed milk, some cocoa and water crackers.

Despite her straitened circumstances, Grandma Essie was always gracious and well mannered. Her middle-class training and values always prevailed, and she passed them down to her children and also to me. I must say how indebted I am to my grandmother and Aunt Vera who gave me succour during those rough early days. They fed me, clothed me and cared for me at a time when I was practically an orphan, without ever making a fuss about it. That has always been the benchmark of a real family as far as I'm concerned.

We lived across the street from the home of a nationally renowned cricketer, Collie Smith. I knew his mother, whose funeral I attended, and his sister and two brothers. Collie was about fourteen and I was about ten or eleven when we met. He went to Kingston College. I used to play cricket with Collie and his brother Patrick on a nearby open lot on Saturdays. Another brother, Linden Wright, was a baby and he had a sister, Jean-Ellen. Collie would bat all day and never get out, and then would return the next day expecting to continue, but we never allowed him. I like to think I could have become a great bowler because of those experiences bowling at him, but as they say, hindsight is always twenty-twenty. This was around 1945.

Sometimes we would sneak off to a lot in the community inhabited by Revivalists. We would watch them through the zinc fence, dancing around with their gowns swinging and their faces contorted as if in a trance. Captivated as we were by the energy of it, we kept visiting the area over and over again. I also used to follow Collie and his brother to Boys' Town to watch and play football, even though Grandma Essie and the rest of my guardians never approved. She didn't want me to develop any of the habits of the "bahout" boys or the "oil gals" in the neighbourhood. The bahout boys were the push-

CHAPTER 1: THE EARLY YEARS

cart boys who made a living transporting goods for whatever price they could negotiate. The oil girls sold coconut oil in downtown markets. Needless to say, neither group had much in the way of social graces, and my grandmother did not want me to develop any of their 'bad' habits. There was still some of that Campbell pride that made her feel that our family was much better off because of our background, and my future would be spoiled if I got too comfortable with "those people". But I was too young for any of that to matter.

Many people currently say that Denham Town and Jones Town were not as depressed and poor back then as they are today, but that is false. Maybe they were not as overcrowded as today and perhaps the people's behaviour was different, but they were still poor, depressed, underdeveloped communities. Loxley Comrie, writing in the *Jamaica Observer* newspaper on September 20 and 27, 2009 about Collie Smith, referred to the areas of Trench Town, Denham Town and Jones Town as "the Golden Triangle". Speaking about this area on the twenty-first anniversary of Boys' Town, Premier Norman Manley said, "With so many problems to face and overcome, notably these social evils which are inherent in an area overlaid with poverty and appalling housing conditions – Boys' Town has been led by inspired Christian leadership of its director, Reverend Hugh Sherlock." Yes, the area was overlaid with poverty and appalling housing conditions where people struggled against tremendous odds.

On one occasion we went to Boys' Town to play football and they put me on as centre forward to play against boys from another community. I was about nine or ten, playing against boys who were much older and bigger than I was, and although I didn't score any goals I still count that experience as the greatest accolade I have ever received. It was Frank Reckord, a Kingston College old boy, who was in charge of football and other sports who so honoured me. Sometime afterwards we moved from Denham Town to Greenwich Farm. We lived at 17 West Avenue. There I distinctly remember how at night "rat bats" would attack the mangoes of an East Indian mango tree growing in our front yard. You could hear the sound of them thudding into the mangoes, and the impact of the mangoes hitting our roof before they hit the ground. We would just cut out the spots where the bats had eaten, then consume the rest of the mangoes. They were delicious East Indian mangoes.

Aunt Beryl and her family lived at No. 1 Fourth Street in Greenwich Farm. To the right of their house was a sawmill with piles of sawdust and huge unsawn logs. The two-bedroom cottage had a dining-cum-living room. Uncle Allan occupied one of the bedrooms. He became friendly with a lady from the sawmill. She was a DaCosta, fair in complexion, and from this union came my cousin Gloria. The other bedroom was occupied by Aunt Beryl and her children. Her husband, Algeron Gurney Shakes, died in 1947 just after my grandmother's death. Afterwards things became difficult for Aunt Beryl. She sent one of the four children to St. Elizabeth to live with their father's aunt, and eventually got a job in a factory. Whenever I stayed with her, all three or four of us would sleep in the same bed. She was close to my late mother; in fact I discovered later that she was one of the witnesses who had signed my parents' marriage certificate. When I was about to leave Jamaica, she gave me a wallet-sized photograph of my mother – it had been taken at 130 East Street where my parents used to live. It was the only picture of my mother that I ever had. I took the photo to Canada and had the misfortune to lose it at a beach I went to with one of my father's friends. I deeply regretted it, for no one else seemed to have had any pictures of my mother.

Aunt Beryl later joined her daughter in Florida, where she died eventually. One of her surviving sons, Errol (Rally), returned to Jamaica from the United States and we occasionally saw each other. My wife and I invited Rally and my cousins Dorothy and Greta at Christmas 2009 to an informal get-together at our home. Gloria, our other cousin who lives in Mandeville, was unable to join us. Rally kept asking my wife why I was calling the cousins together. Was I alright? She told him I was in perfect health. He then followed her into the

CHAPTER 1: THE EARLY YEARS

house, and asked whether she was keeping anything from him. She tried to assure him that I was fine. On his return to Portland he suddenly died, apparently of a heart attack. On June 26, 2010 we attended his funeral.

Aunt Millie also lived in Greenwich Farm. She lived in a two-bedroom house at 17 East Avenue near to the railway line with her husband and my cousins. She was my favourite aunt because, despite her age, she had a kind of youthful exuberance that endeared her to everyone. She played cricket with us, rode bicycles and just involved herself in everything we were doing; she shadow-boxed, she was like an adult teenager.

She used to fake-box with Bunny Grant, a budding boxer, as he walked past her house in the evenings. Bunny would later become a Commonwealth boxing champion in the lightweight division.

But Aunt Millie had a profound sense of responsibility. During one of my visits to her house, I stepped on an empty kerosene tin and the other end flew up and embedded itself deep into my right shin, scraping the shin bone. It was a bad gash. As soon as Aunt Millie saw what had happened she ran into her house, grabbed a sheet from one of the beds, tore it and then wrapped my shin with it. Then she put me on her back and carried me out to the main road nearby to get transportation to take me to the Kingston Public Hospital (KPH) to have it dressed.

I also remember that as I waited in the emergency area, a lovely nurse came and gave me crackers and a tin of condensed milk. And every time I went back to have my wound dressed she would give me something. I don't know why she did it; maybe she thought I was poor, or maybe she thought I was a cute kid. But whatever the reason, that experience led me to regard the nursing profession with great respect. In fact I've always thought a statue should be built in front of the KPH dedicated to their efforts. None would dispute that they truly deserve it.

Aunt Millie's husband was Charles Thompson, Uncle "T". He rode a bicycle to and from work. He was a mechanic at the Texaco main plant near Rockfort in East Kingston. Of average height, he looked like an East Indian but he was really a mulatto. I saw his mother once. She was a white lady with cotton white hair. Uncle T reared ducks and we would collect the soft eggs that they laid. He had dogs and used to bring home stale bread which would be soaked in sugar and water and fed to the dogs. We children could not wait for him to bring home the stale bread which we enjoyed eating. He also raised pigs in the empty lot next door. One of their friends used to cut my hair in the backyard. One day I saw him eating some nuts and I asked him if I could have some. He said sure, and I ate some of the nuts; they were castor nuts from which castor oil is made. I need not mention their potent laxative effect. Those were happy days, carefree days.

I had a special liking for my cousin Dorothy, who always stood up for me. She was Aunt Millie's daughter. She was like my sister. Aunt Millie also had a son called James, but we called him Jimmy. When he was five years old, Jimmy had tonsillitis and enlarged adenoids. He was taken to an English doctor who had set up practice in Jamaica, and the doctor performed an operation on Jimmy right there in his surgery. But what was intended to heal Jimmy only made him worse, because he lost his voice and never spoke again.

Jimmy was a handsome youngster who had an excellent talent for drawing. They sent him to St. Christopher's School for the deaf in Brown's Town, St. Ann. We were very close, and I learnt the double alphabet in sign language to speak to him. Later in life I tried to learn the single-language alphabet, but my timetable didn't permit it. Sadly, Jimmy's young life was marked by continuous acts of cruelty from others around him, as they made fun of his handicap. Whenever people in the community saw him they would start knocking two stones together – a way to annoy deaf people. Eventually Jimmy started to hang out at the top of East Avenue and Spanish Town Road every day, doing nothing in particular. Over time he just seemed to waste away, until his untimely demise.

CHAPTER 1: THE EARLY YEARS

My grandfather had been a sort of street entrepreneur, and I am told that he would go downtown to the waterfront and translate Spanish for locals doing business with shipping crews that came from Central America or Cuba. Unfortunately he died before I was born. I would really have enjoyed meeting the man who had convinced my grandmother to fall in love with him. Things took a turn for the worse after my grandfather died. My grandmother ended up straddling the poverty line for most of her life, a real fall from grace for her, because I'm sure she never envisioned that kind of life for herself. I don't think Grandma Essie ever let her family know her real circumstances whenever she paid visits to them. She kept her pride.

The Campbells, my great-grandparents, owned many acres of land in St. Ann. I vaguely remember being taken as a child to view what used to be their land holdings. They stretched somewhere from the vicinity of York Castle school for some twenty minutes driving by car. The graves of my great-grandparents could be seen from the roadway. I also remember a large tree that had a huge iron ring embedded in it. I was told that this was where some of my ancestors would tie up defiant slaves.

My grandmother's brothers, Charles Campbell (Baba Charlie or Uncle Charlie) and James Campbell (Maas' Beau), were accused of selling off the lands over a period of time. Uncle Charlie was a "village lawyer". I have seen some of the documents which he drafted. I was impressed by the competence he displayed, considering his lack of formal legal training. On a Saturday after church my grandmother would sometimes take some of us grandchildren from the North Street Seventh Day church to visit Uncle Charlie and his wife Aunt Kathie in Allman Town. Although they welcomed us they would often make comments about us. On one occasion Uncle Charlie remarked with some surprise how well I used my knife and fork.

Despite Uncle Charlie's attitude towards dark-skinned people, I have a feeling that Aunt Kathie was of mixed ancestry. She was a Wilson. There was a family story circulating that Monsignor Gladstone

Wilson, the erudite Roman Catholic priest, was a relative of hers, but she once refused to see him – presumably stating that they could not possibly be related. Monsignor Wilson was a black man. I am sorry I never met Monsignor Wilson – for I would have asked him if they were in fact related.

Still, our side of the family had their own prejudices too. Aunt Vera was told once that her cousin, the Most Honourable Marcus Mosiah Garvey, was being hailed as a national hero and the story of his deeds would be on television. She angrily replied, "He is no cousin of mine, he is too black. And anyway, he's a communist [troublemaker]." It was a reflection of the prejudices they held. But I have to admit that this attitude was a little more prevalent among the Campbells, and as a result our social interaction with that side of the family was limited. Later on in life someone told me that the Campbells would probably recognize me as a relative in spite of my colour because of who I had become.

Whenever Uncle Charlie came to visit there was always some tension in the house. Uncle Charlie was of average height and slim in appearance. He had not inherited the 'fat gene' prevalent among the Campbells. Uncle Charlie for the most part looked white. My grandmother was a bit darker than Charlie but they had soft, silky hair, which they probably inherited from their father whose photograph we have. He was a Scotsman. Little is known of their mother who was probably of mixed ancestry.

One day at 17 West Avenue, Greenwich Farm, after Uncle Charlie had exchanged his usual pleasantries with the rest of us, he and Grandma Essie went off aside to a corner for a private chat. I was standing nearby, when I heard Uncle Charlie say, "We sold the land, Essie, but we didn't get too much for it. But anyway, hold on to this." I turned around in time to see him hand her a two-and-sixpence piece. Grandma Essie took the coin without uttering a word. In the days of my great-grandparents, parcels of family land were not left by wills as they are today; the owners would simply give instructions

CHAPTER 1: THE EARLY YEARS

to their relatives and friends saying who was to get whichever parcel. Whatever was the real value of Essie's inheritance from my great-grandparents, it doesn't take a stretch of the imagination to see that what Uncle Charlie gave her could never measure up, nor was it meant to. It was conscience money, but of the most paltry kind.

After he left and my grandmother and Aunt Vera were discussing what had happened, Aunt Vera said, "Mama, you shoudda fling it back in his face," and grandmother, Christian lady that she was, looked Aunt Vera in the eye and said, "Vera, he's my brother." That was the end of the story. My grandmother was no fool. She knew she was being taken advantage of, but that statement at the end of it all was classic Essie, and even then in my pre-adolescence it registered on me and gave me volumes of respect for her. I have no hesitation in saying that this was the most defining moment in my relationship with her. That night I learnt what true forgiveness looked like, and I have always striven to emulate it ever since.

The incident with my grandmother and Uncle Charlie happened while I was attending what was then known as Greenwich Farm Elementary School, which was not far from my home at 17 West Avenue. In fact we could get there by walking through the backyard barbed wire fence and then over the lands of the Water Commission where the sewage farm was located. It was constructed as a waste-water treatment plant, which mainly involved the separation of suspended solids from the liquid portion of the wastewater. The dry dung was often burnt. This was the state-of-the-art technology. Subsequently the plant fell into a state of disrepair, resulting in inadequately treated effluent being discharged into the Kingston Harbour. This facility was closed in April 2008 after a new waste-water treatment plant was constructed at Soapberry in St. Catherine.

Large water pipes, big enough for a man to crawl through, used to be located on the lands at Greenwich Farm. Winston McFarlane who had married my cousin Curly (Inez McFarlane) and a relative, Eric Beckford, were employed to go through these pipes, chipping off the rust and then refurbishing them. You could hear the sounds, the cacophony, miles away. When those water pipes had been cleaned of the rust and cankerous material, they would be refurbished by being painted black with a tar-like substance, both inside and out. Now as good as new, the pipes would be re-used. On those lands they taught me to make springes and 'calabans' – traps to snare little birds – made with the spine of the coconut palm leaves.

On my first day at Greenwich Farm School I was joined by my cousin Harry (Harold Mallett) whose residence butted up against the back fence of the school. Their house was the official residence of the superintendent of the sewage farm, who happened to be his father. On that first day, Harry and I were the butt of a serious prank by our classmates. Both of us, descendants of the Campbells that we were, always had our trousers well pressed, shoes polished and hair neatly combed whenever we went out, including our attendance at school. To the other boys, I imagine we must have seemed like a pair of 'dandies', looking and carrying ourselves as we did, so they decided to teach us a lesson.

They told us that classes were being held for half a day only as it was the first day. In our naivety we believed them, and as soon as we thought that school was over we headed off with our slingshots to the bottom of the property adjacent to the school. We were having a great time, when suddenly the face of our headmaster, Mr. Robotham, appeared above the fence separating the two properties. He was a tall, dark man with a carbuncle on his neck. "What are you boys doing there?" he asked sternly.

Innocently we replied, "Just shooting birds, sir."

He glared at us for a few moments, then simply said, "You should both be in school," and strode away.

The headmaster and most of the staff were well acquainted with Aunt Vie and her husband the superintendent. By the time we got home the news of our escapade had preceded us, and Aunt Vie was not amused. She gave Harry a good spanking with a flat hairbrush, while I got away with a tongue-lashing. To this day, I don't think that Harry has ever forgiven me for that episode, as we were both blameworthy.

CHAPTER 1: THE EARLY YEARS

I did not stay at Greenwich Farm School for long. I was transferred to the Seventh Day Adventist School on North Street opposite St. George's College. School was held in a large hall which accommodated four or five classes without partitions.

Among the teachers was Miss Gordon, a frail old lady, who it was alleged had been married several times. She taught the most junior class. One day she said to me, "You are not a bit like your mother." I don't know whether she meant in appearance or behaviour. Then there was Miss Brown who taught the senior class. My teacher was Miss Mars, a plumpish, round-faced, near-white lady with greyish-green eyes, typical of many Jamaicans who hail from the parish of St. Elizabeth.

One day during the recess, some boys were gathered in the school yard. At the school gate sat a vendor selling 'asham' – parched corn crushed to a powder, sweetened and served in a funnel-shaped brown paper package. At the far end of the school yard, away from the front gate, were located the school toilets, surrounded by zinc sheets about five feet high, through which entrance was gained like a garden maze. Although one could not see into the private area, objects and other missiles could be thrown at the person using the toilet. The game of the day was to fill the empty paper funnels with water drawn from a nearby standpipe and hurl them like a basketball player over the zinc fence partitioning the girls' lavatory.

When I returned to class after the break, Miss Mars summoned me to the front of the class. A little vixen of a girl with greyish-green eyes and a similar complexion to Miss Mars had apparently reported that I had been throwing water bombs into the girls' lavatory. I suppose she might have seen a head rising above the enclosure of the zinc fence as the person rose to hurl the water bomb. I would never pretend to be always well-behaved, but on this occasion I could truthfully say it wasn't me.

In front of the class Miss Mars asked, "Why did you do it?"

I said, "I did not."

She kept repeating the same question, and I continued to deny the accusation. In between each denial she struck my hands with a leather strap. I suppose all I had to do was admit it, perhaps say I was sorry, and the strapping would have stopped. But I would not be beaten into submission, for I was not guilty. I had stopped my denials, tears streaming down my cheeks, my heart swollen with hurt and anger. After some twenty-two lashes, I am told, for I was not counting, my bigger cousin Dorothy, who was in a senior class, came over and just took me from the class and led me out of the school.

There was a boy named Delroy who might have been regarded as having a slight resemblance to me, and I surmised that it might have been a question of mistaken identity. Walking out of school like that could have had serious consequences, for it could have become an impediment to getting into another school. As we walked out of the school literally in the middle of the day, by sheer coincidence we met our grandmother Essie, who was accompanied by her niece Enid Campbell. Cousin Enid was a tall, robust lady with a kind of discoloration of the cheeks which was referred as a 'mulatto blast': it was as if the cheeks could not decide whether to be light or dark in complexion – not uncommon with people of mixed ancestry. She was an imposing figure, with an arrogant and superior look, though really quite approachable and courteous.

Cousin Dorothy began explaining rapidly what had caused her to rescue me and led us to walk out of the school, and how Miss Mars had called us a bunch of rebels. My grandmother and cousin Enid marched us back into the school to confront her. Grandma Essie asked, "Sister Mars, do you remember why Moses did not enter the Promised Land?" Her understanding or interpretation was that Moses had said, "Drink, ye rebels." How therefore could she call innocent children rebels?

Cousin Enid, towering above her, said, "If I didn't find you as nice a lady as you have been, I would have struck you as many times as you strapped my little cousin." Miss Mars began to cry. I started to feel sorry for her. The whole episode had a lasting effect on me. I now knew what it felt like to suffer an injustice; as much as I tried I could not let this incident go.

CHAPTER 1: THE EARLY YEARS

It haunted me for years. I knew I had to somehow confront Miss Mars and settle this issue. On my return to Jamaica decades later, I enlisted the help of a friend and a Seventh Day Adventist member, Princess Lawes, to locate Miss Mars. I learnt that she had received her master's degree, had taught in Trinidad where she had undergone unsuccessful surgery on her back and was confined to a wheelchair. Later she went to live with her sister in Lluidas Vale, St. Catherine. I arrived at their cottage and was introduced as Senator Harding. After I related the incident that had occurred some thirty years before, she said to me, "Did I do that, Senator? If I did, would you forgive me?" I felt like a fool. That was not my reason for going. Why had I made that journey anyway? I don't know. I had long since forgiven Miss Mars, but that is what some people call closure. Some months later I attended her funeral and still remember word for word "A Psalm of Life" by Longfellow which she had taught me.

After that incident at the Seventh Day Adventist school, my father was not pleased. He advised the head teacher that he would take me out of that school and would "send me to the best school in the island". That turned out to be Kingston College, where I stayed until I emigrated to Canada, at the behest of my father. I was ten years and eight months old when I sat and passed the entrance exam to Kingston College. I remember it well. A passage was dictated to us which we then had to express in written form in our own words. This clearly required the skills of writing, spelling, punctuation and comprehension. I still remember that Nick Hardy sat beside me. He became a hardware merchant. He was fat and I was skinny. For years I called him "Fat Hardy". A friend of mine used to call us Laurel and Hardy after the famous comedy team in the movies. Later in life Nick told me that we sat beside each other because we were placed in alphabetical order. He remembered me wearing tweed pants which were very expensive. In fact my father had sent them from abroad.

Kingston College had only about four or five hundred boys then, not the mammoth school that it has become; but it had a spirit, an esprit de corps that has lasted – even grown. We developed a special adoration for our school. KC became a fraternity, a kind of brotherhood which persists even after you have left school. I have often thought, "If only our country had that emotional glue." I caught a glimpse of that feeling when Jamaica qualified for the football World Cup finals held in France in 1998.

KC's pride was not mere bluster. The institution provided some seventeen headmasters for schools all over Jamaica. KC won the athletics championship cup nineteen times in twenty-six years, including fourteen consecutive years. (See *The Brave May Fall But Never Yield: History of Kingston College 1925–2006* by Anthony S. Johnson.) In 1931, KC entered seventeen boys for the Cambridge School Certificate; amazingly, they were all successful. Perhaps my father had indeed sent me to the best school in the island.

Our class went to Tinson Pen on Victoria Day, a national holiday to commemorate the birthday of Queen Victoria; it was not then an aerodrome. There was a bungalow surrounded by a railed verandah. On that day it was raining, and as we stood singing in the rain "Rule Britannia – Britannia rules the waves", the purple dye from my school cap kept dripping on my khaki school uniform. It was certainly not Gene Kelly singing in the rain. I had visited these grounds before, but then it was an agricultural show with foreigners from New Zealand exhibiting their goats. When I recall being drenched on Empire Day I feel humiliated, but those were colonial days and it seemed quite natural – though it did plant in me seeds of resentment.

I will always remember my encounter with the founder and long-serving headmaster of Kingston College, Percival Gibson, who was to become the first native Lord Bishop of Jamaica. Though of slight build and small stature, he was a man of outstanding ability and tremendous presence, known to us boys simply as "Priest". He was endowed with a resonant voice and superb diction. He often wore his frock coat and bishop's leggings. I was awestruck by him, perhaps even a little afraid of him. I arrived late to school one morning and was sent by the head prefect to him, presumably for a caning. I was terrified. He simply looked at the scrawny little boy before him, and,

CHAPTER 1: THE EARLY YEARS

whether out of mercy or being too occupied with more important matters, dismissed me with a warning in his precise, articulate style: "Go to your class and never be late again." I was never late again.

It was while I was at McGill University when "Priest" came to receive his DD degree that we would meet again. I was now a grown man, no longer awestruck or afraid of him. He was an ascetic who genuinely cared about the welfare of his countrymen. I was even more convinced that this was an extraordinary Jamaican, an extraordinary human being. In an article published in the *Gleaner* of February 12, 2003, Anthony Johnson had this to say:

> *Bishop Gibson became a national symbol during his lifetime. To the end his fiery sermons criticised any aspect of political, civil or social life which he felt was unbecoming. He was particularly harsh on immoral behaviour, and called for reform, often stating: "Kingston is the wickedest city on Earth." In his lifetime no one ever dared to challenge him, but he never received a Jamaican civil honour. He resigned his duties in 1967 and passed away on April 3, 1970.*

Many interesting people have walked the halls of Kingston College. I remember two of my classmates, Michael Bronstorph, a white Jamaican with very blond hair, and Cliff Lashley, an articulate, dark-skinned, small-bodied boy. I saw both of them as being elitist. Their detractors often referred to them disparagingly as "the whiskey boys", after the brand of whiskey that featured a pair of black and white terriers on its logo.

I recall seeing Michael and Cliff having afternoon tea on the lawns of Kingston College, enjoying their finely trimmed cucumber sandwiches and seeming quite unperturbed by their surroundings. I found the whole thing disturbing: their manner of speaking, their air of superiority. They were always immaculately dressed from head to toe. My shoes were often scruffy from kicking footballs, tin cans and other objects, my shirt-tail out of my pants – despite the well-pressed and laundered khaki uniform that Aunt Vera always made sure that I had. I could not stand either of those boys. Was it jealousy? Was it what I later came to understand as "projection" – in other words, transferring one's own desires onto another person? What was it? Years later, after I related the story to my wife, she asked, "What's wrong with eating finely trimmed cucumber sandwiches?" "Nothing," I replied, "but not at that age."

As it turned out, Cliff and I would meet later in life and become good friends. It all started in London. It so happened that there was an exhibition of ancient pottery at the Albert and Victoria Museum, and because of my consuming passion for ceramics I had to see it. And who could I ask to accompany me but the erudite and well-read archivist Cliff Lashley? The visit was an exhilarating experience. He was able to point out some interesting details that I had not observed.

When some of the ladies at the High Commission wanted to go shopping, he was a superb escort. On the occasions when I accompanied them to the dress department in the stores, there were those large hassocks on which we would sit awaiting their exit from the changing rooms. When they emerged, Cliff would often exclaim, "Oh, no no, dahling, absolutely not you," or "Ahh – divine, just you, my dear." He later returned to Jamaica after he had qualified as an archivist. Cliff had acquired the largest collection of West Indian novels – perhaps more extensive than the collection at the University of the West Indies. Knowing Cliff, he would have read them all. On my return to Jamaica we ran into each other on several occasions. He had become affiliated with the Eagle Group of Companies via an educational trust, and I was an Eagle director.

Cliff had promised me a personal donation for an election campaign, but he died before our meeting. He was brutally murdered – dismembered – and his remains were reportedly found in a gully along Lady Musgrave Road in Kingston. His partner allegedly had killed him. I say partner, for Cliff was gay. Despite what some may think of his lifestyle, with his death Jamaica lost one of her brightest sons: an erudite, well-read, delightful person with so much to offer future generations.

CHAPTER 1: THE EARLY YEARS

The tall figure of Jonathan Crick loomed large at Kingston College. A Barbadian by birth, he taught Latin and English. He had an unusually broad nose and was very sensitive about it. If you did any unnecessary sneezing in his class, you could end up in detention. In my class were Kamal and Rudolf Shoucair. Their younger brother Edward Shoucair was to become a lifelong friend. The Shoucair brothers were friendly and amusing. On one occasion I was being examined by Mr. Crick at his desk. At the end of the questioning he entered a mark of 80 in the column beside my name. The Shoucair brothers started their antics at the back of the classroom and I erupted into a fit of uncontrollable laughter. Mr. Crick immediately changed the mark from 80 to 60. I felt he could have punished me otherwise if he thought that I was disrespectful.

One day in English class Mr. Crick asked us to compose a rhyming couplet. I hardly knew what a couplet was, let alone a rhyming couplet. Maxi Johnson, brother of Ambassador Anthony Johnson and Wally Johnson, rose to the occasion. "KC has a good reputation and that was a true speculation," he improvised. Later in life when we spoke, Maxi had no recollection of the incident. He studied law and sociology in London where he subsequently passed away.

Many years later when I was chairman of the Nuggets for the Needy campaign – a marathon call-in programme organized by the Kingston Jaycees to raise funds for various charities – I attended a meeting of school principals at Mico Teachers' College in Kingston. I was appealing to schools to participate in the programme and was seeking the assistance of the principals. Mr. Crick was there, for he was now headmaster of Cornwall College. After the formalities he began telling all assembled that I had been his student and expressed pride in my academic achievements. My mind flashed back to that classroom incident when he had reduced my marks which could have had adverse effect on my academic achievement; but by then I had long since forgiven him.

In 2008 I attended a graduation ceremony at Kingston College. As I watched the proceedings, I wished that I could be back in my class for just one week. So many memories came flooding back – not only of the friends I had made there, but of how proud Grandma Essie had been when I passed the entrance exam. Those were happy school days which would prepare me for further education. To my school mates, I repeat our school motto – "Fortis", my brethren.

At some point during 1946 Grandma Essie's health began to fail and it gradually grew from bad to worse. She had been the mainstay of the family for decades and had guided us through many challenging times. On the whole her health was fairly good, but she had a heart condition which grew worse with advancing years. On the night of her death I was sitting on a trunk at the foot of her bed, clinging to the iron railings and watching Aunt Vera and Cousin Curly attend to her. They had sent out messages about her failing health, and several family members began to arrive. As I sat there watching her, she suddenly gave a loud gasp and her lower jaw jutted forward. She had drawn her last breath. By the time Aunt Milly arrived, Gandma Essie was dead. I still recall Aunt Milly's entry into the room, with both hands on her head as she kept wailing, "Mama! Mama!"

It was the first time I had seen someone die. The drama of the moment was certainly gripping, and I knew that Grandma Essie had left us, never to return. She was buried in the Seventh Day Adventist lot in May Pen Cemetery where other members of the family were interred. She was seventy-four years old. With her passing, my father decided that it was time for me to join him in Canada.

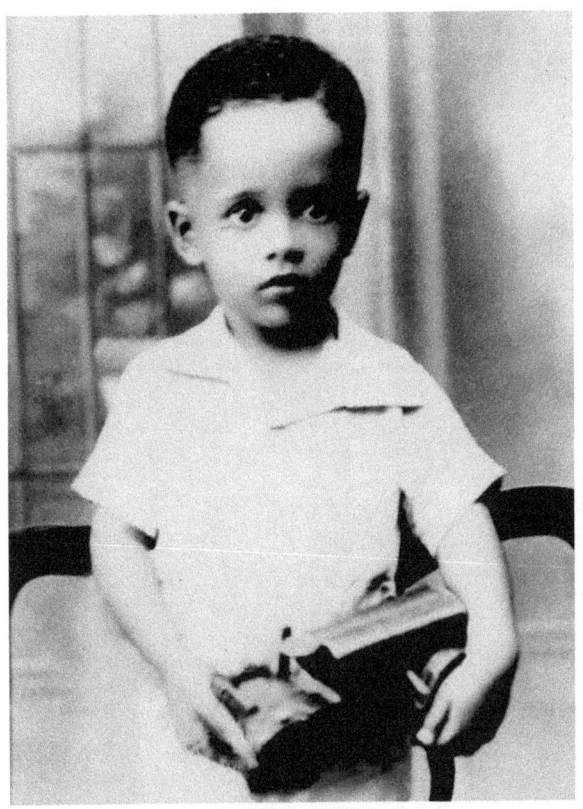

Ossie, aged 3, 1938

Top and Above: Ossie, 1945

My grandmother Asenath (Essie) Isabel Levy nee Campbell, 1945

Cousin Dorothy Thompson, 1945

My father Sylvester Alexander Harding, 1963

Sylvester Alexander Harding

Uncle Charlie Campbell, 1954

Two-storey house where I lived up to age 3 at 47 Asquith Street, Jones Town (where my mother died) picture taken on my return to Jamaica, 1963

Madam Bailey's infant] school, Asquith Street, Jones Town, 1965

CHAPTER 2

On to Canada

I was almost twelve years old. It was time to leave for Canada. I had to apply for a passport. My father had sold a Ford motor car to Reverend Menzie Edward Williamson Sawyers, a Baptist minister whose church was on Price Street in Jones Town. Aunt Vera took me to him to have the passport application certified, for at least he knew my father. He declined to sign the passport form, claiming that if I was to commit any offence abroad or get in trouble with the law it would reflect badly on him.

Aunt Vera was distressed but undaunted. She took me to Mr. Lewis, a justice of the peace who operated a gas station across from Bumper Hall and May Pen Cemetery near to McGregor Orange House. He may have known some of my relatives but he really did not know me. He asked my name, looked at the passport pictures and certified the passport form. Near the gas station was an East Indian village with many circular dwellings made of wattle and daub and plastered with cow dung. We used to buy callaloo and Indian kale from the villagers. I really appreciated the fact that Mr. Lewis certified my passport form although he didn't know me. His action was in direct contrast to the unhelpful attitude displayed by Reverend Sawyers, who actually knew my father. Whenever I recall this incident I think about some of the indignities the poorer people continue to suffer in Jamaica.

I was leaving my friends and family behind. What would it be like where I was going? Would there be a pot of gold at the end of the rainbow? Maybe not. But my father would be there. In my earliest recollections of him I was being carried on his shoulders, as we visited friends on Hanover Street not far from where the Sutton Street Resident Magistrate's Court is now located. It was a residential area with some very nice houses. Yes, I was going to see my dad. Aunt Vera took me to the Palisadoes Airport, now the Norman Manley International Airport. The propeller plane took off from what appeared to be a hangar – I think this building may still be there. My first stop was Miami, Florida. In those days it was called a "cracker town", which meant that racial discrimination was rampant. I remember just going up and talking to people in a friendly manner without any self-consciousness.

I arrived in Canada the day before my twelfth birthday in November 1947. The timing was deliberate for had I been twelve, my father would have had to pay the full plane fare. After meeting me at Dorval Airport in Montreal, my father took me to 1432 St Antoine Street where I boarded with the Caldwells, a Jamaican family. It was in the "negro district". Mr. Caldwell was barely literate, and his daughter's formal education was limited, but they were a very welcoming family. Two other Jamaicans boarded there as well: Ken Russell, who used Noxzema face cream each night and who always slept in a stocking cap – the object of which was to keep his hair smooth – and Clifford Scarlett, who had a cyst on his forehead. They both worked as sleeping car porters for the Canadian Pacific Railway. They worked on the train two or three times a week, sometimes for two days or longer. I would occupy Ken's or Scarlett's bed whenever they were away. I did some sightseeing and started to get my bearings in

CHAPTER 2: ON TO CANADA

Montreal. My appetite increased in the winter months and my weight shot up from 110 to 150 pounds.

In the negro district there was a nightclub called Rockheads. It was owned by an ex-porter who had made money during the prohibition period. It was alleged that he had smuggled whiskey across the American border wrapped in the used bed sheets from the train. Many of the uptown people would come to Rockheads to enjoy the black entertainment.

My father married a white English-speaking Canadian. She had two daughters from a previous marriage, and they were away at boarding school. My parents were married by a black parson in the negro area in 1949 at the Union United Church, 3007 Delisle Street, Montreal. I did not attend the wedding, but Ken was a witness. Shortly afterwards we moved north to a French Canadian area called Ahuntsic.

We lived on the third floor of a new apartment complex at 9195 Berri Street. Our landlord was a French Canadian, Mr. La Plante. My new mom urged me to get out of the apartment and play with the children in Christ-Roi Park, which was in front of the apartment. They all spoke French, of course. They were friendly, but I must have seemed strange to them. One day we were horse-playing around and I saw the park attendant coming and I wanted to alert them. I said, "La police s'en vient." They laughed at me because he was not a policeman and I did not know the French word for park attendant. So began my teenage years. I was adjusting to the new climate. I had never experienced snow. I tried ice-skating but without much success, so I quit before I could even stand properly on the skates.

As soon as I arrived, my father began his search for a suitable school. We went together to Loyola College where I was interviewed by the headmaster. It seemed like an acceptable school and I was all set to continue my education there, but for some reason my father changed his mind. I don't know whether it had anything to do with the fees or the fact that he came to realize that it was a Roman

Catholic institution. He was a staunch Anglican. In Jamaica he had been an acolyte at the Kingston Parish Church and a member of the Boys' Brigade. Perhaps he was concerned that I might convert to Catholicism. Dad's devotion to the Anglican Church led to his acquaintance with L.A. Henriques, who owned a jewellery store on King Street just below Kingston Parish church. Not only did Mr. Henriques support the church financially, he was also a major sponsor of the Boys' Brigade. Whenever Dad came back to Jamaica as an adult, he would take me along to call on Mr. Henriques, who invariably invited us to lunch at the Myrtle Bank Hotel on Harbour Street. I remember being impressed by the choice cuisine and elegant surroundings. The hotel was demolished in 1968 to make way for government projects, but the site remains undeveloped to this day.

Eventually I was enrolled at the High School of Montreal, one of the premier schools in the city. I did not know at the time, nor would my father have known, that the High School of Montreal was founded in 1842 and incorporated on March 17, 1843 by the Provincial Legislature with the motto "Corpori, Menti, Moribus", and became associated with McGill College in 1853. The British North American Act of 1867 and the formation of the Dominion of Canada had placed education under provincial control, and the Education Act of 1869 secured to a large extent the demands of the Protestant minority. The Protestant Board of Schools took over the school in 1870.

The High School of Montreal followed the tradition of the best schools in Scotland: half the time was dedicated to the classics, the rest to English, scripture and mathematics. The Scots were particularly influential in the settlement and growth of Canada, and formed the third largest ethnic group in the country after the English and the French. My school was housed in a six-storey building on University Street near Milton, across from McGill University. One wing of the building housed the High School for girls. I entered Montreal High towards the end of November 1947, a few weeks before the Christmas term ended. I had missed about two and a half months. It was difficult

CHAPTER 2: ON TO CANADA

to catch up. They decided that it would be best for me to repeat the year. I was only twelve years of age in any case.

The school had several streams: A for classics, B for the sciences, C for general studies and other streams for woodwork, mechanics and other vocational studies. In order to assess where I should be placed, I was given an IQ test. I was never told the result, but I was put in the A stream. There was a locker room at the back of the classroom where students would deposit their personal effects such as winter coats and winter boots. The first day I went to my locker, someone purposely bounced into me. There was a physical altercation and soon the other boy was on the ground and I was on top of him. I was never attacked again. The pecking order was established. When I resumed classes after the end of the next summer, my class was predominantly composed of Jewish boys. There were three Cohens, Shiposnick, Shalensky, Allan Naimark, and Peter Walkovitch, to name a few. On Jewish holidays I did not need to take lunch; I ate matzos and hard-boiled eggs provided by my classmates. There was harmony in the class and I fitted in well.

From the long association with McGill University, Montreal High supplied many students to the university's arts faculty. To enter McGill University from Grade 11 you needed to pass ten subjects. My class was taking eleven subjects. I decided in Grade 10 that I was going to drop physics. I was quiet in class, gave no trouble, and did the minimum required of me. During the very last physics class I turned around to Allan Naimark and simply said, "Allan, lend me your pen." My physics teacher, Mr. Revard, caught me talking. He upbraided me in no uncertain terms, wondering aloud why I did not exert myself despite having so much ability. I had come third in the school's public-speaking contest, and in Grade 10 I got eight distinctions. I dropped physics and got the ten subjects that I needed to enter McGill University. Perhaps that was a mistake, because later in life I became very interested in theoretical physics.

My classics teacher was Mr. Thomas Kear, a Scotsman, who had a first class honours degree in classics – I remember him always for the phrase "a hay me doots" which meant "I have my doubts". Mr. Leonard Unsworth was the rector (headmaster) when I was in school. Although I do not recall the context in which he said it, I always remember him saying, "Be good or be bad, but be something." In my final year, I was pleased that I got 92 percent in my oral French and 89 percent in my written French. Grandma Essie, you would have been proud.

In the summer, I participated in a programme in the park and won a first prize for a little art work I had made. The next summer I got a job nearby in the Paramount Pad factory where they made shoulder pads for suits and dresses. I was the cutter and had to cut an endless number of shoulder pads. I earned seventeen dollars a week. After some time we moved to 722 Champagneur Avenue in Outremont. This was nearer to town and was a more developed residential area. On Park Avenue in Outremont I was confirmed in the Church of the Ascension – an Anglican church.

There I met many young people in my age group. Many of us played tennis on the small tennis court there. We entered a classic play called *I Claudius* and won a place in the competition. I sang and I acted. The group included Charlie Bennett, Don "Skippy" McGowan who became a popular television personality, and Richard DeLorme, now a minister of religion with whom I am still in touch. Many years later Charlie Bennett came to do charity work in Jamaica and he located me. He paid a visit to my wife and myself, and it brought back fond memories of the years I spent in Canada. On August 28, 1988, I visited the High School of Montreal with Mr Astley South, a Jamaican, and my son Jeremy who was then at McGill. The school had closed in 1978 and was now operating as an Art Academy.

In Outremont I met George Geroux, Alfy Malin, Anne-Marie, the Crosby brothers and Ronald Coleman, whose father was the verger of the Church of the Ascension. Another member of the group was Keith LeBrun, who would remain a lifelong friend. LeBrun was a tall, skinny kid, whose forebears came from the Isle of Man. It was a

CHAPTER 2: ON TO CANADA

happy time, a wonderful time. He and I developed a lasting friendship. We would frequent a little shop near to our home where he would have a Pepsi and a cake called a Mae West. Then we would go to the afternoon movies where there was a triple bill – meaning three movies – for twenty-five cents. He used to deliver the local newspaper for which he earned about two dollars a week. Often we would go to his house – sometimes his brother Graham would be there. We frequently played table tennis on his mother's dining table. He knew my parents and I knew his. Keith called me about one-thirty one morning to tell me that he had popped the question and Margaret said yes. I was the best man at his wedding.

I made many friends in Outremont. I felt fully accepted and well integrated. I was from a different country, but the difference never mattered. My dad continued to work at the Queen Mary Hospital as a medical clerk, for he had worked in a medical unit during the war. My mom worked at a neighbourhood restaurant as a waitress. My parents were happy together. It was at Champagneur Avenue that my sister Sheila was born in 1949.

One day I was playing a record, "It only takes a moment to fall in love but it takes a lifetime to forget," and my dad agreed. It was clear that he had been very much in love with my mother. My stepmother overheard the conversation and was most upset.

I got along well with my new sisters Donna and Sonia. They would often come home from boarding school. In February 2008 my stepsister Donna, who now lives in Florida, came to visit us in Jamaica with her husband Charles Knowles and their son Michael and his wife.

During those teenage years I got a part-time job at a theatre near Atwater and the Forum, which had a large skating rink. This was the venue for some of the matches played by "Les Canadiens de Montréal", a professional ice hockey team that was the toast of Montreal. I was an usher at the theatre which featured live shows. One evening when an American singer, Joni James, was performing there, I observed a man standing partially in the aisle. Armed with the authority of my flashlight, I marched down the aisle and ordered the person to move – he was about five feet five inches tall and very slender. Turns out it was Sammy Davis Jnr, who was performing in Montreal with the Will Mastin trio.

At the theatre I saw Billy Daniels, that "old black magic man" and the great Duke Ellington, personable and an articulate African American. Who could forget him with his full head of hair well coiffed, and his large, baggy eyes, a master composer and arranger with such songs as "Take the A Train"? Then there was the new sensation Johnny Ray with songs like "Cry" and "Little White Cloud that Cried". He literally wept during every performance. I was fascinated by Louis Armstrong, the great jazz trumpeter. One night a visitor from Europe came to see Mr. Armstrong; when I went to him backstage he was wearing boxer shorts, a handkerchief tied over his head, as he listened to the playback of his music on a large tape recorder. When I told him that he had a visitor, he simply said in that famous gravelly voice, "Send him on in, son."

There was also a magician called the Great Morton who not only did tricks but also hypnotized people. When I went back to my young people's group at the church, I tried using the same formula used by the hypnotist on stage. I tried it on one of the girls . . . and it worked! For a moment, however, I was frightened and in a state of panic for it suddenly occurred to me that she might not wake up, and I wasn't sure that I had learnt that part of the trick. Fortunately she did wake up under my instructions.

In 1951, at age sixteen, I entered McGill University, a most congenial and welcoming atmosphere, but it felt good to be reunited with West Indians in general, and more specifically, with my own Jamaican people. I was younger than most of my compatriots. Often when the fellows were going off campus for an evening out they would simply say, "See you later." In front of the Arts Building, which was like the centre of the campus, there was a ginkgo tree. It was said that the limbs grew parallel to the level or slant of the ground around it.

CHAPTER 2: ON TO CANADA

Although no one sat under the ginkgo tree, perhaps figuratively the whole campus was under the ginkgo tree. In Jamaican folklore we would sing about being "under the coconut tree".

Soon after entering university, I was inspired by stories about the great achievements of West Indians who had preceded us: Dr. I.K. Melville, who reportedly led his class in medicine, studied at the Pasteur Institute in Paris and became head of the Department of Pharmacology at McGill; Dr. Phil Edwards, Trinidadian expert in tropical medicine, who competed in the 800 metres in the 1936 Olympics and won a bronze medal for Canada. Then there was Dr. Evelyn who became a full professor of physics at McGill University. He was the son of Reverend Austin Evelyn and his wife Maud, who was the sister of Alexander Bustamante. Impressive achievers on the campus also included Elrie and Eric Tucker from Trinidad who both became medical doctors. Their sister Rae Tucker who was chosen campus queen, and Neville Linton became editor of the *McGill Daily* newspaper which published one of my poems, printed below. Neville was from British Guiana which would change its name to Guyana after gaining independence in 1966.

Terrestrial Turmoil

This war-torn world of sweat and toil
This bloody world of hatred, spite and greed
Lust upon the souls of men like crows upon a carrion feed
Was the earth always like this?
Piled with filth and slime
Scraped from the utmost depths of hell
To spread upon one's short space of time
Cancerous things to dread
There were other unpublished poems of mine, such as:

When in the Autumn of my life
And the youth from me doth fade

GRANDSON OF ESSIE: A JAMAICAN AUTOBIOGRAPHY

I will remember thee
But now, now, in my embryonic state
Sow ye now your seeds of concern
and compassion and I will remember thee.

The winter and the snow had returned. My coat was looking a bit shabby. As a stylish young man of nineteen, I bought a double-breasted fawn-coloured alpaca coat. It was handsome and it was warm. During rush hour, as is natural in a crowded train, passengers would unintentionally bump into each other. On my way home on the train one afternoon, someone bounced against me; my hand was in my pocket, but then I became aware that a hand was slipping through my arm. I became uneasy. As I turned my head slowly, I noticed that the arm linked in mine belonged to a beautiful French Canadian woman of about thirty. What to do? Was I being kidnapped, arrested or being picked up on the train? Then I looked across from me and saw a man beaming from ear to ear, which made me even more uneasy. I said to myself in Jamaican, "Wha fi do?" Then I noticed that the amused man was wearing a similar alpaca coat. What a relief! I had reached my stop – clearly the woman had mistaken me for her husband because of the coat.

On weekends we would go to Belmont Park where there were Ferris wheels and exciting games. I did not fancy those towering machines. My friend Keith LeBrun said I was chicken. On one occasion we ate hot dogs and Keith drank a Pepsi Cola before taking his favourite ride. When he got off the Ferris wheel his stomach continued the spinning motion and he disgorged his meal. I thought it was funny, but I kept a straight face. We enjoyed attending Saturday night dances with our dates. Every Saturday night I wore a different bow tie and danced the night away. These days I rarely wear them, except with a tuxedo.

As a student I made a visit to Detroit and thought that the most affordable place to stay would be the YMCA. I wrote some weeks

CHAPTER 2: ON TO CANADA

before, made a reservation and received confirmation. On arrival in Detroit I took a taxi to the location. I entered the building, introduced myself at the front desk and showed my reservation. I was abruptly told that I had no reservation. I could not understand. The attendant shouted at me: "You have no reservation! Try down the road." Fortunately the taxi was waiting outside. I was directed to another YMCA and then discovered that there was a "white Y" and a "black Y". On entering the second building I was appalled at the filth and the smell of urine. I hurried outside, dismissed the taxi and tried to find some other accommodation. As I walked down the street there were some layabouts sitting on the sidewalk with their backs against the wall and their legs stretched out before them. They asked if I had any cigarettes. I reached for my pack of cigarettes and gave them all I had, quaking with fear and revulsion.

I finally came to an intersection and saw a sign that said "Rooms for Rent". I entered the building and paid two dollars for the night. The room was upstairs and had no drapes or curtains. There was only a light sheet on the bed. Neon lights from outside kept flashing into the room. Then came a thunderstorm accompanied by flashes of lightning which intensified the nightmarish scenario. I have no idea how I slept through it, but I awoke the next morning in a daze. I hurried to the station, got on a train and headed back to Montreal. This was my first experience of racial discrimination. How was I to know that there was a "black Y" and a "white Y"? In my naivety I took the name literally: "Young Men's Christian Association." I never had the occasion or desire to visit Detroit again – the big D as they called it.

I participated in activities on campus – the African Society, the Psychology Club, the International Club, the Debating Club, and I became president of the West Indian Society. In this capacity I represented P.J. Patterson, President of the Guild of Undergraduates, University of the West Indies, at the 21st Congress of the National Federation of Canadian University Students (NFCUS). P.J. would succeed Michael

Manley as prime minister of Jamaica in 1992 under a People's National Party (PNP) administration. Years after leaving McGill I remarked to P.J. that the NFCUS Congress was the only time I ever represented him. My allegiance to the Jamaica Labour Party is a matter of record.

Wills O. Isaacs, the well-known PNP politician, visited us at McGill. At the time we were all concerned about the West Indian Federal Government. I asked him, "If Norman Manley was not going to the Federal Government or Dr. Eric Williams, what would happen?"

He replied, "Men don't make situations, situations make men; when the situation arises, the man will arise." As history would show, Sir Grantley Adams was the man who arose, and the rest of that story has already been written.

My contemporaries on campus included Jackie Minott, now of Standard Products and High Mountain Coffee in Jamaica; O.K. Melhado, formerly of Desnoes and Geddes beverage manufacturers; Sybil Smith (Mrs. Randel) of Paisley College; Paul and Martha Pink of Mandeville; Stanley Moore of the Ministry of Agriculture and Credit Union Association; Peter Moss-Solomon of Grace Kennedy; Lloyd Philpotts Brown, affectionately referred to as LP (for Long-Playing); Frank DaCosta; Trevor Foreman; Neville Gray, who led us in singing Jamaican folk songs such as "Chi chi bud oh"; George Eaton, later Professor at York University; Teddy Warmington, an established builder in Jamaica; H. Denny Repole, eminent architect in Jamaica; Irena Wisniewski (Mrs. Cousins), Honorary Consul for Poland; Peggy Mair (McBeath); O.C. Hutchinson (dentist); Daphne Ramsay; Patricia Marks; and Julius Garvey, son of Marcus Garvey.

The West Indian girls on campus lived at RVC – Royal Victoria College – which was located at Sherbrooke and University Streets; in fact all female students, whether in or off campus, were members of RVC. The residence was an imposing building with classical steps leading to the entrance. After climbing the steps to the building, you were confronted by an enclosed foyer. Beyond that were locked glass

CHAPTER 2: ON TO CANADA

doors. It was an ordeal to go there to collect anyone. Sybil was perhaps the most senior of the girls. She was their undisputed captain and gave guidance to many of the younger ones. In Jamaica we would have said she was the "mother hen".

To invite out one of the girls at RVC was a tortuous affair. If you telephoned the RVC it would be at least four or five minutes before you would be connected to your party. Often you could hear the shouting in the background as someone tried to locate the girl you were calling. Cellphones – bless them – had not yet been invented. Finally, when you were able to converse with the person and you invited her out, more than likely you would be met with a reply that went something like this: "I am not sure what we will be doing later in the week; perhaps you could call back." Call back! Not likely. Whenever you invited out a Canadian girl there would be a clear answer – whether in the affirmative or negative. Consequently the invitations to West Indian girls became fewer and fewer. The non-dating of West Indian girls became an issue and was discussed at the West Indian Society.

Although the RVC was a fortress, what were known as "panty raids" occasionally took place. Some male students – not any West Indians, to my knowledge – would find ways of entering the girls' dormitory, perhaps assisted by someone on the inside, to collect ladies' undergarments. Of course, if they were caught it would result in immediate expulsion. I never understood the point of this game, but I suppose the risk of being caught and the danger involved might have given the 'high' or adrenalin rush.

In my late teens or early twenties, I did not yet understand the ways of women, not that I am now in any way the wiser. There was a buxom, round-faced girl, not very dark in complexion, with a thick head of hair. I'll refer to her as A.A. We would have brief conversations whenever we met. On one occasion we met in front of the library and curiously, she asked me, "Do you pluck your eyebrows?" What a question! Was she implying that I looked gay or that my eyebrows ought to be plucked? Was this an effort to destabilize me?

On another occasion the West Indian Society had a get-together at McDonald College, the out-of-town campus where agriculture was taught. The men had gathered in a corner and were engrossed in deep conversation, not really paying attention to the girls sitting around in the chairs nearby. Someone suggested that we ought to ask them to dance. I asked A.A. if she would like to dance, and she readily accepted. As we moved to the music she enquired in her most caressing voice, "Where did you learn to dance?" I felt she was paying me a compliment. A little embarrassed, I said coyly, "Oh, here and there," to which she responded dryly, "I thought so." Was this another effort to put me down? Perhaps I was not reading the cards right.

There were some Indian girls on campus from British Guiana, as Guyana was known then. One of them always wore a sari, though I was told that this was not their daily wear at home. Was it Indian pride or was it a way of not identifying with us? Finding these girls very charming, I invited one of them out and she accepted. She had a sister and a brother-in-law in Montreal, but the brother-in-law forbade her to go out with me. I was bewildered. I later learnt that it was nothing personal, but because I was not Indian I was not acceptable. I acquired my first car from Keith Blake who hailed from St. Kitts-Nevis. He became a dentist and years later I tried to locate him when I visited St. Kitts, but he was off the island. The second-hand car was an Austin A40, convertible all-aluminium body. The great advantage of this vehicle was that you could hear it coming from a distance. Needless to say, owning a convertible in a cold country was not a great idea. For one thing, the top of the convertible was not practical in winter. My friend Stan Moore taught me to drive using this car. He constantly had to remind me to keep both hands on the steering wheel. I later sold the car to a neighbour and heard that the transmission fell out on the highway while he was driving to the country!

We often frequented a little restaurant on Milton Street near the campus. It was known as "the greasy spoon". We would go there to have hamburgers and French fries – sometimes only French fries.

CHAPTER 2: ON TO CANADA

When someone had no money he would join the group and then ask for some hot water – the waitress would think that he was going to make a cup of tea with the tea bags on the table; instead he would add globs of ketchup to the hot water and make tomato soup! I was more fortunate, for I was then living at home.

Those who had left us on the lower campus and had gone to medical school would often come to visit or really to show off, especially during their first term. On one occasion a new medical student came down in his white coat, one hand in his pocket; he then extended his hand to greet a young lady; the only problem was he literally left his hand in hers. She fainted, for it was the hand of a cadaver.

Another medical student, probably from Eastern Europe, was crossing Milton and University Streets with a shopping bag. He stopped a while, waiting to cross. A policeman also happened to be at the crossing when a human skull came through the shopping bag soaked by formaldehyde. The student was immediately arrested. I don't know whether he was ever charged – the charge could have been suspicion of murder, but that was not the case: he had borrowed the skull because he could not afford to buy one. He was immediately expelled – but I think that the faculty took pity on him and allowed him to return.

Engaging in a sporting activity was a requirement of the university. I took up boxing. I weighed 180 pounds which put me in the heavyweight class. I started to spar with Jimmy, who weighed about 220 pounds. I did not know then that he was the Golden Glove champion for Montreal. After coming out of a crouching style, he landed an overhand left hook to my jaw. I decided then and there that football was a much safer sport.

I graduated with an honours degree in anthropology and successfully completed the first year of the master's programme before changing disciplines. McGill was a happy place, as happy as its successful musical play – *My Fur Lady*.

The Canadian Pacific Railway (CPR) ran passenger trains across Canada and also to New York and Detroit in the United States. All the sleeping car porters were black – from America, Canada and the West Indies. Through my father's friendship with some of the porters I got a summer job at CPR. I did a couple of weeks' training, learning how to convert the Pullman coaches and transform them into sleeping cars. On one trip I got a "special"; this was not a regular passenger trip but one which started in St. Jean, Quebec, to pick up a contingent of female air force troops. Each coach consisted of about twenty units which were converted into beds. There was an overhead compartment in which the mattresses and pillows were kept. The double benches facing each other were broken down to form the base of the beds and the overhead compartment became another bed. As the train was pulling out, the trainman, who carried the signal lantern from the end of the train, said to me, "I don't know about you, but I have to go forward through the [sleeping] car."

Grandmother Essie had brought me up to think that boys were rough, boisterous, daring and untidy. Girls, by contrast, were gentle, well mannered, tidy and modest. I was seventeen. As I turned around to go through the carriage I saw about twenty young women in various states of undress. Some were fat, some were skinny, some flat-chested, some with buxom breasts. One young woman stood straddling two benches, completely nude, playing a risqué version of "Old King Cole was a merry old soul" on her guitar. She paused to ask the sergeant, "Who are these men floating around here?"

The sergeant replied, "They work here." She resumed her singing, quite unperturbed.

I was traumatized. Although I think I relate well to members of the opposite sex, I am not so sure that since then, subconsciously, I am comfortable in a crowd of women. But I was to learn more that summer. On several occasions I saw men and women who boarded the train at different points meet and go to bed with each other then get off at different stops as if nothing unusual had happened.

As a sleeping car porter, part of my job was to keep the washrooms tidy. Behind the door to the washroom there was an inner curtain in

CHAPTER 2: ON TO CANADA

a crescent shape which was to give some privacy when the door was opened. It was after midnight as I entered the ladies' washroom to tidy it. I knocked, pressed the buzzer and then pushed aside the inner curtain, only to see a woman with her upper half naked. I said, "Sorry, madam" and withdrew.

As I withdrew she said, "It's all right, porter, when I have my work to do, I have to get it done – go right ahead."

Apart from my embarrassment, I had better sense. Train inspectors would board the train at odd hours of the night. What kind of explanation could I offer – cleaning the ladies' restroom with a half-naked woman present?

What shocked me, Grandmother Essie, was their lack of modesty. Some of the women were so untidy they would leave soiled napkins during their menses in the little semi-circular baskets. I soon started wearing a pair of gloves. They were like garden gloves made from a rough white material with strips on them – somehow they reminded me of cricket batting gloves. They were quite useful in other respects as well. Part of the service was that passengers could leave their shoes out to be cleaned. I didn't mind the occasional passenger who would leave a pair of shoes out for cleaning. But sometimes this train was filled with soldiers – they would leave their boots out to be cleaned, though I am sure the army had its regulations. After the soldiers had been on a march, the stench emanating from those boots was stifling – but at least I had my garden gloves.

On one occasion I was lucky to get a special – a group of French Canadian members of the Alliance Française. They were a cultural club that went on excursions; I would be on the train for at least twelve days. On these trips two sleeping cars would have their bell systems connected. One porter would go to bed at midnight, and if a passenger rang the bell, the other porter would answer it. The porter on duty would wake up his colleague at 3:00 a.m. and then sleep until 6:00 a.m. Each porter got three hours sleep per night. At the end of the trip I was suffering from sleep deprivation, but I had volunteered for it. I benefited from this trip in two ways. I have never needed an alarm clock all my life for I learnt when to get up, and even when I travel, the hotel wake-up call is really a backup. Secondly, I made enough money to have kept me throughout the next year at university – long working hours plus the gratuities.

That summer a French Canadian friend and I ended up in Vancouver, British Columbia, to see the Commonwealth Games. As we were on our way to the stadium, a glamorous blonde drove up beside us in a convertible and offered us a lift. She was stunningly beautiful. How could we refuse? I believe she thought we were athletes. It was at those games that I saw the famous race between John Landy from Australia and Roger Bannister of the UK. Both had broken that impossible barrier of the four-minute mile – Landy had the faster time but as he turned to look back, Bannister breezed by.

I used to go to Winnipeg, Manitoba, quite often; this was a good-paying trip because of the hours. When we arrived in Winnipeg we would have breakfast at a restaurant across the street from the railway station. This was Portage Street – about four lanes wide; we would have a steak about two inches thick with chips and a few slices of tomato for two dollars. Then we would go to the bunkhouse where we would stay overnight before taking the train back to Montreal the next day. In the bunkhouse the men would gamble away their tips. I always took a top bunk so I could look down and watch the game. Gambling never interested me. Often someone would borrow money from me which I never got back. They could never induce me to enter the game. I have never had an inclination to gamble.

I did a lot of growing up that summer. I have since formed the view that in everyone's life there is a period, a time when there is an awakening. It is probably during *that certain summer*, if you are in college, or when you see the world differently. Perhaps you fell in love or lost your virginity or you started to smoke or drink – but something dramatic occurred in your life – and you changed or saw the world from a different perspective.

CHAPTER 2: ON TO CANADA

After two summers as a sleeping car porter I got a job as a redcap. These were the porters who carried the luggage on or off the train. At the entrance of the railway station was the taxi stand where we would unload the baggage from the trains. In this job I did not have to go out of town and the tips were almost guaranteed. While he was at McGill, Denny Repole used to drive a cab in the summer. We became good friends. Whenever I came off the trains with bags I would look to see where he was in the line. If I had three loads, I would pass the one-bag load to the first cab and maneuvered the distribution so that Denny would get the best load – perhaps three or four bags. This would mean more tips for him. Thus we formed an alliance. I had forgotten this little manoeuvre until Denny spoke about it during his opening remarks at an art gallery in Jamaica many years later.

While working at the railway station, I met one Jean-Pierre Guillemot, a Frenchman who, it seemed, would do anything to be black. He had black friends and tried to ape their accent and speech. We often used to watch the girls go by in the station. I remember a Barbadian, Mr. Blackman, saying to us, "Boys, you see them, you going to die and leave them, you can't have all of them." Jean-Pierre eventually married a black nurse and ended up in New Jersey in the United States.

Near to the railway station was the Alberta Lounge, a restaurant and night club. Oscar Peterson and his trio used to play there. He became one of the foremost jazz pianists in the world. I believe his family came from Barbados – his brother Chuck had one arm and played the trumpet, while his sister gave piano lessons. Peterson was once refused a haircut in Dresden, Ontario, because of his colour. Near the end of his life he received national honours from the Government of Barbados. French Canadians seemed less prejudiced. They did not seem to mind the colour of your skin, but they would wish you to speak French and be Roman Catholic.

In the summer, the Young People's Association of the Church of the Ascension on Park Avenue would meet to play tennis and stage plays and variety shows. I recently came across a programme from one of those shows, scripted by Nora Lunn and myself. It was a musical comedy presented in the church hall at 5434 Park Avenue, Montreal, January 27–29, 1955. Produced and directed by me, it was a light comedy called *Keep It Gay*. I imagine that such a title would stir robust debate today.

It was at one of these tennis court gatherings that I met Jackie Chew. She was not a member of our group but a friend of one of the members. I would meet her again, as she worked upstairs in the office of the Windsor Railway Station where I worked in the summer. We would always say hello. One day I invited her to lunch. She was a pleasant young woman, with a broad smile and a dimple, short, curly, reddish-blonde hair, slightly built – but not skinny. We started seeing each other on a fairly regular basis. I took her to my graduation prom. She was great fun to be with and I looked forward to seeing her. On weekends we would go for drives in her little convertible Morris Minor. We would be on the highway going to her home, out of town, where she lived with her parents. I can recall the wind rushing through our hair and in our faces. It was exhilarating. Sometimes she made me drive even though I had just got my driver's licence. It was absolutely thrilling.

Spring was in the air. The harsh, cold winter winds that swept across the park in Dominion Square had vanished. The perennial tulips that went to sleep in the winter were now bursting out of the ground. I was to meet Jackie in the park to go to lunch. Some fifty metres away I saw her coming. She was wearing a lime green shirt dress and white sandals. Green is so becoming to redheads. My heart leapt and there were the proverbial butterflies in my stomach. What was happening to me? I was falling in love, for the first time. I guess for me it was *that certain summer*. I took her home. She met my parents. Often she would take me home as she had the car. One night near Christmas we were sitting in the car outside my home and I invited her to have Christmas dinner with us. She declined the

CHAPTER 2: ON TO CANADA

invitation. I asked her if she was going out to dinner. She said no. I asked her if she was having dinner at home. Again she said no. I became confused and angry. I told my parents of her refusal and decided I would invite someone else, but they did not approve.

After I had got over the trauma, one evening she said to me, "I am a JW, you know."

I did not understand: "What is a JW?"

She replied, "A Jehovah's Witness."

"So what?" I countered. "What difference does that make?" But then I learnt that they do not celebrate Christmas or Easter or many of the rituals that we observe. Over the next few weeks she revealed her poignant story. She had met her husband while they were both serving in the military. Unfortunately, the marriage did not work. They lived off base somewhere in rural eastern Canada. She said he was cruel to her. When he left her she delivered a child in the cabin by herself. A doctor came some three days later. I was to meet her daughter who was called Kippie. She was beautiful, a lovely child. Jackie had lost another child when her husband had pushed her out of their car and she fell to the ground.

After all these negative experiences, she found comfort as a JW. They did not have a church but a Kingdom Hall. To me it made no difference. I was in love. But when the time came for me to leave Canada, I realized the problem of being saddled with a wife who already had a child. We both knew it wouldn't work. The day I left, she was the only friend who didn't come to see me off at the pier. I was hurt. Later when we corresponded she said she simply could not come to say goodbye. My mother had a relative who was a member of her faith. While in England, I would enquire about Jackie through her. The messages got fewer and fewer. I learnt that she married a French Canadian and they lived on a farm. But Jackie was unfortunate to have found a second cruel husband. The beautiful little girl Kippie went horseback riding and fell off the horse, but one leg was caught in the stirrup. She hit her head on the ground as the horse galloped along. Although she survived, her mental faculties were impaired. It was heartbreaking news, but that chapter in my life was closed.

I learnt a great deal growing up in Canada and I became a man. It was time to move on. I did not accept the offer to go to Dalhousie University, and enrolled instead at the London School of Economics. I took the Cunard Line to England; the voyage lasted five days and four nights, as I recall. I had been given all sorts of advice about how to deal with seasickness and I took my Gravol tablets with me. The trip was pleasant, if uneventful. I never got seasick. When I arrived at Southampton the graffiti read "Go home, niggers". After a few hours on the train I arrived at Waterloo station. I had written to the British Council and had secured a place in the hostel at Hans Crescent near the famous Harrods Store. At the hostel there was a quota for each nationality. The West Indian quota was full, but having applied from Canada I apparently got in on that basis. But when I got there I certainly wanted to be counted among the West Indians.

Dad and his new Buick, June 1963

Alex and Eileen Harding, 1963

Young Ossie in Montreal, 1948

My sisters Sonia (left) and Donna, at Christ-Roi Park, Montreal, 1954

The High School of Montreal, 1952

High school graduation photo, 1967

With Jackie Chew, prom night, 1961

In the play 'I Claudius', Montreal, 1955

Young people's group, Church of the Ascension, Montreal, January 1955

McGill University, October 1955 – gingko tree in background

Jackie Chew in 1992

Jackie Chew and I

CHAPTER 3

A Foggy Day in London Town

A foggy day in London Town
Had me low, and had me down
I viewed the morning with alarm
The British Museum had lost its charm
How long, I wondered, could this thing last?
But the age of miracles hadn't passed
For suddenly, I saw you there
And in foggy London town
The sun was shining everywhere

—Original lyrics and music by George Gershwin

My first residence in London was at the British Council hostel at Hans Crescent in Knightsbridge, near to the famous Harrods department store. This was a preferred area in London, not far from Hyde Park and the West End. A fellow student at McGill had given me the address and phone number of a cousin of his, and told me to give her a call. About a month after I had settled in, I came across the telephone number and the address. As it turned out, she lived diagonally across from the hostel. I called her and she invited me over for tea. I found her very gracious and well mannered. I later discovered that she was a debutante: a young woman of upper-class background who is presented to society, usually at a formal ball.

I arrived wearing a grey suit with a tartan tie. We engaged in pleasant conversation and spoke of her cousin in Canada, and then the doorbell rang. Three visitors arrived. There was a white-haired, middle-aged woman whom I would describe as a dowager; an Englishman who had worked for the BBC and who seemed pleasant enough, and a tall Englishman with hair curling about his ears. He wore a dark pinstriped double-breasted suit. He spoke like a public school boy. It reminded me of the advertisement that often appeared in the *Times* newspaper: "Public school boy seeks job". It did not seem that any other qualifications were required.

The visitors appeared surprised to see this foreigner so comfortably seated in the debutante's flat. I was very sensitive to the situation and hurriedly explained that I was a friend of her cousin's at McGill University. We all conversed well enough for a while. The fellow from the BBC seemed well travelled and had met lots of foreigners. The dowager seemed quite at ease. She said, "I hear that you studied anthropology; I suppose that had to do with little bugs."

I replied, "No ma'am, you are thinking of entomology."

She let out a quick, hearty laugh: "Of course you are quite right, how silly of me!"

We engaged in superficial and harmless banter until the tall Englishman said, "I notice you have a beard; do you all wear beards in Canada?"

"Not all of us," I replied. "But some have beards in my faculty here."

And then the next salvo came. "I see you are wearing a tartan tie; are you Scottish?"

CHAPTER 3: A FOGGY DAY IN LONDON TOWN

I did not miss the undertone in that query. "My great-grandfather was a Campbell, but this is not the Campbell tartan," I replied. The dowager invited me to join them for dinner at the Berkeley. I thanked her but declined, saying I had an assignment which was due the next day.

The police in our neighbourhood had detained a suspect who was accused of snatching a lady's purse in Hyde Park. The accused was a black man. They came to the hostel to find volunteers for the identification parade. Horace Patterson, who later became a lawyer, and Martin Wright, who became a High Court judge, were among the group that volunteered, including myself. We were hoping that one of us would have been chosen, because we had impeccable alibis.

When we arrived at the station the accused was in custody. The police officer informed him that he could stand anywhere in the line-up. The victim arrived. She appeared to be in her sixties. The police invited her to inspect the line-up and she promptly walked over to the suspect and said, "That's 'im." The police again invited her to inspect the entire line-up. She repeated, "That's 'im," looking directly at the suspect.

As we were leaving, the accused said, "Is awright, ol' man, is awright," in a broad Jamaican accent. There is a saying that to the English all black people look alike – in short, they were indistinguishable. Unfortunately for the accused, the victim was a retired nurse who had worked in the Bahamas and certainly could distinguish people of colour. I always wanted to remind Mr. Justice Wright before he died of the day we stood together in an ID parade.

Many volunteers were invited to the hostel to assist us in our adjustment to British life. On one occasion there was a lecture on how to eat hard-boiled eggs. We were highly amused and could hardly contain ourselves – perhaps there were students who came from countries where eggs were not eaten? We will never know. On one occasion we had a visit from a female volunteer. She was clearly a lady of some social standing, well-meaning and sincere. She enquired where we were from and made small talk with each of us.

Arasarathnam advised her that he was from Malaysia. She stumbled over the name and swallowed the latter part of it. She then asked him, "Do you play the piano?"

"No ma'am," he replied. "I knew a Malayan once; he played the piano." I started to learn the art of small talk.

At Hans Crescent the atmosphere was congenial. Students from far-flung regions of the Commonwealth, including the Caribbean, had lodgings there. It was an all-male hostel with double rooms, each accommodating two students. My first roommate was a Sikh whose name was Singh. He wore a traditional turban which consisted of a piece of muslin five or six yards long wrapped around his head. The hair is not cut nor the beard trimmed. The beard is coiled around a string placed under the chin leading up the side of the jaws. The first night when he took off his turban and flashed his long tresses it was momentarily frightening as he looked a bit wild. As time went on I helped him prepare his turban: we would face each other across the room, fold the cloth twice over, and then approach each other folding the muslin as we went along. After this procedure the turbans would be stacked one upon another. I learnt of the five k's: (1) Kesa – the long hair which is never cut; (2) the Kangah – comb; (3) Kacha – short pants (not suitable in England); (4) Kare – metal bracelet; and (5) Kirpan – the ceremonial dagger. This was my first encounter with a truly foreign culture.

Another roommate was from the Delta State in Nigeria and he worked at Port Harcourt. I would retire at about ten o'clock, but he would study until late into the night. He was nearing the completion of his studies and seemed likely to get a promotion on his return home. He seemed concerned about his status. One night after I had retired to bed, I was suddenly awakened by my roommate. In his strong Nigerian accent, he said, "Harding, I have a great idea. I think I am going to write to my wife to get me another wife."

As a Westerner this was amazing to me; a multiplicity of wives was one thing, as I knew of Muslim plural wives as was their custom,

CHAPTER 3: A FOGGY DAY IN LONDON TOWN

but what was unique was to make such an application to one's wife – this would be anathema to a Western wife. Soon, however, I began to see the wisdom of this approach: it made sense for the new wife to have the approval of the senior wife. I don't know what eventually happened, as he left the hostel before I did. But I am still slightly annoyed that I was so rudely awakened from my sleep to hear of that brilliant idea.

It was not easy to get summer jobs in London. In Canada you would write in the spring to various firms seeking summer employment, and more often than not you would get one or two favourable replies. I had exhausted my funds and was two months in arrears at the hostel. My friend David Bacchus (whom I nicknamed D.B.) was from British Guiana, as Guyana was known then. He was also in arrears, and together we had to cope with the overhanging threat of expulsion. He got some money from home and paid the arrears for both of us. This was a favour that would bind us together.

I was offered a job as a dispatch clerk at the Schweppes soft drinks company. However, at five pounds per week, when I deducted transportation costs and lunch, I would have had to pay myself to keep the job. An African friend of mine at the hostel told me one evening that he knew where we could get a job, but I was not to disclose this to anyone, and we had to leave early in the morning. When I asked whether 7:30 a.m. would be good enough, he said, "No. Early." I wondered what job could begin that early. We got some sandwiches made the night before and took some hard-boiled eggs, for the canteen would not have been opened that early.

We set out at daybreak, walked for some distance then got a trolley bus to Acton. We were third in line at the Acton Labour Exchange. As the queue lengthened behind us we sat on the low curb wall in front of the building. Eventually someone came out of the Exchange, unlocked the front gate and said, "Nothing for you boys today." My African friend sighed and was about to depart. But I had the Jamaican temperament. I could not have got awake that early, come all that distance and be dismissed so lightly. I stayed in the line and entered the building. In the meantime a few people who were at the end of the line, maybe Hungarian refugees, were being given little green cards and sent on jobs. I believe they were being sent to Walls where they made pork pies and the like.

As the line progressed and I reached the counter, the clerk asked me, "What can I do for you?" What would anyone be doing in a Labour Exchange? I said I wanted a job. The reply was that the only job available was for an engineer. An African student who was studying engineering shouted, "I will take it!" The hall roared with laughter.

To me this was no laughing matter. I desperately needed a job to survive. I would not yield. A staring match developed between the clerk and me. He eventually asked, "Do you have a driver's licence?"

I said "Yes", and he gave me one of those little green cards.

I went into Acton where I met a kindly-looking middle-aged lady in front of what appeared to be her business place. She asked whether I had a driver's licence. I replied in the affirmative. She said, "Do you see that truck over there? Do you think you could drive it?" I said, "No, ma'am." The job being offered was to drive the truck delivering fish to various parts of London for a chain of stores called Mack Fisheries. The point is, if I could have driven that truck I would have had a job. It showed perseverance on my part.

Indeed it was a foggy day in London Town, for I could see no financial light. Gershwin's lyrics kept haunting me. I fervently hoped I would get a job, which would mean that "the sun was shining everywhere". D.B. and I were getting more desperate. It was not likely that we would get any more money from home. We went walking in Hyde Park near to the Serpentine – an artificial lake – when we saw a young man handing out tickets to some people going out on little boats. He looked like a student. We wondered where he would have got such a job. Ah . . . there must have been a Parks Department. So D.B. and I headed for the Parks Department of the London County Council.

CHAPTER 3: A FOGGY DAY IN LONDON TOWN

In preparing ourselves for a possible interview, D.B. asked me if I knew anything about gardening. I didn't, but I used to watch the gardener at my Aunt Vie's house in Jamaica. The gardener knew how to bud plants and trim them. Before we could go into any long story, the man in the Parks Department gave us two little green cards with instructions to attend at Ravenscourt Park, West of London. And off we went on the train.

When we arrived at the park, the workmen were having tea in the workmen's shed. We handed in the green cards. The foreman gave us each a stick with a sharp metal spike at the end. The object was to impale pieces of garbage and dispose of them. We were given the task to clean up the entire park. We could barely see each other from either end of the park when we started. It must have been several acres, perhaps the size of National Heroes Park in Kingston.

There was a laundry somewhere in the park. Every morning a number of West-Indian-looking women would pass us on their way to work. Whenever one of them said, "Mawnin'," I would say, "That is one of mine." At lunchtime I would lie down flat on the park bench while D.B. continued to dribble his tennis ball. I thought that would make him even more exhausted, but it seemed to relax him. Although the fog in London Town was lifting somewhat, my job was excessively tedious. There was the long train drive to the park, then the routine garbage collection. By chance, I visited the London School of Economics (LSE) and was looking at the notice board where they advertised rooms for rent, second-hand books for sale and so on, when I came across a notice that said, "Temporary Probation Officers wanted." I decided to go for an interview at the Home Office.

The applicants were asked to sit on a bench outside the room where the interviews were taking place. We sat beside two large stained oak doors some ten feet high. At last it was my turn, and the doors opened. I saw a table with three Englishmen sitting behind it. It seemed as if the table was about fifty metres away, but perhaps it was much nearer. I walked up to the desk and remained standing until I was invited to sit. The interview began with the man whose hair was totally white. "Are you a Christian?"

"Yes."

"Practising?"

"Yes."

I never discovered the relevance of the question. The next interviewer began, "Suppose you went to a house to get an interview for a probation report and they slammed the door in your face because of your colour, what would you do?"

Another interjected, "Well, it would be like throwing a brick at you."

"Yes," I said, "but it would depend on what you did with the brick."

They said in a chorus, "Yes, yes, indeed," as if I had said something very clever.

I got the job. The fog was definitely lifting. I announced to D.B. with a pseudo-British accent, "Sorry, old boy, but I have to leave you and Ravenscourt Park." I was assigned to Lambeth Magistrate's Court. I now had an office and I took over the case files of each probation officer as they went on leave. My first case required me to go to a council flat to interview a family. As I entered the foyer of this housing complex, I could smell urine. Obviously people were accustomed to relieving themselves in the foyer. I went up the stairs, knocked on the door and identified myself. The mother of the boy whose report I had to prepare opened the door and invited me in. She immediately offered me a cup of tea. Considering this a hospitable gesture, I accepted. As I began to read the file, I realized that the family had several episodes of tuberculosis. As I wrote down some information, I lifted my cup several times to my lips, but my mouth never opened. As I left the building I thought to myself, "And this is the mother country." I had never experienced this in the colonies.

I had many interesting cases. I recall the case of an old couple who wanted a divorce. They were perhaps in their late seventies. This retired couple went to the park every day. En route to the park

CHAPTER 3: A FOGGY DAY IN LONDON TOWN

they would often stop to buy candies which they would eat as they sat on the park bench feeding the birds. One morning a dispute arose. The husband complained that his wife deliberately bought hard-centred candies although she knew that he ate only soft-centred candies. In a fit of anger he took out his denture and threw it at her. This was intolerable, so now she wanted a divorce. We had to call in their children to help us resolve the matter. I thought, "Funny how little things can turn a dollop of feeling into a deluge of emotions."

I worked as a probation officer for three summers. Next in the survival kit was supply teaching. Like the probation service, this meant substituting for teachers who were on leave. You had to be a graduate, preferably with a university degree. In the first few weeks, an inspector would visit your classes to see how you interacted with the children and how you conducted your class. I was soon certified as a qualified teacher by the London County Council, and this led to my appointment at various schools.

I was assigned to Poplar Boys' School in a tough east London neighbourhood. A colleague teacher explained that some of these boys had been in borstal – a custodial institution for young offenders. I was the junior master and assigned to teach religious instruction (RI). Council rules required that RI had to be taught a certain number of hours each week. I arrived in the classroom to begin my class and I was thoroughly ignored. Some responded, "You are not serious, sir, we never do RI."

I had to assert my authority and gain control of the class. I stormed out of the classroom, went to the staffroom and returned with a cane. There was a young man at the back of the class who had his back to me and kept on talking, as if I wasn't there. I shouted, "You! Come here!" His body slowly uncoiled as he got up. He was well over six feet tall. I told him to bend over and he complied, surprisingly enough. I whacked him with the cane. It splintered, perhaps desiccated from years of lying unused in the staffroom. There was dead silence. I announced, "Genesis Chapter 1," and we began.

I was always comfortable with the Book of Genesis. Incidentally, as junior master I had no authority to cane students.

I had to take the boys on Saturday mornings to Hackney Marshes to play football, often in the fog. The boys would smoke in my presence and I would say nothing, as they were not on the school premises. I developed a kind of bond with them because of these extracurricular activities. This was not a grammar school and I soon learnt that the approach was more like, "Alright, men, get out your T-squares."

I continued teaching during my years at the LSE. Being a full-time student, I was required by the regulations to attend tutorials. I had a class in the afternoon a couple of times a week with Professor Wheatcroft who taught the Law of Trust and Equity. I had to be on time. There was a bus stop about two hundred metres from Poplar Boys' School. The bus was scheduled to leave at 3:30 p.m. If I missed that bus I would not make my connection to the underground and would be late for my tutorial. Some afternoons I literally had to run to ensure that I did not miss that bus. Dr. Vernon Meikle from Mandeville also taught at Poplar Boys' School. Years later I discovered that he was a cousin of General Colin Powell, secretary of state in the administration of George W. Bush, the forty-third president of the United States.

In Poplar I went into a local restaurant one day and ordered a hamburger and a glass of milk. I was ignored. I could not understand why I was not served. It turned out to be an orthodox Jewish restaurant and I soon learnt that their dietary laws did not allow eating meat and dairy products at the same meal. There was more information about Jewish traditions that I would discover when I taught at a modern secondary school, Robert Montefiore, in east London. The students were mostly Jewish. A beautiful little brown-eyed boy asked me one day, "Sir, when is Hanukkah?" I didn't know. If a child had asked you about Christmas and you didn't know the date, wouldn't you look silly? At the break period I consulted a Jewish colleague and was able to sound knowledgeable when I returned to

CHAPTER 3: A FOGGY DAY IN LONDON TOWN

the class and gave the right answer. Tom Theobalds, who became a lawyer and subsequently worked at the Bank of Jamaica before his retirement, also taught at that school.

Another institution where I taught was the Sedgehill Comprehensive School in Kent. It was a large school; the physical education department had about fifteen male and female staff members. I taught the first-year students who were about eleven or twelve years old. They were a pleasure to teach. This was a well-organized school and the children were well-behaved. As far as I was concerned, the fog in London Town had finally lifted. My efforts to find a suitable job had paid off. I recall one of my aunts in Jamaica asking me in a letter what I was doing in England. I facetiously replied that I was teaching English to the English, which was true. My teaching experience in London was not unlike the atmosphere described by E.R. Braithwaite in his book *To Sir with Love*.

The LSE, a college of the University of London, contrasted strikingly with McGill University. There were no lawns, no ginkgo tree, and no subterranean tunnels to escape the winter snow. This was an urban campus with buildings connected to buildings; elevators constantly in motion, students moving from lecture to lecture, to the coffee bar, to the Three Ton Pub across the road. All these activities in the heart of the great city of London, near to the High Courts, near to Fleet Street – the capital of the newspaper empire, near to the Strand with the classic and famous Savoy Hotel, near to the Royal Opera House, to Covent Garden, near to everything.

The LSE was a cosmopolitan institution in which every nationality could be found: Asian, African, European, Caribbean people and nationals of the Middle East countries. Among the Caribbean students were P.J. Patterson, Shirley Meikle (later Miller), Jackie Farrell (later Zewenes), Angela Lewis (later Hudson-Phillips), Shirley Field-Ridley (later Patterson), Dunbar McIntyre, Leroy Taylor and David Simmons. For the law students, London University provided an inter-college system: some lectures were given at University College, others at King's

College and the LSE. Shirley Meikle was a year ahead of me at the LSE. She was a very slim girl who had come to the LSE on a scholarship from Jamaica. She was a very determined, serious student. I was the only Caribbean student in my year. I was elected by my class as president of the Law Society, the organization for law students. I was also on the board of *Obiter*, the legal publication compiled by law students.

Angela, Jackie and Shirley were in my year but they were at King's College. Shirley Field-Ridley was a pretty, bright-eyed girl from British Guiana who later became the wife of P.J. Patterson. This would be her first marriage. Patterson won the Sir Hughes Parry prize and was expected to enter the world of academia. But that was neither his inclination nor his destiny. Every summer he would return to Jamaica. I could not even afford a single trip. It came to my knowledge later that he was campaigning with Norman Manley, the leader of the People's National Party. P.J.'s eyes were focused on politics. He would later become the longest-serving prime minister of Jamaica, finally demitting office in 2006.

Angela Lewis, whose father was Sir Arthur Lewis, chancellor of the University of the West Indies, married Archie Hudson-Phillips, a medical doctor. Angela specialized in taxation and resided in Jamaica. Jackie Farrell married Kwesi Zewenes, a law student from Ghana. Leroy Taylor gained a doctorate in econometrics, the first such degree granted at the LSE. Shirley Field-Ridley would eventually leave Jamaica to enter the political arena in Guyana where she served as a cabinet minister before her untimely death in 1982. Dunbar McIntyre became a banker in Trinidad; David Simmons became chief justice of Barbados and the first Caribbean person to receive an honorary LLD from the London School of Economics.

A bleak dawn broke in London on March 21, 1960. Indeed, it was a bleak day in South Africa, and I daresay a bleak day in the world. It was the day of the Sharpeville massacre, when South African police shot at a crowd of unarmed black South Africans. As the news

CHAPTER 3: A FOGGY DAY IN LONDON TOWN

broke, the students at the LSE began assembling in the main lecture theatre. They decided to have a protest march, what the English sometimes called a "demo". It was quite spontaneous, unlike the Aldermaston marches organized by the British anti-war Campaign for Nuclear Disarmament (CND) in the 1950s and 1960s. Those protest demonstrations took place every Easter weekend between the Atomic Weapons Research Establishment at Aldermaston in Berkshire, England, and London, over a distance of fifty-two miles.

I never took part in the Aldermaston marches. To me they were local matters, although the question of atomic bombs was certainly universal. But the shooting of unarmed, oppressed, defenceless people was an entirely different matter. It tore me up inside. The hurriedly made cardboard placards were stuffed beneath our jackets and "macs" as we began trooping along the Strand toward South Africa House – their High Commission, near Trafalgar Square. The action was spontaneous. As we got near to South Africa House the police arrived. The British "bobbies" shouted, "Move and keep moving!" We kept moving until the marchers began to encircle the building. As we reached the front of the High Commission, the chorus went up with voices in unison shouting, "Murderers! Murderers!" The police appeared jittery and reinforcements arrived. My Ghanaian classmate and friend Kwesi was on my left towards the street. I glanced around in time to see the police in a well-rehearsed wrestler's neck hold bundling him into the back of a squad car. As the police repeated, "Move and keep on moving," I kept on moving, perhaps a little more quickly than before. Kwesi was arrested and charged.

The following day, L.C.B. Gower, the famous academic lawyer and chairman of the law department, appeared on behalf of Kwesi in the Magistrate's Court. The magistrate, an old grey-haired man who appeared arrogant, intolerant and impatient, asked Professor Gower, "Are you a solicitor or a barrister?"

"Solicitor," replied Professor Gower.

"Very well then, I will hear you." Kwesi was fined. We became very worried, for to have reached this far in one's career and to forfeit being called to the Bar because of a conviction, what a punishment! Subsequently, at his Inn, the Benchers enquired into the incident and implicitly supported the students' action. Kwesi was admitted to the Bar. I heard he got letters of commendation from President Kwame Nkrumah and other international personalities. He married Jackie Farrell and she accompanied him home to Ghana. Sometime in the 1990s, P.J. Patterson, Angela and Archie Hudson-Phillips, Kwesi and Jackie Zewenes, and my wife Marigold and myself had a little reunion when the Zewenes passed through Jamaica.

We had now outgrown hostel life at Hans Crescent. In any event the hostel was a stopover to accommodate new arrivals and allow them time for integration; it was never intended to be a permanent residence. We found a flat on Goldhurst Terrace in the Finchley Road area in North West London, an acceptable area. My flatmates consisted of David Bacchus (British Guiana), Leroy Taylor (Jamaica), Milo Butler (Bahamas) and Colin Major (England). I was the fifth member of the group. Leroy Taylor always had to have the single room; the rest of us shared double rooms.

The flat upstairs was occupied by three English girls, some of whom were schoolteachers. Colin Major eventually married one of these young ladies and left the flat. Milo Butler married a girl from Liberia and also moved out. A group of beer-guzzling Australians lived in the flat below us. Crates filled with empty beer bottles were always piled up outside their front door. We lived at another time in Woodbury in the north of London and at Buckland Crescent near the Swiss Cottage underground station. At other times the sharing partners were Enos Grant of Jamaica and Samuel E. Wilson of British Guiana.

In the same neighbourhood lived Anthony "Tony" Spaulding. On a Sunday we would gather at one of the flats where we would listen to jazz music. Leroy Taylor was a fan of Ahmad Jamal. Tony was also a music lover. If we got a bottle of rum we would all share

CHAPTER 3: A FOGGY DAY IN LONDON TOWN

it until it was finished. Tony Spaulding was very disruptive, always criticizing and disagreeing with the choice of music. Sometimes he would walk around the flat barefooted. We would meet again years later in Jamaica. He gained fame as a criminal lawyer before serving as minister of housing in the PNP administration of the 1970s under Michael Manley. He died in 1998 at the age of sixty-four.

In 1969 I attended a conference in Guyana and met with Sammy Wilson. He was now a practising lawyer. The profession had rules about advertising, but perhaps they were not applicable in Guyana. Sammy Wilson's office had a huge sign – "Samuel Eustace Wilson". We had a wonderful reunion as he attended some of the official functions with me. Sadly, sometime afterwards Enos Grant referred me to a news item in the *Gleaner* newspaper where it was reported that Sammy had been murdered in his home. Apparently he was the victim of some domestic tragedy.

In 1987, Enos Grant died under tragic circumstances in Jamaica. At a Commonwealth Law Conference in 2002 at the Ritz Carlton Hotel in Montego Bay, a judge from the Bahamas told me that Milo Butler had died. His daughter had visited me at the Mona campus; we took pictures together but I never received copies of them as promised. Dr. Leroy Taylor returned to Jamaica and worked at the Institute of Social and Economic Research on the Mona campus, but he subsequently retired and went abroad. David Bacchus remained a bachelor in London, but eventually migrated to New York where his relatives were living.

When we were sharing a flat in London we also shared the chores. We all learnt to cook and made our own meals. One Christmas it was my turn to cook the turkey. I realized that if I failed on that occasion I might have to face the hangman's noose. Fortunately it went well. D.B. used to cook on a Tuesday. His specialty was minced meat. Some years later when I visited London he had me over for dinner. As a bachelor he was still doing his own cooking. It was a

Tuesday. Would you like to guess the menu? It was minced meat. I never knew what conclusion to draw.

The flat-sharing arrangement fell apart as some members got married; others had completed their courses and returned home. I had now joined the Foreign Service and was gainfully employed, so I began to search for my own accommodation. A classmate of mine at the LSE, Armour from Rhodesia, assisted me. A friend of his, an architect from Rhodesia, was giving up his flat in the same Swiss Cottage and Finchley Road northwest area. The flat consisted of a bedroom, a kitchen and a large living room, where half-finished pieces of sculpture and carvings were displayed. But the outstanding feature was that it had central heating – a boon in cold, damp, foggy London Town.

My friend Armour directed me to the house agents in Kilburn High Road, Barton and Cohen. I presented myself and announced that I was the person who had called about the flat. A one-sided conversation ensued, with the agent simply saying "yes" and "yes". Eventually I asked whether he would like a bank reference – the English always seemed to like that. "All right," he said.

After this most unsatisfactory encounter I reported to my friend what had transpired. He called the house agents. They reportedly said, "Mr. Harding is a very charming fellow, but he is a Jamaican, you know…I have nothing against Jamaicans, but the other tenants…you know . . ."

My two Rhodesian friends simply advised me to move in and to continue paying the rent. So I did! When I moved in I discovered that the ground floor was occupied by two Canadian lesbians. One was an actress and the other a wardrobe mistress. They were wonderful people; they took me to Kent to see Sir Laurence Olivier perform in one of Shakespeare's famous plays. We became great friends. I was on the first floor. Above me was a Hungarian refugee who was employed in the kitchen at the Savoy Hotel. On the top floor lived Lino, a French-speaking North African along with his wife, a little girl, and

CHAPTER 3: A FOGGY DAY IN LONDON TOWN

a Russian-speaking mother-in-law; his best friend was a Chinese Malaysian doctor who gave up medicine and became an entrepreneur. Some of his endeavours included manufacturing plastic toys which were put into Kellogg's cornflakes boxes. All these tenants had nothing against Jamaicans.

There were lots of parties, theatre-going, dining out on Greek Street in Soho, or visiting night clubs. Sometimes I would meet Ken Abendana Spencer – the renowned Jamaican artist. He was a man about town. He had free passage throughout London, including the underworld, it was alleged. One late night, or perhaps it was early morning, he took me to a club in Soho where musicians would go to jam after they had finished their gig. A bearded, cast-eyed Spencer was sporting a well-worn beret. As we were about to go down into the basement where the music was playing, a voice shouted from below, "Youse musicians?"

Spencer replied, "Yes, we is, man." They invited us to come on down. I must have been the most unlikely-looking musician. The atmosphere was choking, and it was not cigarette smoke alone – it was suffocating, but I heard the most heavenly sounds you could imagine. They were playing for themselves, free-form jazz, sounds that could never be replicated. The music was celestial.

Ken Abendana Spencer was an interesting man. He created his own legend. He was reported to have sired some twelve offspring, including one allegedly with an English duchess. According to him, he was descended from an outside child sired by a member of the Royal Family who had visited Jamaica as a young man. Strangely enough, he bore some resemblance to Edward VII. Spencer was once given an eviction notice from a council flat in which he was living in London. When he went to court the order was not only reversed, but he was given an indefinite extension. We would meet again in Jamaica years later.

The late Keith Gilfillian in his bachelor days had many parties at 21 Frognal Avenue near to the Finchley Road subway exit. The girls were mostly Continentals. These were fun parties, sometimes a little risqué but never obscene. On one such occasion when I entered the flat, I noticed that there were ladies' panties hanging in the entrance as if on a clothes line. I thought, "How untidy! Surely they could have removed them before the guests arrived." I later discovered that before entering, all these ladies' unmentionables had to be removed and hung on the line. Nothing untoward took place, but the realization that all our female dancing partners had removed their undergarments created a titillating atmosphere. In the bistro nearby was Ram John Holder from British Guiana singing and strumming his guitar. Eventually he appeared on a weekly British television comedy about West Indian life in England. The setting was a barber shop. It was called *Desmond's* and starred Norman Beaton.

Among some of the new friends I met in London was a young Englishwoman named Margaret Tynski who appeared to be estranged from her immediate family. The fact that she was pregnant for a black man, a Jamaican musician named Joe Harriott, no doubt accounted for this estrangement. Because of her dilemma, three of us – Enos Grant, David Bacchus and myself – virtually adopted her. Born in 1928, Joe Harriott had attended Alpha Boys' School which produced a number of prominent Jamaican musicians, many of whom migrated to the UK in the 1950s. Joe became a pioneer of free-form jazz, his principal instrument being the alto sax. He died in Southampton in 1973. Margaret gave birth to a son whom she named Zachary, and I agreed to be his godfather. She changed her name to Renata and subsequently married a West African named Hutton-Mills who became Zachary's stepfather.

Over the years Renata kept in touch with me, and I learnt that Zachary eventually joined the Royal Tank Regiment of the British army. He was stationed in Germany, where he would meet his future wife. He always expressed the desire to find out about his father's roots, and pursued this mission when he visited us in Jamaica in 1975. I took him to Alpha Boys' School where he was thrilled to meet

CHAPTER 3: A FOGGY DAY IN LONDON TOWN

Sister Mary Ignatius and to hear the stories she recounted about his father Joe Harriott. In the summer of 2010, Zachary's daughter Nadja came to spend some time with us and wanted to meet some of her grandfather's relatives, but we were unable to make contact with them. Her visit was a most enjoyable one for us all until she left to continue her studies in Spain. I am still in touch with her grandmother Renata.

Numerous friends kept dropping by my flat in London. Although this staved off loneliness, sometimes it may have been better to be alone. There was a Jamaican friend, simply called Smith, brother of the then powerful A.B. Smith, chief personnel officer in the Jamaican civil service, and Fifi Smith, secretary to the governor general of Jamaica. He came to London to study but did not complete his course, and ended up becoming an alcoholic. It was embarrassing and inconvenient for me, because whenever he visited I had to make sure that all alcoholic beverages were hidden. He would ring my doorbell at two or three o'clock in the morning. I soon learnt to stuff the doorbell so that whenever someone rang it, it would not register. On those early-morning visits he was not boisterous, but maudlin. He and his brothers had attended Kingston College, and he would relive every cricket match he had played with his brother Fifi, describing each stroke and how many runs were made off each ball. Frankly, I found Smith's sentimental reminiscences boring. His brothers in Jamaica were always asking me if I had heard from him, but I lost track of him after a while.

Then there was Ellie Kissonergist and my Greek Cypriot friends. I became like a member of the family. I started to learn modern Greek. But life was too complicated, and because of my yearning to go back home I had to avoid any personal involvement. Years later, after I returned to Jamaica, my housekeeper advised me one day that I had a visitor from "foreign" who was next door at a house party waiting for me to come home. It was Ellie, unannounced. She claimed that she had written from New York, but I had not received any correspondence. I was very busy and was going off the island, so I asked a friend to show her around. I was later told that she had married a Greek banker and was living in Cyprus. She was a beautiful person inside and out: her father was Greek and her mother Ethiopian.

While we were students in London there was a member of the group who dropped out of sight after a while. I did wonder what had happened to her. Perhaps she had gone back home. I think she was either from Bermuda or the Bahamas. One day, much to my surprise and pleasure, my telephone rang and there she was. She had got married and now had a baby. She invited me to come over and have lunch with her and her husband. I was delighted, not only at the thought of seeing her and her new family, but lunch or dinner was always a welcome invitation from student days.

She had told me nothing about her husband except that he was a journalist from Nigeria. To my surprise, perhaps shock, he was an albino – someone we called a "dundus" in our native Creole. He was charming, eloquent and friendly, but all through lunch I could not help constantly glancing at him through the corner of my eyes. I thought he looked raw – but rawness is olfactory rather than visual, and I did not smell anything. When reliving the experience, I later remembered the movie *Guess Who's Coming to Dinner*, starring the Bahamian/American black actor Sydney Poitier and Spencer Tracey as his fiancée's father. I then wondered whether that was the feeling white people would have if we came to dinner. It was prejudice, totally unfounded and irrational. My power of reasoning made me overcome this prejudice. Many years later in the Jaycees movement, I met an albino girl who was quite pretty and charming; when she was to receive an award presented by me, I hugged her and kissed her on the cheek. Clearly I had overcome my prejudice against albinos.

While I was at the High Commission in London, Brother Sam Clayton, a Rastafarian who was later associated with the Mystic Revelation, came to see me. He was travelling with other Rastafarians

CHAPTER 3: A FOGGY DAY IN LONDON TOWN

passing through London on their way home from Ethiopia. They were a little short of cash and might have got stranded in London. They had some animal skins which they had brought with them and I was able to find a merchant in London who bought the skins from them. Much later I was told that permission was required to take the skins out of Ethiopia. I got on very well with the Rastafarians. Some of the staff at the High Commission had negative attitudes towards Rastafarians and felt that my having a beard perhaps explained my affinity for them. I readily discovered that I had no prejudice against Rastafarians. In fact, I too was not a pork eater.

Because of my interest in art I became associated with many persons who were probably gay, though I did not know for certain. Many of them I found very artistic, very creative, and often very talented. I had a good friend who, like myself, had antiquarian interests and who shared my passion for good wines. He had been married and had a son. One evening while we were tasting some of his excellent wines he told me that he was bisexual, and when he began showing me some pieces from his collection he brought out a painting that had a message written on the back of the canvas. I have had paintings endorsed in presentation to me and my wife, but the words on that canvas would have made a dancehall queen blush. They were in direct contrast to those little love letters we may have written in our school days to our favourite girl. I found that I did not have any prejudice against bisexuals or homosexuals, although I abhorred their lifestyle.

I also knew several people who smoked ganja (marijuana). I never indulged, not for moral or medical reasons; I was simply not interested. It was the same with gambling; I just found no attraction to that lifestyle. I always thought gamblers were fools. You can never beat the banker – short-term gains perhaps, but in the long run – never. I have no prejudice against gamblers. In life there are times when one has to take calculated risks, but that is different from habitual gambling. Confronting one's own prejudices gives a deeper insight into one's own being and reveals who we really are.

Being presented to the Queen Mother, London School of Economics, 1961

At English High School after being called to the Bar, 1963

Opening of the Jamaican High Commission, London, 1962

CHAPTER 4

Homeward Journey

At the Jamaican High Commission, in 1963 I was promoted to Second Secretary diplomatic in charge of consular affairs. In those days, official delegations from Jamaica would stay at the Savoy Hotel located in the Strand, central London. It was a traditional hotel, very conservative and dignified. I went to the Savoy to welcome Clifford Campbell, the Speaker of the House, who was returning from a Commonwealth Parliamentary meeting in East Africa. My impression of him was of a very modest man, one might even say humble. He was the epitome of a rural Jamaican schoolteacher. While we were at the Savoy, one Lord Denham, an equerry of the British Royal household, came to escort Mr. Campbell to Buckingham Palace. I helped him dress for the occasion. I lent him my cufflinks, and off he went in a state carriage. I had no idea why he had been invited to Buckingham Palace. When he returned he was Sir Clifford, Jamaica's first native governor general. I had no idea that he had been nominated as governor general.

I had to see to the governor general's attire. We were sent to a shoemaker in Haymarket, somewhere below Piccadilly Circus. His feet were measured on brown paper and traced with a pencil. This measurement was for his boots – created in a traditional way dating back many centuries. I then had to ascertain the appropriate uniform for a governor general. After consultation with the Commonwealth Relations Office, a uniform in black facecloth material such as that worn in Australia seemed appropriate. But it turned out to be unsuitable. The seventeen-ounce facecloth material was much too heavy for the tropics. I had to search for another uniform. This time I chose white, somewhat like the uniform of an officer from the Jamaican Coast Guard. But in the end there were several complaints echoing from Jamaica. It was said that Sir Clifford's stomach protruded in the lightweight material.

(Later, when I returned to Jamaica in 1965, I called on him and met Lady Campbell, a most pleasant and charming lady who gave me an anthurium plant which I used to embellish my bachelor home. "Sugar Head" was Sir Clifford's nickname, the origin of which remains a mystery to me, but it all came back in 1991 when I attended his funeral at St. Andrew Parish Church.)

In 1962, Miss Jamaica, Carole Joan Crawford, won the Miss World crown. One of the judges was Sir Leary Constantine, the well-known West Indian cricketer from Trinidad and Tobago. He told me he had given her full marks in every category. I was there the night of her coronation. I was later to accompany her on a European tour to promote Jamaica. A member of the delegation was Suzanne McManus, who at the time of writing was still working in the hotel and tourism sector in Jamaica and presently with the SuperClubs organization.

Carole was a petite beauty of about five feet three inches. She was easy to work with. While visiting France she appeared on a television programme and was asked to name her favourite French personality. She looked at me and I prompted her. "Maurice Chevalier," she replied, and that went down very well. That same night in Paris we had reservations at the world-famous Maxim's Restaurant. I was given the honour of selecting the wines. There were so many of my favourites:

CHAPTER 4: HOMEWARD JOURNEY

in the reds there were Nuits St. George; Chevalier Montrachet; Chateauneuf du Pape; and among the whites were Chablis Grand Cru and Pouilly Fuissé. For the first time, I understood what the expression "like a child in a candy shop" meant. Then came time for dinner and before us was a menu featuring some of the most exotic dishes, a gourmet's delight. Carole's mother, who accompanied us on the tour and who was nicknamed "Mutti", asked flatly for "roast beef well done". With all the exotic choices before her, her selection was underwhelming. When we arrived in Berlin, there were several cars waiting to meet us. We were whisked away to a hotel where the press was waiting – we did not realize it at the time, but we had been kidnapped. That was not the official party but a press crew, and they got a scoop on Carole's visit.

Mrs. Crawford was in constant wrangling with the *Gleaner's* Myrth Swire – complaining that Miss Farm Queen had got more publicity than her daughter. Myrth simply reported everything Mutti said in the *Gleaner*. We were all proud of our Miss World. She sent me a special First Day cover; I believe it is called – with the first issue of our Miss World on the Jamaican stamp. I never saw her again; I heard she got married and now lives overseas.

As the officer in charge of protocol at the Foreign Service, I had to meet many officials arriving at the airport, sometimes at an early hour, often struggling through thick, pre-dawn fog. Adolph Ramgeet, a Jamaican of Indian descent, was employed to the High Commission and he was my driver on these occasions. We had many conversations during these trips and he became a companion and friend. Ram was also celebrated for his ability to mix excellent Jamaican rum punch.

Jamaica's Independence Day was usually celebrated with a large cocktail party. Invitations were issued to officials of the host country, other accredited diplomats and members of the Jamaican community. Ramgeet and his wife lived in the South London area called Brixton, which was largely populated by West Indians. Some of the community leaders received their invitations, but Ramgeet and his family were overlooked. Because he worked at the High Commission, this snub embarrassed him and caused him to lose face in the community.

David Reid, an executive officer who knew of Ram's talent for making rum punch, asked him to make some for the party. Ram charged a fee of five pounds for doing the job. The High Commissioner then was Sir Laurence Lindo, a tall bald man of fair complexion. He was a chain smoker and had a pronounced stutter. Sir Laurence had gone to Oxford University at Keble College. I was told that he once acted as governor for the West Indian island of Dominica. I believe he had also worked in the Colonial Secretariat which was the pinnacle of the Colonial Civil Service. He was a gentleman, but somewhat autocratic. When Sir Laurence heard of such "impertinence" from Ram, he spoke to me about it, and although Ram had come to the hall with me to deliver supplies, Sir Laurence stuttered, "Ramgeet is not to come in here, and that is an order!" When I saw the look he gave Ram, it struck me then that the Government Service was strangely akin to the military. And so the High Commissioner and his guests were left to enjoy the rum punch prepared by a faithful co-worker who was barred from entering the hall where the function was held.

In between his work at the High Commission, Ramgeet often visited an Indian restaurant and learnt how to cook Indian food. He retired to Jamaica and opened an Indian restaurant. It began well, but faltered in the end. I last saw Ram when he came to seek legal advice on some family issue, but he passed away before I could help him.

Another person I remember fondly from my days in the Foreign Service was Deputy High Commissioner Allan Morais, who formed the Association of Deputy High Commissioners in London. He was a man of style and decorum, a connoisseur. He once took me out to dinner and sent back the wine after tasting it. Clearly he found it of inferior quality. The maitre d' apologized and sent a complimentary bottle to the table. When I first arrived at the High Commission, Mr. Morais sat me down and gave me a long list of abbreviations which

CHAPTER 4: HOMEWARD JOURNEY

I should learn, e.g. BU – bring up, KIV – keep in view, and so on. The junior officer would write a rather detailed note on a file. The senior person would write less, and the highest in command perhaps only one word – "approved" – with his initials. Mr. Morais unfortunately died in office while in London.

I learnt from Bertram "Billy" Powell, senior officer in charge of trade, that you should have only one file on your desk at any time. I tried to emulate him. I never succeeded with the one file – but I did reduce the number of files I dealt with at a time. There were also Clive McMorris, Don Brice, S.A. (Tommy) Stimpson, Hosford Scott, Patsy Pyne (Mrs. Robertson) and Arthur Bethune from the consular section, who died in a motor car accident. It was a great crew, and we set Jamaica on the map in diplomatic circles and in England.

I recall that during this time Kingston College won the Schoolboy Athletics Championships (Champs), scoring more than 100 points, a first in the history of the competition. There was a banner headline in a Jamaican paper that read, "The Glorious Purple and White," and I posted the tear sheet on my office door. No one spoke to me for the rest of that day. Except for Hosford Scott and Allan Morais, all of them had attended either Jamaica College or Wolmers.

As passport officer, I kept the staff working some evenings until 10:30 to 11:00 p.m. issuing Jamaican passports to persons surrendering their colonial passports. They took pride in their new blue national passport. "Sister Walker", an office attendant, made tea and sandwiches for us while we worked. I am told that she returned to Jamaica and retired in Portland or St. Mary. Also in the Consular section were Don and Fay Goring, Ramón Gordon, Peter King and Allan Rickards who became president of the All Island Cane Farmers Association. Peter King became an expert in trade and an assistant to that famous Jamaican Minister of Trade and Industry, the Honourable Robert Lightbourne.

King and I would meet several times years later in Jamaica. We often spoke about Cecil Baugh's pottery. His aunt, a retired nurse, had left him a large collection of early Baughs. We also spoke about his coffee farm and the day his new pick-up truck caught fire. I was to see Peter for the last time at a function at the French Embassy in Jamaica one Friday evening in 2006. We reminisced about our days at the London High Commission. He died that weekend under tragic circumstances.

Fay Goring (née MacDonald) turned out to be a relative of mine. My grandfather Edward Levy and her grandfather Clem MacDonald were brothers of the half-blood Elizabeth Garvey who had married twice, once to MacDonald and once to Levy. She was Marcus Garvey's aunt. The nearest that I have been to Marcus Garvey was standing beside his coffin in 1964 after he was disinterred as a result of the efforts of Edward Seaga to have him buried in Jamaica's National Heroes Park.

Another colleague at the High Commission was Rupert Miller, a retired teacher. He had also taught at Kingston College where some of the boys nicknamed him "Hawkeye". He acquired that name because he was totally deaf, but this deficiency was compensated by his excellent vision. He could see every movement or action right to the back of the classroom. Although he was forced to wear a double hearing aid, he was studying German, Italian and French well into his retirement years. Rupert Miller was an extraordinary person. I recall two of his favourite sayings: "I would prefer to wear out than to rust out," and "Always remember that the people you meet on your way up in life are the same people you will meet on your way down."

The 1962 Commonwealth Prime Ministers' conference was held in London at Marlborough House. Alexander Bustamante, Jamaica's prime minister, was in attendance accompanied by Lady Bustamante. I was assigned to Sir Alexander as his aide-de-camp. It was on that occasion that I got to know the man who was to become Jamaica's first national hero during his lifetime. We were often together alone and I got an insight into this great human being. He displayed a genuine concern and love for people. He was incisive in his observations but also very endearing.

CHAPTER 4: HOMEWARD JOURNEY

We paid a courtesy call on Harold Macmillan, prime minister of Britain, at Admiralty House. On leaving, Bustamante said to me in his inimitable way of speaking, "Son, what do you think of Mr. Macmillan?" I replied, "I think he is a very conservative gentleman, sir." Busta snapped, "Conservative? Macmillan, Macmillan is a snob!" Later that day I had occasion to speak to one of the English drivers assigned to our delegation. He said he used to drive for Mr. Macmillan who travelled with a male secretary, and whenever the prime minister wanted to give the driver instructions he would speak through his secretary. Of course I have no idea whether the story was true, but if it were, perhaps Mr. Macmillan was indeed a snob.

On one occasion, Sir Alexander and I were travelling to a meeting, and as we were passing Trafalgar Square we noticed that a public meeting was in progress. He asked me what kind of meeting it was. I said I thought it was a Common Market meeting. He asked, "For or against?" I replied that I thought it was against. He said, "Let's stop." I knew he loved crowds. The security officer alighted from the front of the car; he did not seem very comfortable and he loosened his jacket. I thought I saw a firearm: a head of government going into a crowd in a public place was not to be taken lightly. I was comfortable until I saw the unease of the officer. As Sir Alexander began to enter the crowd, a cameraman was almost struck by a vehicle as he tried to take a photograph. Looking elegant in his bowler hat, Bustamante was featured on the front page of the *Daily Mail* next day above the caption: "Commonwealth Prime Minister attends Anti-Common Market meeting". Busta was to say subsequently that the Common Market was like a dagger at the heart of the Commonwealth.

At the conference Bustamante sat beside Sir Raphael "Roy" Welensky, prime minister of Rhodesia and Nyasaland – today's Zimbabwe. Rhodesia operated a racist regime somewhat akin to apartheid. Dr. Eric Williams, prime minister of Trinidad and Tobago, was addressing his Commonwealth colleagues. He spoke extensively on the Common

Market. In fact, one might say he gave a lecture to those present. Bustamante was clearly bored. Dr. Williams' intervention lasted for more than an hour. Busta turned to Sir Roy and said, "I am going to send that man to your country", and Sir Roy simply smiled. Then Bustamante said to him, "Is it true that in your country three black men's votes are only equal to one white man's vote?" I was astonished, but then I recalled the question allegedly posed by Busta to Her Royal Highness Princess Margaret (when she visited during Jamaica's Independence celebrations in 1962), "How is your sister?" To which she replied, "Do you mean Her Majesty the Queen?" He supposedly said, "Yes, your sister." However, Sir Roy did not seem offended by Busta's question. In fact, both men ended up arguing afterwards about who would travel in whose car at the end of the meeting.

At this conference, I also met Sir Alec Douglas-Home who was later to become prime minister of Great Britain. He was a most affable man. He met me in the lounge and perhaps noting my discomfort, asked me whether it was my first conference. He put me at ease. Among those attending the conference were Jawaharlal Nehru of India, John Diefenbaker of Canada, Liaquat Ali Khan of Pakistan and Kwame Nkrumah of Ghana. The young cabinet ministers Ken Jones, Dr. Herbert Eldermire and Clem Tavares, who were part of the Jamaican delegation, seemed to have been organizing something for that evening. But the prime minister had other ideas. He said we were having dinner at the Spanish restaurant Martinez on Swallow Street near to Piccadilly Circus. Bustamante spoke some Spanish on entering the restaurant, but it sounded to me like street Spanish.

He was very quiet during dinner. The ministers were talking about the day's events. They spoke about the grand entrance that Kwame Nkrumah of Ghana had made, accompanied by outriders and all. He greeted his African brothers with a kiss on both cheeks. However, when he came to Eric Williams, he kissed him on one cheek only. They jokingly wondered whether that meant Williams was half-African.

CHAPTER 4: HOMEWARD JOURNEY

Bustamante suddenly asked me, "Where is the driver?" An Englishman had been assigned to us to be our driver for the duration of the conference. I said, "I don't see him, sir, it is difficult to get parking around here." He still seemed a little uneasy. A few minutes later he again asked about the driver. He then got up, with me in tow, went over to the maitre d' and said, "My name is Bustamante, there is a uniformed man coming in here. Feed him." And then we returned to the table. Bustamante began to have his meal only after he saw the driver come in. I was impressed by his humanity – this was not about vote-getting, he was genuinely a caring person. I was convinced that this was a good man, and I would always support him and what he stood for.

One afternoon Bustamante received a letter from one of our countrymen in Birmingham, complaining of police brutality. He said, "Call the little girl for me." He was referring to Lois Clarke, senior secretary at the High Commission, whom we called "Dot". He then asked me who was responsible for the police. I said Mr. Ralph Butler, Minister of Home Affairs. Protocol allowed a Commonwealth minister or prime minister to write directly to his counterpart in another Commonwealth country.

He said to Dot, "Take a letter." It began, "Dear Minister…We have had complaints by our people in your country of police brutality. We do not treat your people like that in our country and we don't expect you to treat our people like that in your country." When some of the members of the delegation arrived, including Mickey Hendricks from the Jamaica Broadcasting Corporation (JBC), and heard of the letter, they tried to recast it suggesting that perhaps Bustamante should say "allegations of police brutality" and so on. Bustamante looked at Dot and said, "Read the letter for me." When she had finished reading the letter as originally dictated by him, he said, "That's just what I want," and he signed it.

I said to myself, "This man is different." Once again he was incisive and direct; there was no vacillation. But most of all he showed concern for the little people wherever they were – in Jamaica or England, whether a Jamaican or an English chauffeur.

When Pope John XXIII died on June 17, 1963, I accompanied High Commissioner Lindo to the funeral at St. Peter's in the Vatican, Rome. We were in the Sistine Chapel. As the cardinals in their scarlet robes went around the catafalque incensing the body, reciting the Pater Noster with the rolling "r's" so characteristic of Italian Latin, suddenly we heard a high-pitched, nasal Pater Noster minus the rolling "r's". It was the American cardinal. That evening, we had dinner with some of the cardinals. When they learnt that I was from Jamaica they asked if I knew Monsignor Gladstone Wilson. They remembered him well because they had played friendly football games together in Rome some years before. They asked me to convey their greetings to him. I did not know Monsignor Wilson but I had heard great things about him. Unfortunately he died before I could convey the greetings from Rome.

Many years later, in 2009, I presented Archbishop Don Reece with a copy of the Pope's funeral service of 1963 for the archives, and related to him the story of the cardinals and their greetings to Monsignor Gladstone Wilson. His contemporaries in Rome had reached the status of cardinals. I am told that the Monsignor, in addition to being very brilliant, was fluent in many languages. Was it his race that had retarded his advancement in the church?

I recall an incident involving Sir Egerton Richardson while I served as protocol officer at the High Commission in London. Sir Egerton was a powerful civil servant, a former financial secretary, a black man who had scaled the heights of the colonial system. He had worked in the Colonial Secretariat, been made a permanent secretary, but never fulfilled his ambition to become governor of the Bank of Jamaica. A kingmaker in his own right, he was Jamaica's ambassador to Washington and a personal friend of Hugh Shearer who would later become prime minister of Jamaica.

Sir Egerton had arrived from Jamaica for an official visit to Germany. The High Commission had not yet acquired an official car and the

CHAPTER 4: HOMEWARD JOURNEY

car company from which cars were rented would hire an old Rolls-Royce to take officials around. On that occasion, the rented car had a partition separating the driver from the passengers in the back seat. Dawn Bitter, a young lady from a well-known Jamaican family, asked me if she could get a lift to Bisley where they had the annual rifle competition in which Jamaicans always competed. Bisley was not far from the airport. I asked Sir Egerton if I could give a lift to the young lady and he agreed. She rode in the front section with the driver, separated from us by a glass partition, while the ambassador and I sat in the back so that there was no inconvenience to him.

When we arrived at the airport we were taken to the VIP lounge and I went in search of the Lufthansa official. I was told by the receptionist that the passenger agent was on the tarmac and would soon come to attend to the Ambassador. In my absence someone apparently told him that he was in the wrong lounge, that this was the arrival lounge, not the departure lounge, so he should go back outside to enter the departure lounge. When I returned there was no sign of Sir Egerton in the VIP lounge. With some trepidation I called the High Commission immediately and spoke to Deputy High Commissioner Morais. I was quite worried about the possible cancellation of an official trip, and knowing the influence of Ambassador Richardson I thought that I would get a good dressing-down, although I had followed the instructions of the passenger agent to the letter.

I found out later that the hired car transported Sir Egerton to the front of the airport to access the lounge. As he alighted from the car, however, the liveried chauffeur closed the door and inadvertently smashed the tip of an expensive umbrella which the ambassador had acquired the previous day. This was the last straw. In a rage, Sir Egerton threw down the umbrella, jumped back into the car and returned to London, where he announced in high dudgeon that he would no longer be making the trip to Germany.

Surprisingly, Morais simply said to me: "Don't worry about it. I know Richie." Subsequently I heard that Sir Egerton had complained that I had given a lift to Dawn Bitter. The next day I had his umbrella repaired. They simply replaced the tip. He asked me how much it cost and I said two shillings and sixpence. I was never refunded. I was therefore surprised to learn that when I was subsequently appointed as a chargé d'affaires to Mexico Sir Egerton had inquired who I was, whether I was married or had any children. I could not believe that he did not recall that incident.

I will never forget the day I bought a Rolls-Royce. It so happened that Fred M. Jones, landowner, farmer, and philanthropist from Portland, Jamaica, visited London during my tour of duty there. I suppose in the old days he may have been called a planter. I later came to learn that he was the father of the twins Keith and Ken Jones. Ken became a minister in Bustamante's administration. The Joneses were the founders of the Happy Grove High School in Portland.

Fred M. was on his way to Australia to attend a cricket Test match. He asked me if I could buy a Rolls-Royce for him. I agreed and he left the necessary papers and the bank arrangements with me. I went to a Rolls-Royce dealership at the end of Bruton Street and Berkeley Square – the one immortalized in song by American jazz pianist Fats Waller who made a hit about the nightingale singing in Berkeley Square. Of course, there had never been any nightingale in Berkeley Square – but that is another story.

I entered the car showroom and started looking around. A well-dressed salesman approached me and with an upper-class English accent asked, "See anything you fancy, sir?"

"Yes," I replied. "That Rolls-Royce over there."

He escorted me to the car and we inspected it. I said, "Very well, I will take it."

"Your address, sir?" the salesman asked. I gave him the High Commission's address at Bruton Street.

A few days later some of my colleagues at the High Commission called out to me with great amusement, "Harding, there is a man downstairs asking where he should deliver your Rolls-Royce."

CHAPTER 4: HOMEWARD JOURNEY

I shot back, "Damn fool, he is to ship it to Jamaica." Of course, my colleagues were dumbfounded. Within a few days the car salesman wanted to sell me a small car "to run around London", but I did not need one. To me, what was most interesting was that if a gentleman said, 'I will take it', that was the end of the matter; the item was sold.

The Rolls-Royce reached Jamaica safely. I learnt that later it was bought by the Hon. Russell Graham, Custos of St. Andrew. It was used in a movie scene here in Jamaica and ultimately ended up in the United States. Years later I was able to relate the story to Mrs. Mary Langford, Fred M's daughter. Truth be told, I did buy a Rolls-Royce, even though it wasn't mine.

When I returned to Jamaica in 1965, I was almost a stranger in my own land. I made arrangements to stay for a while with Stan Moore, my friend from McGill University, and his wife Sheila. I woke up the morning after my arrival, looked out the window and found myself in a Technicolour world – the reds, the oranges and the pinks were vivid, for I had become accustomed to the browns, greys and sombre tones of England.

It was a Sunday morning, and we had to have a traditional breakfast of ackee and saltfish. Stan and I went to a market at Three Miles on the Spanish Town Road to buy ackees. As we arrived there were two women vendors, known as higglers, in some sort of altercation – arms akimbo – engaged in what is locally called a tracing match. "Lemme go! Lemme go!" they were both protesting while being held back by others. It was clear that despite the bravado of their "lemme go's" they both wanted to be restrained. I sighed and said, "Yes, I am back in Jamaica."

I was assigned a government house on Palmoral Avenue in Mona Heights. It was sparsely furnished and looked across to what is now a hockey field. My car was at the wharf. A shiny black Fiat 2800 with the latest features, including an alternator instead of a generator, fancy lights in the side of the front doors and an overdrive. All I had to do was clear it. The vehicle attracted duty, for I had no diplomatic privileges in Jamaica. I was to learn the rigmarole and vicissitudes of the customs department. The customs officer, one Mr. Cespedes, did the valuation. I thought it was excessive. Perhaps it was not. Welcome home! Through a friend, I was sent to a senior civil servant who referred me to another customs officer. Yes, I had to pay the duty, but it was reduced. After all the paperwork and going to so many departments, I learnt my first lesson as a returned resident: If you need to clear something at the customs, engage the services of a customs broker.

The caretaker of the government houses at Mona Heights found me a household helper. The houses were designed with a separate room out in the backyard which was the helper's quarters. I was introduced to Madelaine, a tall, extremely thin girl. She kept the nearly empty three-bedroom precast house clean and arranged for a gardener to cut the grass. She made the beds and did some laundry. I found her satisfactory.

An incident occurred with Madelaine which is forever etched in my memory. As part of my ceramic collection, I was given one of a limited edition, a large round ashtray, signed by Picasso. The signature itself was of great value. On returning home one evening I noticed that the ashtray was missing. I asked Madelaine where it was. She simply replied "It broke, sir." I was always struck by her language. Of course she did not break it; it obviously broke itself. I asked her for the pieces, thinking perhaps I could mend it. But she had disposed of it in the garbage – and wouldn't you know it, the garbage collector, who was always late, who sometimes missed his day – had been right on time, this time. Madelaine could not understand what all the fuss was about since it was only an ashtray. She suggested that I deduct the cost from her wages. I told her that I did not believe in indentureship.

CHAPTER 4: HOMEWARD JOURNEY

My house was close to Mona Road, a main artery leading to the University of the West Indies (UWI). There was a bus stop two blocks away. I would pass people waiting at the bus stop on my way to work. On one particular morning there was a slight drizzle, and I offered a lift to a young man at the bus stop. He was tall and looked half-Chinese. He was a draughtsman in an architect's office. From then onwards I would offer Owen Yuen a lift whenever I saw him at the bus stop. One morning he was in the company of a young lady; apparently they lived in a house further up from my residence. She was tall. In high heels she appeared to be about 5 feet 10 inches, and had a slightly oriental look. He introduced me to this beautiful girl as his sister, Marigold Yuen. I would give her a lift whenever I saw her. There was something about her that caught my attention. We became friends. Whenever she passed my house on her way home she would leave a flower in the gate so I would know she had passed by. My father came from Canada to visit with me and I introduced her to him. He said he knew instantly what would transpire. In a short while it seemed that she was his daughter and I the son-in-law.

On returning to Jamaica, I decided that I wanted to practise my profession and was transferred to the Attorney General's Department where I worked under the supervision of the Honourable Victor Grant, QC, and Attorney General. While at the Attorney General's Department I took a short course at Harvard Law School. When I had successfully completed it and was on my way home, my class visited the World Bank and other international institutions. The World Bank selected me and a few others from the group to see if we might have been interested in employment. I was told what salary would be paid and that an allowance for children would be part of the emoluments. I had no children, but in any event I had no interest, because I was keen to return to Jamaica. The World Bank called me in New York indicating that they would pay my airfare to return to Washington for an interview, but I declined the offer.

While in New York I was joined by a fellow international law student who was from the Philippines. Feeling somewhat bored in the hotel, we decided to go out on the town. He asked me if I was familiar with New York and I told him I wasn't. I had heard of a neighbourhood called Greenwich Village and I thought we might go there. Much to our surprise, it was not a little village as we had imagined. We went from one bar to another, what in England we used to call a pub crawl. Many drinks later, we entered yet another bar at 2:00 a.m. Here we found barrels filled with roasted peanuts in the shell. Along with the beer one would crush peanuts and throw the empty husks on the floor. A few peanut shells would look untidy, but with so many shells on the floor it was like litter in a hen house.

There were only two other customers in the bar sitting with their backs to us. We decided to approach them and they accepted our offer to buy them a drink. They were actually two African American women – one was an assistant wardrobe mistress in an off-Broadway theatre, the other a schoolteacher. They asked my colleague where he was from. He said Manila in the Philippines. One of them engaged him in conversation, saying her brother was a G.I who had been in the Philippines. After a while one of them turned to me and asked, "Where are you from?" On hearing that I was from Jamaica, she declared, "You are those guys who don't think you are black, eh?" It was not immediately clear what she meant, but I did not regard it as a compliment.

As the conversation progressed there was much talk about "black is beautiful", a popular slogan at the time. At the first opportunity I had to re-enter the conversation, I let her have it: "Where I come from we knew we were beautiful long before we knew we were black!" Touché! A perfect squelch. Of course, we never fully understood the indignities that African Americans had to suffer. They faced problems in the schools, problems in housing, problems at the workplace and problems of self-esteem. We had problems, but our world was different. The overt racism they had to confront was not our experience.

I was quite settled in the Attorney General's Chambers acting as Crown Counsel, and I thought the Foreign Service was now behind

CHAPTER 4: HOMEWARD JOURNEY

me. But I was summoned to the Ministry of Foreign Affairs and told that Prime Minister Donald Sangster wanted me to go to Mexico to open an embassy there. If the prime minister so requested, I really had no option. I told Marigold that I was going to Mexico and asked if she would like to accompany me. She said yes. Of course it was clear what was implicit in my invitation.

We were married at Up Park Camp by the Reverend Orland Lindsay, chaplain to the Army, a Kingston College old boy who later became Anglican Archbishop of the West Indies. We decided that we would not invite anyone except two witnesses – Stan Moore, my long-standing friend, and Kathleen Kennedy, a cousin on my mother's side. Both the bride's parents decided that they were coming, as well as two of her brothers who were in Jamaica and a number of other uninvited guests. The wedding was followed by an informal family reception at our house in Mona Heights. We ended up hosting an open house at Jacisera Park, home of the Jamaica Civil Service Association. Then off we went to begin our Mexican adventure.

CHAPTER 5

To Mexico and Back

There was a feeling of excitement, but some apprehension, as would be expected when one ventures into unknown territory. My three-year tour of duty at the High Commission in London had helped to hone my skills in foreign affairs and diplomacy, but I was quite unfamiliar with Latin American culture. I had been one of the first employees when the High Commission opened its doors in 1962, but now I would be in charge of setting up Jamaica's embassy in a Spanish-speaking country.

Sir Egerton Richardson was Jamaica's ambassador to Washington with responsibility for the Embassy of Mexico. I was chargé d'affaires and reported to Kingston on consular matters.

Apart from the routine business of dealing with Jamaicans either passing through or resident in Mexico, there is a particular incident that I recall. A Jamaican painter named Stanley Barnes came to Mexico to study art restoration. When we met at the embassy he seemed somewhat indifferent, even brusque, but we extended to him the usual courtesies that we provided to all our nationals. We did not hear from him for a long time until he suddenly contacted us one day by telephone. His manner was extremely friendly, in complete contrast to his behaviour at our first meeting. He even addressed me by my Christian name although we were strangers. I would soon learn the reason for this transformation.

He explained that he was in a spot of trouble. According to his story, the water in his bathroom had overflowed and leaked into the apartment below his. The neighbours downstairs had called the police. He was afraid that if he ended up in jail he might be transferred to another location and could get lost in the prison system. He was really worried, especially as his knowledge of Spanish was very limited. Our accountant Lawrence Brown, who also had consular responsibilities, went to the rescue. The matter was resolved to the satisfaction of all.

On October 26, 1967, I had the privilege of signing amendments to the Treaty of Tlatelolco on behalf of the Jamaican government. This was a treaty for the prohibition of nuclear weapons in Latin America and the Caribbean. The treaty was further ratified by Jamaica on June 26, 1969.

The first week I arrived in Mexico I was invited to the Club Reforma, where many of the diplomats would hang out. It was expected that since I was Jamaican I had to know how to play cricket. I was immediately introduced to the batting side. I struck the ball and got a single. My partner hit a single and I went back to face the bowling. I got another single, but before I could reach halfway down the pitch, I felt as if someone was choking me. I could not breathe. A bearded Englishman, the nephew of the well-known English Labour politician Sir Stafford Cripps, came over to me and said, "Take it easy, old boy, it's the altitude." I eventually adjusted to it, but Marigold never did.

My sister Sheila paid us a visit and decided to stay on for a while. I found her a temporary job at the embassy. Despite being capable and reasonably efficient, she was accustomed to reading well into the night and arising late in the mornings. As a consequence, she was

CHAPTER 5: TO MEXICO AND BACK

always late for work although the embassy was immediately next door to the residence. This pattern of late arrivals was most unlike my father and myself, for we were both early risers and punctual.

Sheila's late arrivals were particularly embarrassing since she was my sister and was not setting a good example. I instructed our accountant Mr. Brown to adjust her salary accordingly. Sheila was most upset at this turn of events. When I came home that evening, I heard her saying to Marigold, "I don't know how you can stand that man; he is just like our father." I took that as a compliment, because my dad was principled, responsible and diligent in all his undertakings.

Sheila was interested in the entertainer Janis Joplin and wanted to learn to play the guitar. I bought her a guitar which she took with her on her return to Canada. I never heard anything more about the guitar or any attempts at music lessons. We would not see each other again for several years.

Marigold and I lived at the Hotel del Prado for six months until we found a suitable location for the embassy. Naturally we knew the menu by heart. The maître d' was so concerned that he would often bring us items from the local market. During our stay at the del Prado, someone recommended a local hairdresser and Marigold decided to try her out. She returned home in tears. The hairdresser had washed her hair in a sink usually reserved for washing dishes, and Marigold could say nothing as she spoke not a word of Spanish. When she came back and complained to me I asked, "Why didn't you go to the hairdresser in the hotel?" She decided to do just that, and so had her hair done twice in one day. I don't know whether this was the reason, but she looked like a movie star after the session. She was as beautiful as any woman could ever be.

We were very happy in Mexico. We became extremely popular with members of the diplomatic corps. We were at all the informal gatherings; they christened Marigold "Maria de oro". Cantinflas, the famous Mexican comedian who appeared the film in *Around the World in Eighty Days*, was present at one of these functions when each embassy had to perform an item. I sang Tony Bennett's signature song, "I left my heart in San Francisco". The Japanese ambassador's wife was so moved that she got all teary-eyed. It was her husband, along with Ambassador Chen (from Taiwan), who tried to encourage me to take up golf. He would tell me, "Never mind Chen and his custom-made golf clubs. Just get some clubs and let's play." Years later, after we returned to Jamaica, Chen passed through and gave us the sad news: the Japanese ambassador had collapsed on the golf course one day and died of a heart attack.

We invited guests to a reception at the embassy to celebrate Jamaica's national day in August 1967. The occasion was enlivened by the presence of a dance troupe from Jamaica who thrilled the gathering with an exciting performance. Their arrival had been arranged by Sonia Pottinger, Jamaica's first female music producer, who also provided the traditional bandana costume that Marigold wore with stunning effect. We were featured on all the front pages of Mexico's national newspapers, some in glorious colour. Newspapers are strange creatures, we soon learnt; you cannot buy the front page, but you cannot avoid being there if they deem it important. (It was with regret that we would learn in Jamaica, many years later, of Sonia Pottinger's passing on November 3, 2010.)

It was a pleasure to encounter once again a Mexican friend, Juan Barona, whom I had met at Harvard University when we were studying international law. Juan and his wife Conchita invited us to visit the pyramids on one occasion. Juan and I started to make the ascent, having left our wives at the base of the pyramid. I was unaware at the time that Marigold had decided to follow us. We were nearly at the top when someone going down called to us. Apparently Marigold was about to faint. The climber was an American and he told her to put her head in her lap so the blood would flow back to her head. The steps on the pyramid were very narrow and it would have been a real tragedy had she fallen. She had difficulty coping with the altitude, as I indicated earlier.

CHAPTER 5: TO MEXICO AND BACK

Our premises at 32 Euken Avenida were owned by a retired Mexican army official, General Anayo. When we first moved in, he had asked where was our *mozo* (houseboy). As we did not have one he sent us a young Mexican private in the army. The soldier stayed in the garage downstairs and would not enter the house. The only time he left the premises was when he had to *pasar revista* – that is, to report to the army for inspection.

The general asked whether we had a car. We did not. He asked his driver to lend us his Ford car, but it was not available. He suggested another car, but that was in the garage, and yet another one was being used by his daughter in Cuernavaca. In the end we drove to the border with Texas and bought a car for the embassy. Then there was our Mexican staff: Esperanza, our cook, and her husband Antonio who was our driver. They were devoted retainers who gave us a pen and pencil set when we left the country. There was also Freda, our helper whom we had brought from Jamaica. It was only when we applied for her passport that we realized she was over sixty.

While at the embassy, we were approached by a Frenchman who had personal contact with various vineyards in France, and who seemed to be an authority on wines. He was well known in the diplomatic community. After we placed our usual order, he told us about a new wine which he said was excellent, and encouraged us to buy a case. This special wine took quite some time to arrive. During the waiting period Freda heard us talking about the long delay for the delivery of this special wine. Finally it arrived, and we thought we would have an informal dinner with some of our friends to introduce this excellent wine. It was good, but not as extraordinary as we had imagined.

The residence was like a Spanish castle. A winding staircase led to the staff quarters located upstairs. During the dinner Freda was obviously enjoying the special new wine. She seemed to have had her own wine-tasting. At the end of the function she was a little intoxicated. Before going to her quarters she came to Marigold and said, "Ma'am, it's nothing like our good old Jamaican Porto Pruno."

So much for our 'great' wine. Freda was barely able to ascend to her quarters. Porto Pruno was a well-known Jamaican wine sometimes used in making a punch or, more often, in making cakes. It was a strong inexpensive wine, not served with dinner. Freda was clearly not impressed with our new wine. When we relocated to Jamaica she returned to her house somewhere behind the Kingston Public Hospital. We never saw her again.

On the street immediately beside the embassy there was a little native Indian woman, her black hair well greased upon her head, selling her tortillas from a small wagon. She was a little scruffy, with large cracks in the heels of her bare feet. We were urged to have her removed from the side of the embassy. This I stoutly resisted. After all, she had occupied that spot every day before the embassy had been located there. I certainly did not want to create a diplomatic incident. In any event our Mexican staff, Esperanza and Antonio, would go out and buy her tortillas as they seemed unconcerned about her cleanliness or lack thereof.

After spending an enjoyable year in Mexico, I was to be transferred to Geneva. It seems "Richie" had his candidate for Mexico. Many years later, my friend Thomas "Tommy" Stimpson, whom Sir Egerton had first sent to Mexico when I was transferred, related the following in a letter:

> *Ossie Harding had not been Sir Egerton's choice for the post to Mexico. It seemed to have been the choice of Mr. Hector Wynter and Sir Donald Sangster. As soon as Mr. Hugh Shearer became Prime Minister and elevated Sir Egerton as ambassador to Washington, the latter decided to replace Harding with someone of his choice.*

The ambassador to Geneva was Ken (K.B.) Scott whom I had met in London on his various visits. He somehow adopted me and would give me advice whenever he passed through. He once asked me if I had any life insurance. Although I asked him why I needed it, I then

CHAPTER 5: TO MEXICO AND BACK

took out my first life insurance policy. On another occasion he asked me whether I was a member of the civil service Thrift Society, a credit union. He indicated that on my return to Jamaica I might need to borrow money to purchase motor car tyres or something, so I joined the Jamaica Mutual Thrift. I wondered if it was because of this relationship that Ambassador Scott had requested that I join him in Geneva.

Marigold and I were enjoying home leave in Jamaica before going to Geneva. I recall a vivid picture of Henri Poincaré, the French mathematician who solved a theorem as he stepped onto a tramcar in Paris. As we were crossing the train lines in May Pen coming from Milk River bath one day, like Poincaré I was struck by something, and there followed a strange conversation.

"Darling," I asked Marigold, "do you want to go to Geneva? I'm not so sure about it."

"I don't think I want to go," she replied.

"Well," I said, "if you don't want to go, we don't have to go." A career decision was taken that we would not go to Geneva. I am sorry if Ambassador Scott was disappointed. I was perhaps somewhat arrogant, maybe rightly so. Why should men like Sir Egerton, though he was an excellent civil servant and a highly intelligent person, determine my future?

I went to Victor Grant, the attorney general, and asked if I could have my old job back. He jokingly said that big diplomats like me would not want to work in the Attorney General's Department. Mr. A.B. Smith, the chief personnel officer, said there was no vacancy in the department. Were they trying to force me to go to Geneva? By this time I had learnt how to play the game. I went on leave. When they realized that I was firm in my resolve, I was returned to the Attorney General's Department. But it would not be for long.

The reports I later received were that "Richie's" candidate was a disaster in Mexico. He was not in the Foreign Service – in fact, he was not even a civil servant. It is said he was studying for his PhD, but I don't know if he ever completed it. His wife, a New Yorker originally from Jamaica, chose to remain in New York, and his alleged flirtations in Mexico were frowned upon within the diplomatic circles. That was my replacement, Lloyd Wright. But that was not the last we would hear of him. We had moved to a house in Jacks Hill with more land space so that Marigold could indulge in her horticultural pursuits. The house in Hope Pastures was sold to a Jamaican chef who worked in the Bahamas. He rented the house to "my replacement", who came and almost evicted us.

Subsequently we heard that Lloyd Wright was rearing goats in the country and was making goat's milk cheese. I later became aware of an unexpected family connection. I discovered that my aunt Gladys Wright, who was my father's 'sister by the half-blood', was also the aunt of "my replacement", as she was his father's 'sister by the half-blood'. So Lloyd Wright and I had an aunt in common although we were not related. I have discovered that these interconnected relationships are a common feature of Jamaican life.

As far as I was concerned, this was definitely the last thread to Mexico. So my narrative stated, so I believed; but fate has its own energy, its own force, and its own determination. We were, after some forty-three years, destined to return to Mexico. I was invited to attend the Doha Development Round in Mexico City from May 20 to 22, 2010. We were not sure what to expect on our unplanned return. On our first visit we had lived in the Hotel del Prado for six months while trying to find premises for an embassy and residence. We had spent our honeymoon at the del Prado, so there were sentimental memories galore.

On our second visit we discovered that the Hotel del Prado had been destroyed by an earthquake in 1985. The premises had been rebuilt with the assistance of Japanese technology according to anti-earthquake standards and now housed the Mexican foreign ministry. I had lunch there with the official major and members of their foreign ministry staff. As I was occupied with the conference, where I was

CHAPTER 5: TO MEXICO AND BACK

asked to chair one of the sessions, I was unable to visit Xochimilco with Marigold, as we had done in the distant past. Xochimilco was a lake where flowers grew, and native women in their little canoes sold flowers. Although the scene was picturesque, the odour of the water was not too pleasant. From what I could remember, it was just a huge canal with canoes going from one end to the other.

With her undying love for flowers, Marigold had to revisit Xochimilco. She was accompanied on this occasion by Señora Navarette, the wife of the president of the Mexican Senate and their party – security, translator and a photographer. Xochimilco was now a tourist attraction, I was told, and populated with water lilies. It was beautiful and quite charming. We then went to see 32 Euken Avenida where the embassy and the residence had been located. Although the main buildings were still recognizable, they had been expanded and joined, and the street had become a gated community. We stopped and took pictures and a security guard waved to us.

Our visit to Mexico after so many years evoked a feeling of nostalgia. We did not expect to find the world we had left, but almost in the words of the old song, we had taken a sentimental journey and renewed old memories.

But this was still not the end of the story. Fate would intervene again. I had declined to go to Geneva after our stay in Mexico. But shortly after my second visit to Mexico, destiny said I must now visit Geneva. On July 19, 2010, I attended the 3rd World Conference of Speakers of Parliament in Geneva, accompanied by Marigold. We took a boat cruise on Lake Geneva, and while I was in meetings she took a train ride high into the mountains where she could see the snow-capped peaks and could look across to France.

Marigold was introduced to fondue, a local communal dish of melted cheese eaten by spearing cubes of French bread and dipping it into the melted cheese. This was not unfamiliar to me. Then there were the souvenirs of cowbells and Swiss chocolate and hearing the Swiss horns. We took the opportunity to visit the Ariana Museum, which housed the headquarters of the International Academy of Ceramics of which I am a member. We found Geneva a very attractive city, beautifully laid out. It was a city with a plethora of international organizations, but did we regret not accepting the diplomatic appointment there? I don't think so.

Let me now go back to the point in my life when I returned to Jamaica from my diplomatic assignment in Mexico. By this time Marigold and I were living at 11 Keble Crescent in Hope Pastures. One of our neighbours was Jackie Minott, the sales manager of a beer company. We knew each other from McGill University. Apart from Stan Moore I had few friends in Jamaica. Many of my schoolmates had emigrated, and being away so long I would not know where to find the others. Jackie was a member of the Junior Chamber of Commerce, otherwise called the Jaycees, and his wife Bev suggested that I join up too. I took her advice and became a member of the Jaycees, and there began my reintegration into the Jamaican society. Many of the members were my age; some were in business, some young professionals – in short, a group compatible with me. The Jaycees became my link with the commercial world and private enterprise and my re-entry into Jamaican society.

In the Jaycees movement I became general counsel on the executive of Jaycees of Jamaica; Deryck Gibson was president. Later I served with Steve Touzalin, a lawyer from St. Mary. I became president of the Kingston Jaycees in 1971–72 and president of the Jaycees of Jamaica the following year. I was appointed JCI Senator #13436, which signified a life membership in the international movement. The Jaycees included members like Arthur "Turo" Zaidie, Anthony Levy, Eddie Shoucair, Tony Capleton, Norman Wright, Herbie Gaunlett, Vincent Matross-McIntosh, Ryan Peralto, L.G. Gooden, Joe Bryan, Les Brown, Ronnie Nasralla, Raymond Jackson, Wesley Chang, Jackie Minott, Sonny DaCosta, Roy Barnarsee and Pat Phillips. Members from other chapters joined with the Kingston chapter to create a vibrant

CHAPTER 5: TO MEXICO AND BACK

organization. Ronnie Nasralla and Raymond Jackson became Olympians and represented Jamaica in fencing at the Olympics.

There was an earlier set of Jaycees such as Adrian Foreman, R. Danny Williams, Manley McAdam and Donald Davidson. They had brought the first trade fair to Jamaica. In collaboration with the radio and TV station JBC, the Jaycees of Jamaica put on a national radio telethon, Nuggets for the Needy, that raised large sums for various charities. The Jaycees had the franchise for the Miss World Beauty Pageant. It produced Jamaica's first Miss World, Carole Joan Crawford, and beauty queens such as Mitsy Constantine, later Mrs. Edward Seaga, before the franchise was acquired by the government.

While I was at the Attorney General's Department, R. Danny Williams, Donald Davidson and Adrian Foreman, all members of the Kingston Jaycees and insurance agents for North American Life Insurance Company in Jamaica, wanted to transform it into a Jamaican company. They were looking for a young lawyer. I was later appointed Company Secretary and General Counsel of Life of Jamaica Limited (LOJ), its first employee. My colleagues in the Attorney General's Department cautioned me: it was a new company and might not succeed. Furthermore, they said if I remained in law, one day I was sure to become a High Court judge. I went anyway. Later two of my contemporaries, Clarence "Billy" Walker and Lloyd Ellis, did become Supreme Court justices. I have often asked myself whether I missed anything by not becoming a High Court judge. I don't know. In my new position I was introduced to the practice of the world of mortgages and mortgage lending and the world of life insurance. I led the legal team in the mergers of several life insurance companies which were being nationalized at the time. I do not regret the decision.

In the late 1970s Danny Williams, president of LOJ, was appointed a senator and a minister of government under the PNP administration. There was some celebration at LOJ. I was appointed an opposition senator, but there was no fanfare at LOJ. But there I stood across from my boss in the Upper House of Jamaica. Danny did not remain very long in the Senate. I was to complete twenty-eight years, and became the longest-serving senator in the history of Jamaica. I again returned to the senate as president in 2007 for the second time, having been Minister of Justice and Attorney General and Minister without Portfolio in the Ministry of Foreign Affairs. In September 2011, I announced that I would not return to the senate, if appointed. There were no more heights to climb.

I left LOJ in the late 1970s and set up a private law practice with a former law student of mine, Alan Deans, and one or two other lawyers who came and left over the years. We continued to do legal work for LOJ.

I return to 1970. My father had been ill in a hospital in Toronto and came home to recuperate. He clearly wanted to be with us. Marigold was expecting our first son, Jeremy. I jokingly said I hoped for a daughter who would look after me in my old age. Dad used to put his ear on Marigold's large belly to listen to his grandchild. He always said to her, "Don't listen to him about a daughter. You are having a boy, but I will not live to see him." Later we found out that he was suffering from kidney failure, but we were then unaware.

The night before he died, my father was very restless. He kept jumping up out of his sleep. At one time I found him on the floor beside his bed. I sat up in a lounge chair in his room and fell asleep while he was snoring. He jumped up again and I tried to calm him: "It's alright, Dad, I am with you." He snapped at me as if I were once again a child.

His last words were, "You are not with me, I am on my way to eternity."

When I awoke there was an eerie silence. He had passed. I called out to Marigold, "Dad is very low." But I knew he was dead.

CHAPTER 5: TO MEXICO AND BACK

My friend Dr. Louis Lee came and tied up his jaws and called the undertaker. Dad was gone. We tidied his room. When Beatrice our helper came and saw the empty room the next morning, she said, "Oh, Dad has gone back to Canada." I almost couldn't bear to tell her he was dead.

Dad died on December 13, 1970. Marigold was forbidden to attend the funeral, because Jeremy was expected at any moment. Dad was buried at St. Andrew Parish Church on the 16th and Jeremy was born on December 19, 1970. I had gained a son and lost a father; that was a bittersweet time.

My sister Sheila came from Canada for the funeral. Mom, my stepmother, did not. She didn't like funerals or graveyards; she did not even visit my father's grave when she came to see us in Jamaica. My friends Jackie Minott and Elias Fatta from the Jaycees took charge of all the funeral arrangements. They sent me the bills some weeks later. Although I reimbursed them, I am forever indebted to them for their kindness and expert handling of all the necessary arrangements.

CHAPTER 6

My Art and Ceramic World

In the summer programme at Christ-Roi Park in Montreal North, I won a prize at age thirteen for a small relief of a baby done in wood and then painted. In the following year my Hawaiian dancing girl in grass skirt, made from plaster of Paris, also won a prize. At the High School of Montreal, with the guidance of my art teacher Mr. Byers, I made a large bust of a man in clay. It was very well received on Open Day when it was exhibited at the school and highly commended by visiting parents, who expressed the view that I was surely going to be an artist. I am not sure that I had such aspirations, but in any event the circumstances of my life dictated otherwise. Deep down within me, however, there still lingered a desire for some artistic expression, perhaps more for sculptural form than colours. Although I appreciated paintings, especially the expressionist painters, there was something about form that captivated me. It became full-blown in my appreciation of ceramics, which not only had form but also colour and texture.

In 1981, I attended a retrospective of Cecil Baugh (1908–2005), Jamaica's master potter, presented by the National Gallery of Jamaica at Devon House in Kingston. I was enthralled, captivated and awestruck by the beauty and elegance of these ceramic pieces. I had an unquenchable desire to acquire all or at least some of the pieces on display. But in a retrospective all the pieces are already owned; nothing in the exhibition was for sale. I did not know Cecil Baugh or what he was like, but I decided to call him on the phone, and later visited him at his Leitrim Avenue residence in Vineyard Town. He turned out to be a most affable, humble and endearing person. From the moment we met we became instant friends because of our mutual passion for pottery, and a lasting relationship developed. We were never tired of talking about the new pieces that I acquired. I was later to write a monograph on Cecil Baugh – *From Yabbaman to Master Potter*, which I self-published and presented at the National Gallery of Jamaica at the opening of its exhibition *Clay and Fire: Ceramic Art in Jamaica* on 31 July 2005.

I met the late Reverend Phillip Hart, rector of Kingston Parish Church, in the late seventies. He was an art *aficionado* and knew of my interest in pottery. He asked me if I had met Ma Lou, another local potter, and suggested that I should. I located Ma Lou (Louisa Jones) (1916–92) in St. Catherine, in Job Lane not far from Spanish Town. She was one of the few, or possibly the last, of the traditional potters. She had learnt the craft from her late aunt whose tradition had been handed down from her African forebears. She made yabba pots. The nomenclature yabba comes from the Twi language of Ghana. These pots were made of low-fired earthenware clay, not in a kiln, but outdoors. The freshly made pots were surrounded by shards or broken pieces then built over with sticks into a conical shape, somewhat reminiscent of how charcoal is made.

Ma Lou was a person of integrity. On one occasion when I visited her humble home, I saw a few yabba pots which had some dark spots that added variety to the red clay colour. I thought this was different, ideal for the discerning collector. When I tried to purchase them, Ma Lou, as poor as she might have been and in need of money, said she

CHAPTER 6: MY ART AND CERAMIC WORLD

could not sell me those pots, for if she did she "would have sinned her soul" since the pots were underfired and would be porous.

Osmond Watson (1934-2005), painter and sculptor, was a modest and very private man. I was allowed to invade his privacy from time to time, perhaps because we shared certain similarities: we were about the same age and he had grown up in Jones Town, the site of my first school. Osmond was a man with strong likes and dislikes and he was never afraid to express his opinion. When Rastafarians were still being marginalized he depicted Christ as a Rastafarian. He was a devotee of Sai Baba, the popular Indian guru, and whenever I found books on Sai Baba I would bring them for him. I used to see more of him when he was living near to Washington Boulevard. One day as we sat conversing and looking down from his balcony, we saw a group of people going from door to door, led by a white man who seemed to be a foreigner. As they came to Osmond's gate he said, "I am not buying anything today."

The reply was, "We are not selling anything."

Osmond cynically countered, "Aren't you selling religion?" They seemed to have been evangelists. I acquired many paintings created by this outstanding artist.

Carl Abrahams (1913-2005) was a painter whose work included the religious, the mythological, as well as landscapes and cartoons. He lived with his sister at 3 Linstone Crescent, St. Andrew, in the vicinity of Jamaica House, where I visited him on several occasions. He returned the visit one Christmas accompanied by three beautiful young girls. Whenever I visited him, apart from talking art he would always talk about his fellow artist Edna Manley, the sculptor (wife of national hero Norman Manley). I always wondered about this preoccupation. Carl was a very genuine person who was always humorous, as expressed sometimes in his paintings. Many of his works form part of my collection.

I was invited by Jean-Robert Estimé, foreign minister of Haiti, to pay an official visit to that country in February 1986. In anticipating the usual exchange of gifts, I acquired a painting from Carl Abrahams for the National Museum of Haiti. The painting depicted a muscular man breaking free from his chains. My wife and I were scheduled to meet President Jean-Claude (Baby Doc) Duvalier and his wife. But the reaction of our friend the foreign minister made us realize that something awkward had transpired. The president had fled the country on the same day we arrived. Was the image of the broken chains prophetic? Was it that Haiti had now been liberated from the arbitrary rule of Baby Doc? Baby Doc and his wife fled Haiti long ago, but that country seems destined to remain in the grip of poverty and despair.

Ralph Campbell (1921–1985) was a highly expressive representational painter whose works reflected his energy, freedom and vitality. We often visited his studio in August Town not far from the University of the West Indies. To me he was a Jamaican impressionist. He painted a landscape of the hills of Kintyre, St Andrew, looking from the Papine area. He specially inscribed the back of the canvas to Marigold and myself. He always signed his canvases with his national honour – OD (Order of Distinction).

Revivalist, sculptor and painter Mallica "Kapo" Reynolds (1911–1989) was a leading member of the group of self-taught artists referred to as "intuitives". He was an ordained bishop of a revivalist group and founder of St Michael's Revivalist Tabernacle. I visited his home in Waterhouse in the western part of the city, and on one occasion we took a picture together. Many of his paintings and sculptures are on display at the National Gallery of Jamaica, and I am the proud owner of several of his works.

Ken Abendana Spencer (1929–2005) drew his inspiration from scenes of Jamaican life. His early watercolours depicted seascapes, landscapes, vignettes of Jamaican life at the waterfront, in town squares and in the markets. I had met him in London in the sixties. He was a frequent visitor to the basement clubs and jazz bars of the Soho district where I accompanied him on one memorable occasion, as recounted in chapter 3.

CHAPTER 6: MY ART AND CERAMIC WORLD

We saw each other again on several occasions after Spencer returned to Jamaica in 1986. My family and I visited him at his home in Portland. He was constructing a castle in Fisherman's Park in Long Bay, Portland. The building was some six storeys high, with circular staircases and an indoor spit that was large enough to roast a whole cow. I told him that the only thing missing was a moat, for he already had a bridge at the entrance to the building. But there was something else missing: my younger son ran up and down and all around the building, then returned to say that there was only one toilet! I asked my wife when she thought the construction would be completed. "Never," she replied. "This is his life's work."

Spencer was a prolific painter and a great marketer of his works. They adorn the walls of several north coast hotels as well as offices in many commercial buildings. He would often show me several canvases at one time and would invite me to make an offer. I had to remind him that I was a collector, not an art gallery. I once asked him whether he ever got up one day and just painted a picture, not because he wanted an immediate sale. His only response was: "Picasso was a prolific painter."

Albert Huie (1920–2010) was another artist who became our friend. Marigold and I visited his studio and he visited our home. He was especially fond of my wife Marigold. He painted a special bunch of marigolds for her arranged in a pot that had been made by Cecil Baugh, and he insisted on delivering the painting personally. We had acquired an early Huie painting of Isabel Seaton (1941) who had been a member of the Legislative Council, which was later replaced by the Senate of Jamaica. I wondered whether his insistence on delivering the painted jug of marigolds was because he wanted to have another look at this early portrait. He studied it for some twenty minutes, but he made no comment. We were thrilled to have his works in our collection. On February 5, 2010, I joined in paying tribute to him in the Senate of Jamaica on the occasion of his passing.

Barrington (Barry) Watson (1931–2016) painted a portrait of Marigold. She had to be taken by the driver to his studio at Orange

Park in St. Thomas. I had collected some of Barry's early sketches which he had done in England and left with his landlady. I had rescued them, but as I had not paid for them I had to return some of them to him. We had also met in Germany where he obtained a piece of pottery for me from a potter named Eska. Barry's approach to painting was generally academic and realist. He became a popular portrait painter. I also acquired works from both his sons who are sculptors.

Sculptor, painter and restorer of monuments, Fitz Harrack (1945-2013) hailed from St. John, Grenada. As a restorer he was commissioned to restore the statue of the Most Honourable Norman Manley, national hero, located at St William Grant Park in downtown Kingston. He also restored the statue of national hero Paul Bogle, created in 1965 by renowned sculptor Edna Manley to mark the Morant Bay rebellion. The statue was damaged by some local residents who apparently felt it did not look like Bogle. Fitz restored it in 2010 and invited Marigold and myself to view it. We took photographs together in front of the statue.

Fitz Harrack worked in copper, aluminium, wood and cast stone. Many of his copper sculptures are found in commercial banks and in the conference rooms of the International Seabed Authority in Kingston. His work in wood is amply displayed in his "splash form" series, examples of which are on show in the National Gallery of Jamaica. Over the years Fitz became a close friend of Marigold and myself. We are proud to have his sculptures adorn our house and our gardens. He designed and created a magnificent sculpture in bronze and aluminium which adorns the home of my son Jeremy. He was commissioned to carve busts of several well-known Jamaicans.

George Fitzroy Harrack, OD died on January 10, 2013, at home. I gave the remembrance at his funeral on January 30, 2013 at the Garrison Church of the Ascension at Up Park Camp, Kingston.

I met David Pottinger(1911-2007), otherwise called Jack, through Fitz Harrack. Pottinger painted the streets, the lanes, the sidewalks and the backyards of old Kingston; the pushcarts, the higglers, the

CHAPTER 6: MY ART AND CERAMIC WORLD

"walkfoot" vendors: in short, the realities of life on the streets of Kingston. I collected many of his paintings. I particularly enjoy his depiction of Revivalists conducting street side meetings.

And so my art collection began to grow with Van Pitterson, Ralph Campbell, Ken Abendana Spencer, Eric Smith, Alexander Cooper, Colin Garland, Milton George, David Boxer, Paul Blackwood and Roy Reid; the watercolours of Herb Rose and the ink and watercolours of Susan Shirley. There were also paintings by the intuitives Kapo, Tabois, Alan Zion, and Albert Artwell. Then there were the foreign artists: Kyan Moon (Korea), Laurenceau and Ralph (Haiti), Juca and José Saboia (Brazil), Henry Aubrey (France), Sir Martin Reid (UK). To these were added the sculptures of Fitz Harrack, Christopher Gonzales and Edna Manley who were among the leading sculptors of the day, as well as Raymond Watson, Basil Watson and Richmond Barthé – the African American sculptor who once resided in Jamaica, Joseph Richards (J.R.), and the remarkable Ronald Moody.

Ronald Moody (1900–1984) was a British sculptor of Jamaican birth. He went to England to study dentistry in 1923, but was so profoundly stirred by the "irresistible movement in stillness" of the Egyptian sculptures at the British Museum in London that he decided to become a sculptor, and actually taught himself. Not only was he regarded as one of Britain's major modernist sculptors, but his fame spread to Paris where he spent two richly productive years, from 1938 to 1940. In 1964 Moody created the sculpture of Savacou, a warrior bird in Caribbean Indian mythology, which stands on the grounds of the University of the West Indies, Mona. He is the only sculptor to have been awarded a Gold Musgrave Medal for sculpture in Jamaica – Edna Manley's Gold Musgrave was awarded for her contribution to the development of art in Jamaica.

While I was visiting London in 1983 I wanted to meet this famous artist and to collect a piece of his work, if possible. I sought the assistance of Norman Rae who was then Trade Commissioner at the Jamaican High Commission. Norman was a Kingston College graduate and Jamaica Scholar who was well versed in the dramatic arts and art in general. He gave me the address of Ronald Moody. I borrowed the services of the High Commission's driver who spent many hours with me trying to find the address. We finally located it somewhere in Chelsea. Moody's studio was situated on the ground floor of an apartment in a building complex. I had a most interesting visit. He told me how he had escaped World War II crossing over the Alps to Britain. He had exhibited in many places in Europe. The works I saw in his studio were monumental and impressive. I thought that if I could afford even one, it ought to be in the collection of the National Gallery of Jamaica. I saw a small piece in a crouching position. Moody said that he had just come out of hospital and that was how he felt. Although it was the least expensive, I did not have enough money.

I jokingly said to the driver on the way back, "Lend me a couple of quid, will you?" He took me seriously and said he could get the money from his credit union. The next morning he came to me with the rest of the money which, when added to what I had, was just the right amount. He was kind enough to collect the sculpture, and I asked, "How will I repay you?"

"Don't worry," he replied. "When I come to Jamaica I will find you."

He did come to Jamaica, and he did find me. He borrowed a sum of money to repair a place in St. Mary which was more than I had owed him. I never saw him again. But subsequently my wife was in London and he told her that he could not understand why I had spent so many hours driving around London to buy this little sculpture. Had he been farsighted, he would have tried to buy a piece for himself, because Ronald Moody died some months afterwards and the prices for his sculptures skyrocketed.

In 1988 I became a member of the International Academy of Ceramics, headquartered in Geneva. I was nominated and elected *in absentia* at a biennial meeting in Australia, in the category of collectors, after the submission of a number of slides of my collection. At that

CHAPTER 6: MY ART AND CERAMIC WORLD

time there were only five members in that category worldwide. I remained the only member in the Caribbean area. Some ten years later I was pleased to have co-sponsored Norma Rodney-Harrack, artist-potter, who was admitted in the category of ceramists.

The late Cecil Baugh, Norma Harrack and myself spearheaded the founding of the Jamaica Potters Association (JAPA) in June 1990. We had envisioned an association which would have helped young potters, perhaps having a common kiln where they could fire their wares, a small library of ceramics, and encourage high standards for the craft. Our fledgling association was commandeered by a group now called the Association of Jamaican Potters. We resigned and never became members of the new association. In June 2009, however, I was invited by the group to open *The Potters* exhibition at the Bank of Jamaica. I accepted the invitation and was presented with a piece of ceramics by the president, Michael Layne.

During the years since the *Baugh Retrospective* I have kept adding to my collection of ceramics. I attended conferences of the International Academy and the National Council on Education for the Ceramic Arts (NSECA) and visited the local exhibitions. Local exhibitions have been held at the National Gallery of Jamaica, the Edna Manley School of the Visual and Performing Arts, the Bolivar Gallery (Hugh Dunphy), Hi-Qo Art and Framing Gallery, and the Frame Centre Gallery owned by Guy and Charmaine McIntosh. I became a personal friend of Guy McIntosh, whose establishment does excellent framing and minor restorations. Guy and I met regularly at his gallery over the years discussing art and the art community, usually on a Friday morning, which we dubbed the "Coffee Club". Guy McIntosh died on August 8, 2011.

My collection, the Hardingham Collection as it is called, includes significant potters who have potted in Jamaica: the "Clonmel Potters" Belva and Donald Johnson, Phillip Supersad, the two Todds, Gene Pearson, Jean Taylor-Bushay, Michael Layne, Walford Campbell, Allison and David Sinclair, Margaret McGee, Everald Powell, Jag

Mehta, Majorie Keith, Peter Cave, Madge Spencer, Orville Bailey, René Pischar, Norma Rodney-Harrack and others. The collection also includes foreign potters such as Bernard Leach, David Leach, John Leach, Lucie Rie, Michael Cardew, Ladi Kwali of Nigeria; Maria Martinez of San Ildefonso Pueblo, New Mexico (whose daughter incidentally had been in Jamaica as a Peace Corps worker); Ursula and Karl Scheid, and Gerald and Gotlind Weigel, all of Germany; Korean Pots; the Blue Pottery of Delhi; the Yixing purple clay pottery of China and the Gzhel pottery of Russia.

Along the way, I acquired a substantial collection of books on ceramics, including the five volumes of a *Survey of Chinese Ceramics*, in Chinese and English, beginning from pre-historic times to the tenth century, and right up to the present century with contemporary wares. At the time of acquisition, there were only two known sets in the United States. I also acquired the book *Gzhel Ceramics* covering the eighteenth, nineteenth and twentieth centuries, illustrated in Russian and English; books on Bernard Leach, Shoji Hamada, Lucie Rie, Soetsu Yanagi, Lucie M. Lewis (native potter of Arizona), Michael Cardew, and others.

On November 20, 1988, an exhibition of teapots was held at The Frame Centre Gallery in Kingston in recognition of Cecil Baugh's eightieth birthday. *Plates and Platters* would follow in April 1991 at the same venue. But it was the international assortment of ceramic teapots that received much acclaim, and somehow I came to be remembered for my collection of teapots. I have been offered metal teapots, even a wooden one. I have to remind those persons making such kind gestures that I am not a collector of teapots. I collect pottery; the teapots are but a sub-collection.

My quest for ceramics led me on many journeys, one of which occurred in 1984. As Minister without Portfolio in the Ministry of Foreign Affairs I was scheduled to attend a meeting with the Foreign Minister of Costa Rica in San Jose one Monday morning. I indicated to the driver that before the meeting I wanted to visit a potter's work-

CHAPTER 6: MY ART AND CERAMIC WORLD

shop to buy some ceramics. It was the pottery of the Todds. They were an American couple who had potted in Jamaica and had left during the early seventies and settled in Costa Rica.

I had no idea that the pottery was so far from San Jose; we had to leave at about 7:00 a.m. to travel to Paradiso Desamparados and return. When we reached there I looked around the shop, bought two pieces and left in order to keep my ten o'clock appointment with the Foreign Minister. I had never met the Todds, but as a collector I knew of them. After I left Costa Rica, Jamaica's honorary consul told them who I was and that I had visited their studio. Perhaps they were not satisfied with the pieces I had chosen, because they sent me two pieces to add to my collection.

On a visit to India in the 1980s I tried to locate a potter by the name of Singh, but whenever I asked my host to help me to locate this person, it was never convenient. I came to the conclusion that perhaps I was not to visit the neighbourhood where he lived. I then wanted to acquire a piece of the blue pottery of Jaipur, but since I could not fit in such a visit in my official schedule, I decided to settle for a piece of the blue pottery of Delhi. When I located the potter I asked my translator to enquire whether the potter had obtained the blue by using cobalt. She said he would not tell me that because it was a family secret. I insisted and he replied in the affirmative, saying to the translator, "I may as well tell him for he seems to know anyhow." It has been suggested that this form of pottery shows the influence of the invaders who many years earlier had invaded India throughout the north – the Mohenjo-daro Valley – but that has not been definitively established. In 2012, I obtained a piece of the blue pottery of Jaipur through my personal friend and physician Dr. Hafeezul Mohammed who was attending a medical conference in India. He was surprised to learn that the same establishment had potted there for seven generations.

On one of my excursions in Colombia, the police accompanied me into a district to buy a piece of pottery. The potter did not have a kiln but fired his small wares in a kerosene tin. I found that remarkable. In China, on a visit to Shen Yang in the north-eastern province with my wife, who was judging in an international flower and garden exhibition, I stopped in a tea shop where I attended a tea ceremony. I saw a magnificently large ceramic teapot on display. I enquired where I could acquire a similar one, and the owner of the tea shop said, "In Beijing." My escorts suggested that since I was an important visitor and needed to have it; the owner could acquire another one. They negotiated a most favourable price for me. I carried the teapot in my lap from China to Jamaica.

I am indebted to various people who are aware of my passion for collecting works of art. A former government official was travelling in Kwazululand in South Africa when he was struck by the beauty of a teapot in a shop window and felt he had to buy it for me. He travelled all the way from South Africa with the teapot as hand luggage. He arrived at my law office one morning and simply presented it to me. I opened the package and saw what it was: an English-style teapot decorated with traditional native designs from Kwazululand. It was exquisite. To think that an acquaintance, not a close friend, would remember me in this way brought a lump to my throat. I was so choked with emotion that I could barely say thanks. One of the most priceless gifts is kindness, and receiving it is the most humbling of all experiences.

For many years I had hoped to acquire a pot from Ladi Kwali, a Nigerian potter from Abuja. My friend Cecil Baugh said he was going to visit his daughter in Chicago and he thought he knew where he could locate Kwali's work. I gave him one of his own pots to exchange for it. He returned to Jamaica and said nothing about it, and I never asked. Ladi Kwali (1925–1984) had learnt traditional pottery from her aunt. She made large pots which were traditionally used for carrying water or as cooking pots, using the coiling method – from coils of clay and beaten from the inside with a wooden paddle. The pots were decorated with incised geometric or traditional figurative

CHAPTER 6: MY ART AND CERAMIC WORLD

patterns. She had been exposed to the teachings of Michael Cardew, a student of Bernard Leach. She learnt to throw pots on the wheel, glaze and fire at high temperatures. In her recent works we see an amalgam of traditional pottery and Western studio pottery.

Ladi Kwali became well known in Europe, was awarded an MBE, and had a road named after her in Abuja. During the eighties I was visiting London and went to my favourite pottery shop – Gallery Besson in the Royal Arcade. I noticed two pots in a bottom cupboard in the shop – guided by the nose of a collector I always know how to ferret out pots – and I asked the shop assistant if they were African pots. She said they could be but she was not certain. The proprietor was not there. I returned the next day to the gallery when the proprietor, Anita Besson, was in attendance. I am sure she knew why I had returned. We had afternoon tea and chatted about all sorts of things. Finally I broached the subject: "I saw two pots yesterday which appeared to be African, but your assistant was not sure."

"Yes they are," came the reply.

"Are they Ladi Kwali?"

"Yes," she responded. "That one is not for sale, but if you are interested you may have the other."

I unhesitatingly said, "Yes." It was like finding the Holy Grail. Of course, in my anxiety I forgot to ask the price. At that time the gallery did not take credit cards. However, the pot was acquired in the following manner: A friend of mine passing through London paid US$500, I paid an additional sum, and a friend living in London who was returning to Jamaica paid the balance and brought home the Ladi Kwali which proudly stands in my collection. There are unwritten rules which seem to exist with galleries and known collectors: once sold, even if someone offers a higher price, there would be no transaction. On the other hand, the collector's word must be his bond. The legend surrounding my Ladi Kwali pot is that she used to conduct business with a company in England and often settled her accounts by giving pots. That company went into liquidation or was bought out by another company who found these unusual-looking wares and was going to dispose of them when they were acquired by someone else. The pots found their way into the gallery where I had the good fortune to discover them.

I visited Northampton in Massachusetts where the Leslie Ferrin Gallery was located. After meeting the proprietor Leslie Ferrin, I bought a number of teapots and became a friend of the gallery. Miss Ferrin referred me to another gallery which had a teapot exhibition displaying some unsold pots. Many of them were by well-known English potters. I was able to acquire them in one purchase. In my travels I became familiar with the ceramic shop in the Victoria and Albert Museum in London where I acquired many books on pottery in addition to ceramic pots. I met Claire Beck who always directed me to good artists. On one occasion there was an exhibition of English pots in California that she told me about. I was able to acquire some of the pots before they were shipped back to England. The collection included many by Lucie Rie. On another occasion Claire Beck sent me some pottery, labelling the shipment "works of art". Apparently works of art were exempted from customs duties in the United Kingdom, but on arrival in Jamaica that designation only increased the duties. With a heavy heart, I had to return the shipment unclaimed.

In Puerto Rico I met with Jag Mehta – an Indian national originally, but a naturalized Jamaican who worked in the tourist industry. Jag Mehta used an electric kiln in whichever hotel he worked, and that was no different when he was in Puerto Rico. I then visited the Casa Candina in San Juan where I met and collected the works of Bernardo Hogan, Susan Espinosa, Jaime Suarez and Sylvia Blanco. I was able to arrange a scholarship with them for a young Jamaican potter who was an excellent thrower, the nephew of Jamaican potter Jean Taylor-Bushay. Unfortunately he migrated and never pursued the pottery medium.

In Jamaica I met David Leach (1911–2005), son of Bernard Leach, when he visited Cecil Baugh on October 31, 1991. David had been a

CHAPTER 6: MY ART AND CERAMIC WORLD

contemporary of Cecil Baugh at St. Ives, Cornwall. David's son John Leach had visited Jamaica on October 9, 1990, when we met. On these occasions we talked pottery. I was pleased to return the visit to John at his pottery at Muchelnay in Somerset and also David Leach at St. Ives in Cornwall. Both their works are happily featured in my collection. On one of my visits to a pottery fair in Yorkshire I had the pleasure of meeting Bill Ismay, perhaps the greatest single collector of twentieth-century pottery in Britain. Bill Ismay was a retired librarian in Yorkshire who was awarded the MBE for his contribution to pottery. He passed away in 2001.

On October 28, 2009, Norma Harrack held an exhibition of her pottery at the Olympic Art Gallery in Papine near the University of Technology. She exhibited about fifty pieces. It was an impressive show, with a variety of forms and exhilarating glazes demonstrating the artist's exceptional talent. All the pieces exhibited were sold. I was fortunate to acquire three pieces for my collection. I had the privilege of being master of ceremonies for the occasion. The guest speaker was Professor the Honourable Rex Nettleford, who delivered an engaging speech in his accustomed eloquent and inimitable style. I gave him a copy of my monograph on Cecil Baugh. Rex Nettleford was a co-founder of the National Dance Theatre Company in 1963. He was a Rhodes Scholar, a social critic, a choreographer and Vice Chancellor Emeritus of the University of the West Indies. It was the last occasion on which we would meet. The sad news came that he had passed away in Washington, DC on February 2, 2010. One of his favourite pots from the Harrack exhibition was used as the urn at his funeral, and his ashes were buried in the

Chapel grounds of the University of the West Indies, the institution where he had spent his adult life. Rex Nettleford will be remembered for many things. I will remember him as a lover of the arts.

In 1993, through the initiative of Norma Harrack, the Jamaica Postal Services issued four stamps commemorating Jamaican pottery. The pots of Cecil Baugh, Ma Lou, Norma Harrack and Gene Pearson from the Hardingham Collection were depicted on Jamaican stamps and therefore circulated throughout the world. Over the years I have continued my visits to pottery exhibitions in order to acquire new pots. So my deep desires for some expression of art and my appreciation of form were sublimated, while my collection of ceramics kept growing. Collecting works of art has become a passion and a lifetime endeavour for me.

With Marigold, Ceramic Expo, Canada, 1998

Carl Abrahams visits Hardingham at Christmas, 1986

Discussing a ceramic piece with Fitz Harrack, 2009

CHAPTER 7

Political Life

In the common room gatherings at the hostel in London the conversations were varied but frequent. Whatever the topic of discussion, it invariably turned on things back home in our Caribbean territories. Many spoke of the reforms they would make, especially in the political system. After all, we were now well educated, many of us in the professions, and we were on our way home from the metropolitan countries. I listened with great interest and often joined in the discussions, but I harboured no ambition to enter active political life on my return home.

When I was living at 6 Keble Crescent in Hope Pastures I had no political affiliation. Many people thought I was a supporter of the PNP, but I have no idea why they formed that view. If anything I was just civic-minded, though I had a great respect for Bustamante. Most of my relatives supported the PNP; it was middle-class, it was the thing to do. My uncle Allan Levy was the only member of the family who supported the JLP. He had worked at the wharves and Bustamante had fought for improved working conditions for the stevedores. Uncle Allan used to say, "First there is God and then Bustamante."

GRANDSON OF ESSIE: A JAMAICAN AUTOBIOGRAPHY

Between 1972 and 1974, the JLP was hardly functioning. The PNP, swept along by the force and magnetism of Michael Manley, had captured the imagination of most Jamaicans since the party's massive election victory in 1972. I was invited by Les Brown, a Jaycee who was a young entrepreneur, to attend a PNP meeting at his home in Beverly Hills. This was a very upscale area overlooking the city of Kingston. Houses were architect-designed in very fashionable styles. His house was well appointed, luxurious, with a swimming pool and attractive appurtenances. I was told that Michael Manley would be at the meeting, which of course was a drawing card, but somehow I was apprehensive, not having attended such a meeting before. I dropped off my household helper and arrived at the address, where I parked outside at a convenient spot to avoid being hemmed in, in case I wanted to leave early. On entering the premises I was greeted by an impressive sight: several of my Jaycee friends were seated on chairs arranged around the swimming pool. I noticed that the bar was well stocked with Black Label whisky and thought to myself, "If this is socialism, then this is for me."

Michael Manley did not attend the meeting. Present were D.K. Duncan, destined to be a fiery Minister of Mobilization, Maxine Henry (now Wilson) – a future Minister of Education, and MP Desmond Leakey, who was a Jaycee from Trelawny. D.K. Duncan was wearing a short leather jacket, a beret (like Che Guevara, I suppose) and boots with the flaps partly zippered. I was content to enjoy the expensive whisky and had made up my mind that I would not enter into any discussions. I was there to listen.

At the meeting there were two burly brothers of reddish complexion who seemed to have been truck drivers. They asked the question: "What is it in the constitution that you guys want to change?" Desmond Leakey got up to answer. He started by saying that a committee had been set up in Parliament to consider changes to the constitution. The burly brothers repeated, "But what is it in the constitution that you want to change?"

CHAPTER 7: POLITICAL LIFE

When it seemed that Desmond Leakey's response was not satisfactory, Dr. D.K. Duncan rose to his feet. Gesticulating like an orator, he began: "Brothers and sisters, the constitution of Jamaica puts property above the individual."

At this point my patience snapped. I broke my silence. "That is not so," I said. "The constitution grants the right of freedom of assembly, the right to form trade unions, freedom from arbitrary arrest, and freedom of worship, all of which concern the individual." Some in the audience insisted that D.K. was right, and like the chorus in a Greek play they declared in unison that Leslie Ashenheim was responsible. "Nonsense!" I cried. "In Commonwealth constitutions the state can compulsorily acquire lands if necessary, but they must compensate the individual." I had another whisky and stated that Norman Manley, David Coore and Edward Seaga were also members of the team that had drafted the constitution. Emboldened by the whiskey, I exclaimed: "The problem with you people is that you want to confiscate other people's property! Over my dead body!"

The Greek chorus chanted: "Yes! People like you will be dead!"

D.K. Duncan stayed back after the meeting, we chatted and it all ended on a friendly note. But the die had been cast.

At about three o'clock in the morning I returned home. Marigold teased and said: "It took you that long to drop off the helper? Where were you? I could understand if you were caught in a poker game or playing dominoes, but at Les Brown's house discussing politics?"

My reply to her was: "I saw some people tonight who are going to mash up Jamaica."

However well-intentioned they may have been, the radical PNP administration of the seventies confirmed my fears. In our maturing years I ran into D.K. Duncan and told him that it was he who had caused me to join the Jamaica Labour Party. He replied, "Mike Henry told me the same thing."

In 2010 I met a colleague in a restaurant who, unsolicited, raised the matter of the Les Brown meeting at Beverly Hills. According to him, after that meeting Les Brown had been threatened. He left his house and became a Rasta, and my colleague suggested that the meeting may have been recorded and the tape given to Edward Seaga. I was alarmed. I had seen no one taping the meeting, and I had neither the motive nor the desire to do so, if that was what he was implying. In the days when that meeting was held, I had no connection with Edward Seaga or the JLP.

I did see Les Brown after Bruce Golding became prime minister in 2007. He had a low-income project for an area in August Town and was having difficulty getting approval. I simply sent the plans and documents to Prime Minister Golding. I heard nothing further. On entering Medical Associates Hospital from the New Kingston entrance one day, I was hailed by someone whom I did not recognize at first. When he approached I realized that it was Les Brown. He was bearded and seemed a little gaunt. He greeted me and said, "It is good to have good friends." Apparently his project had been approved. I did not ask him about the reported threats on his life as I did not know the story at that time.

In 1973 I became a member of Young Jamaica, the youth arm of the JLP. We did our best to provide the JLP with moral and strategic support. I was asked by the party to assist them in the enumeration exercise in Hope Pastures where I was living. My involvement extended from Hope Pastures to other areas in the constituency of East Rural St. Andrew. After the enumeration exercise I had become familiar with most of the constituency and got to know a tremendous number of people. The JLP asked me if I would represent the party in the upcoming elections. "Why not?" I thought. After all, it was Bustamante's party. In 1974 I joined the JLP.

This was at the height of what became known as the "tam pack" period. The radicals in the PNP wore tams made of wool like the Rastafarians – a style adopted by most of the young UWI economists advising Michael Manley. The radicals were reported to have caused some commotion at the Adventure Inn over in Portmore. They were

CHAPTER 7: POLITICAL LIFE

strident, an irreverent bunch of rebels. The PNP juggernaut was barrelling along at full speed. Meanwhile the shocking news spread among the Jaycees: Harding had joined the Jamaica Labour Party! Apparently this was not what was expected from up-and-coming middle-class "progressive" people. Having been introduced to the constituency, I was made caretaker – the stage before becoming the candidate. I began to travel through the constituency and to meet the voters. I started to attend funerals, christenings, weddings and branch meetings. At these meetings there was a set agenda which included an item called "social and welfare", where problems of some of the members were handled. Branches were the counterparts of what were called groups in the PNP, and being a branch member automatically made you a member of the Labour Party.

After I had been introduced to the constituency, I arrived at a branch meeting one day to find that Abe Dabdoub was present. Apparently he felt that the constituency was up for grabs and he wanted to throw his hat in the ring. I spoke to Edward Seaga about the incident. In turn he spoke to Dabdoub and the matter was resolved. On another occasion Karl Samuda, who was living in the constituency and who had been associated with David Lindo, a former JLP MP for that constituency, decided to make a bid to become the representative. At a meeting in Irish Town, however, my supporters told him in no uncertain terms that they wanted me as their candidate – proudly displaying the slogan "Ossie Harding all the way" which was printed on their T-shirts. Karl Samuda could not prevail. In the end, though, he became a very successful politician, winning his constituency of North Central St. Andrew as a member of both major political parties on different occasions. Samuda was expelled from the JLP in 1990 in the wake of the so-called "Gang of Five" rebellion against Edward Seaga's autocratic leadership style. He joined the PNP and won his seat in 1993 by a slim majority over the JLP candidate, Tom Tavares-Finson. In 1997 he returned to the JLP and successfully defended the North Central St Andrew seat in the general elections held that same year. He has been an effective general secretary of the JLP as well as a minister of government.

Abe Dabdoub, an ardent supporter of the JLP and Edward Seaga, finally won a seat in NE St. Catherine through the courts. He later switched allegiance to the PNP and brought a successful case in the West Portland constituency on a constitutional issue that the incumbent Daryl Vaz had dual nationality and had sworn allegiance to a foreign power. Dabdoub was successful in disqualifying the incumbent but he was not given the seat; the courts ordered a by-election. The Court of Appeal confirmed that verdict and the JLP successfully defended the election with an increased majority. The Dabdoub intervention set off a series of by-elections which ultimately did not find favour with the electorate. The country felt that the political parties should negotiate the position because the by-elections were far too costly.

As I began my campaign in the constituency, my thoughts drifted back to the days at the student common room at the hostel in London, the discussions we had and the dreams we shared. The reality, however, was quite different. The seasoned grassroots politicians were there to tell you what to do, and if you were not careful they would tell you how to do it. I felt that there were some persons just lying in wait for you, as a predator waylays its prey. You were a meal ticket, you were to be fleeced. Some people think that politicians exploit the people and sometimes corrupt them. Although this may happen, the truth is that the experienced grassroots supporters will not only exploit the neophyte representative but will corrupt him or her if they can.

It was Saturday, June 19, 1976. I was at the Holiday Inn in Montego Bay where I was chairing a meeting of the JLP. Edward Seaga was sitting immediately to my right. The party was in election mode and had gathered for a retreat. At exactly 12:00 noon a senior police officer

CHAPTER 7: POLITICAL LIFE

entered the conference room and handed a document to Edward Seaga, who passed it to me. It was a letter from Prime Minister Michael Manley, stating that Cabinet had authorized him to advise the Governor General to proclaim a State of Emergency under the provisions of Section 26 (5) of the Constitution, and that the State of Emergency became effective at noon that day. Mr. Seaga read the letter and asked me, "Is this legal?" After examining the document I advised him that it was legal. It was the first and only time that I ever saw Edward Seaga looking confused and somewhat disoriented. He said, "If it is legal, then I can't call out the people." He thereupon returned to his room and the meeting broke up in confusion. It was not long, however, before Seaga regained his composure and started to plan his response.

I went downstairs to the bar where I was joined by Ferdie Yap Sam – a JLP candidate – and some other colleagues. I told them that I was going back up to my room and would soon return. But by the time I got back downstairs, Yap Sam had been detained and whisked off to Up Park Camp in Kingston. Patrick (Pat) Stephens, a member of the team, was also detained. Ray Miles, chairman of the PR committee of the JLP, was taken into custody. Pearnel Charles was missing and we wondered if they had taken him in, but apparently he had gone to his parents' house near Moneague in St. Ann. Ray Miles was taken to the police station in Montego Bay. The policemen wouldn't lock his cell. He sent out and ordered refreshments. Miles was then flown to Kingston, with a police officer holding a gun to his head the whole time. We subsequently heard that he was released because he had British citizenship. Whether that had any influence or not, the fact is that they had no arrest warrant for him. He was released the following day.

Pat Stephens was approached in the conference room at Holiday Inn and was invited to a police station near the hotel. Accompanying him were Frank Phipps, QC – a prominent attorney – and Abe Dabdoub, also an attorney. They had all been at the conference. The police said they wanted information on "Spy" Robinson, and if Stephens told them what they wanted to know he would be free to go. In the midst of the interview a call came in from a superintendent of police ordering that Stephens was to be detained, although this was not the original arrangement.

Pat Stephens was incarcerated with Yap Sam, Peter Whittingham and Earl Spencer. He remained in Cell 9 at Up Park Camp for five and a half months but was never charged. It was alleged that he was plotting the assassination of a foreign head of state. Two well-known Jamaicans, R. Danny Williams and Oliver Jones, gave character evidence on Stephens' behalf. After a change of command at Up Park Camp his confinement was changed to house arrest, which lasted six months.

The first seven persons detained under the State of Emergency were all high-ranking members of the JLP. Hugh Shearer called the Police High Command and declared: "If you want to lock up the members of the JLP, come and get us. We're all at the Holiday Inn. Stop picking up our people on the streets!" Additional detainees were picked up over the next few days included Pearnel Charles and Olivia "Babsy" Grange who were both leading members of the Opposition. Widespread consternation followed when George Lazarus, a well-known voluntary social worker, was also detained.

I was stopped on the road one day by Howard Aris who was an active supporter of the PNP, and he told me to be careful. I had a strong feeling that I too might have been detained. I knew that I had not committed any offence, but that seemed irrelevant because I was not aware of any wrongdoing by the JLP detainees. After the friendly warning from Aris, I went to the bank the next day and added my wife's name to my law office accounts so that she would have signing rights if I were placed in detention. This action reflected my state of mind, but fortunately my fears would not be realized.

I recall that on three occasions when Pearnel Charles was sent to the Resident Magistrate's Court the charges against him were dismissed, yet he was sent back to "Red Fence", which was what the detention

CHAPTER 7: POLITICAL LIFE

centre was called. It was rumoured that Dr. Michael Beaubrun, the psychiatrist, had recommended that the centre be painted red. I have no idea if this was true or what was the purpose. A popular slogan of the day was: "Red is dread."

I was the first candidate to arrive at the centre on nomination day to contest the seat in St. Andrew East Rural in the upcoming general election. Different times are traditionally set for opposing candidates to be nominated. This practice is observed by both parties to avoid the possibility of clashes among their respective supporters. I was accompanied by my wife and our younger son Zachary. My papers were in order, the correct fees were paid and I had the requisite number of electors from the constituency signing the nomination papers. The nomination took place at the police station in Gordon Town. As I drove southwards from the nomination centre through the PNP crowd, I had left my car windows open. Candidates were advised to do this so as not to appear intimidated.

As the car advanced through the crowd, a young man shook his opened bottle of drink and pointed it in my direction to drench me. I instinctively got out of the car in the middle of the PNP crowd. At the same time, some women in the crowd grabbed the young man and said: "No! You can't do that to Mr. Harding!" Many of them were "crash programme" workers cleaning the verges under the special employment programme instituted by the PNP. Although they were supporters of the ruling party and despite the political tension, they were not hostile to me. I had met many of them before and assisted some of them during my visits to the constituency. They pointed out that the young man was not even from that constituency.

On the way up to the nomination centre, a truck full of PNP supporters armed with sticks and offensive weapons overturned at the foot of the road leading to Jacks Hill from the Papine end. Some of the passengers sustained severe injuries. Dr. Horace Chang, who was then a young doctor at the University Hospital of the West Indies (and would later become a minister of government) and who was assisting my campaign, treated many of the victims at the scene and subsequently at the hospital. The word among my grassroots supporters was that the Lord had struck down "those wicked people".

I returned to the constituency office located on the Gordon Town Road. A disturbance broke out between my supporters returning from the nomination centre and PNP supporters who were going up to nominate their candidate. In the midst of the melee one of my supporters had his ear sliced off. Bedlam ensued. My supporters began to tear off the placards, using the shafts as weapons. I could see the imminent bloodbath. I immediately got in the back of a vehicle and ordered all my supporters to move, and move immediately, down the road and into Maryland, a safe area. When we got there I ordered the preparation of lemonade…and got some very strange looks from the crowd. Grandma Essie always gave you lemonade after you had a fall, a traumatic episode or a shock, and it worked! An element of calm was restored. This was it, the real thing, Jamaican elections!

The following day I went into Hermitage, a community near to August Town below the university. There was some disturbance and stone-throwing between the political factions. I was able to get my supporters to desist. The other side continued the fracas. The police arrived and began to herd my supporters into a van. The soldiers intervened and advised the police that if they took in the JLP supporters they would then have to take in the others as well. My respect for the Jamaica Defence Force grew. They appeared to be professional. I could not say the same for the police personnel present – they clearly signalled their political bias.

My law office was located at 72 Harbour Street – the then Life of Jamaica Building. One day I was told that there was a young man from the constituency who wanted to see me. Although I was a bit busy I decided to see him, even though he did not have an appointment and this was not a constituency office. People would often say: "If you cannot see the caretaker, can you imagine how impossible it will be if he is elected a Member of Parliament?" A young man of slight

CHAPTER 7: POLITICAL LIFE

build, possibly in his early twenties, came in. He was about five feet eleven inches tall, of reddish complexion with copper-coloured hair. His hair was in locks, but I was not sure if he was a Rastafarian, for to some this was just a hairstyle.

He began his speech: "I am from Maryland and I am a true-born Labourite." Maryland was an area in the constituency that showed strong support for the JLP. He continued, "I was the man who did drop dem two yout' at Maryland but the police don't know. You are new in this business; I am going to tell you that the only good comrade (supporter of the PNP) is a dead comrade."

I did not know whether he was telling the truth, in which case I ought to report it to the police, or whether he was trying to impress me that he was a "badman" whose services I would need. Finding the whole thing disgusting and distasteful, I knew I needed to terminate this visit. My impulse was to kick him out, but I did not know what kind of repercussions this might have in the constituency. All I knew was that I had to get rid of this "true-born Labourite". My instinct told me that this type of individual would always need a "bus fare". So, before he could ask, I offered him a bus fare with words which implied, "Don't call me, I'll call you."

Some weeks later my wife had to send out a press release for her flower club. When we arrived at the Jamaica Broadcasting Corporation to drop off a copy of the release, there was a crowd in front of the radio station with placards demonstrating against Pearnel Charles. Who would you guess I saw in the demonstration, carrying the most conspicuous placard, but the "true-born Labourite"? The last time I remember seeing him, he was going up Red Hills Road with a group of Rastafarians of the Twelve Tribes. I have never known Rastafarians to be active in politics. There were others like the "true-born Labourite" who had various violent solutions to suggest, and who would corrupt you if you were gullible enough to let them.

The PNP had switched their official candidate for the constituency – Eric Bell, lawyer and tennis buff – to another constituency. The southeastern part of the constituency had become very violent, especially in the Bull Bay area, with a gang of motorcyclists called the Black Unity Gang. It was alleged that they were controlled by the councillor for that division, Roy McGann. I complained to Eric Bell about it before he left the constituency, but he said he knew nothing about it and I believed him. It was common knowledge that Roy McGann wanted to represent the constituency when Eric Bell left. Bell said he would report my complaints to Keble Munn, the Minister of National Security.

It was said that Roy McGann had been a Labourite. In fact his family supported the Labour Party and one of his brothers actually ran for the Labour Party in a previous election. It is alleged that he became a member of the PNP after he had a falling out with Roy McNeill, JLP MP, over some issue concerning a quarry. I remember meeting Roy McGann for the first time when he was acting mayor of Kingston, when I took an overseas visitor, the president of an international service club, to make a courtesy call. When we entered his office, we encountered a shortish man with grey-brown eyes, swivelling around in a high-back chair, who said to us, "What can I do for you?" I thought this was an inappropriate welcome for a visitor whose arrival had been expected.

In my practice I met a young man whose motorcycle had been seized by the Cross Roads police. It was an unlawful seizure. I got the motorcycle released back to the young man without any charges. He felt beholden to me. He was a huge fellow – well over six feet tall – and had what could be described as a fierce look. One day while we were doing a house-to-house campaign at Ten Miles in the Bull Bay area, my workers became alarmed and began shouting, "Dem a come! Dem a come!" They were alerting me to the invasion of three to four motorcyclists of the so-called Black Unity Gang.

I simply said to them, "We are carrying out a lawful activity." But I was concerned because I never had any strong-arm men. That day my huge fellow with the fierce look had followed us and was parked under a tree watching us go from door to door canvassing support.

CHAPTER 7: POLITICAL LIFE

As the Black Unity Gang started to circle around menacingly, no doubt to intimidate us, my huge fellow with the fierce look simply said to them, "Wha' a gwaan, iyah?" They turned around and left.

Roy McGann and I met in a bar in Mavis Bank while we were campaigning, and I said to him, "Roy, just tell your boys in Bull Bay to cool it." In Jamaican parlance "he didn't carry me nor bring me". In short, he made no reply.

One of the policemen stationed in Bull Bay told me that he said to McGann, "How are you going to beat the young man? The people love him and he is a young lawyer." He allegedly replied, "Harding is a professional. He won't do what I will do."

Douglas Vaz, who later became an MP for the Labour Party, told me that he had spoken to O.K. Melhado, my old McGill University associate and a supporter of the PNP, who said to him, "Wait till you see what they have done to Ossie." This was in reference to the practice known as gerrymandering – manipulating the boundary of an electoral constituency to ensure victory by the ruling party. The PNP took off part of the middle-class area in Hope Pastures and added August Town, a very dense area largely populated by their supporters and allegedly harbouring criminal elements. They were in political control of the area.

The stage was set. On Election Day I could hardly enter the community. First of all it was not an area in which I had campaigned, as it was newly added to the constituency. On Election Day there was unending violence, there was no semblance of order until a Jamaica Defence Force helicopter landed in August Town. Some of my supporters were burnt out; one of them told me he had to crawl on his belly on the Hope River bank to escape. This was literally my baptism of fire. I had to find him a place in Jacks Hill – a semi-rural area – where he could find shelter.

When the ballot papers were being counted on election night, the PNP councillor hung his head in shame. The ballots in some of those areas were not folded but crumpled, as they had been clearly stuffed into the ballot boxes. There were some 17,390 registered voters in the constituency. Though not the largest in numbers, East Rural St Andrew was the largest constituency in size in the country. It touched the parish of St. Thomas in the east and West Portland in the northeast. It combined the hilly regions and foothills of the Blue Mountains down to Papine, Elletson Flats and August Town near the University of the West Indies and Harbour View near to East Kingston and Port Royal. The result was 8,710 for my opponent, 5,925 for me, making a total of 14,635 votes, which represented a turnout of 84.1 percent.

How I wished I could go back to the common room discussions at the hostel in London to tell them what it was really like. McGann won that election. But his demise would come in the next election campaign against Joan Gordon (now Webley). He was shot and killed in Gordon Town Square on October 14, 1980, two weeks before the general election of October 30, when the JLP would claim a massive victory. There were suggestions that McGann had been shot by Labourites, and both Michael Manley and Carl Rattray were on television with a flip chart speculating as to how he might have been shot. This was of great concern to me as I feared that it could have caused retaliation. His killers were never caught. It was said that Roy McGann had been shot from behind, which suggested either by his own supporters or by the police. As the tumultuous decade of the 1970s drew to a close, this tragic event created history: Roy McGann remains the only parliamentarian ever to have been killed while campaigning in a national election in Jamaica.

A commission of enquiry was set up in October 1978 to investigate the reasons behind the declaration of a State of Emergency in 1976, and whether there had been any corrupt action on the part of the political directorate. The PNP had finally caved in to pressure from the JLP, the press, and civic groups within the society. The sole commissioner was the Chief Justice of Jamaica, the Honourable Kenneth Smith. I was one of the attorneys appointed to represent the JLP. Armed with information concerning blank detention orders that had been signed

CHAPTER 7: POLITICAL LIFE

prior to the State of Emergency, I had to cross-examine Prime Minister Michael Manley in my attempt to probe the arbitrary detention of suspects. I asked him whether he would be surprised to learn that these signed orders existed. "Yes, indeed," he replied smoothly. The following morning he returned to the commission with a statement that they had searched the Attorney General's Department the night before and found no such forms. At this stage the cordial relations between Michael Manley and myself in this commission were about to break down, because that was an asinine response. Who would have kept signed blank detention orders that others could locate?

When Keble Munn appeared before the commission, I presented him with a signed blank detention order and asked whether he could identify the signature that appeared on it. He stuttered and went red in the face, because the signature was his. I then reminded the commissioner of my allusions to the existence of such detention orders during my earlier cross-examination of Prime Minister Manley. The commissioner replied, "It is unfortunate that your instructions did not go that far on that occasion."

Sometime after the Smith Commission of Enquiry, I happened to be with Keble Munn in the government departure lounge at Norman Manley Airport, and I asked him about the blank detention orders that he had signed during the 1976 State of Emergency. He told me that a senior police officer had given him the orders to sign as well as the copies, but he later discovered that the copies were blank. Unfortunately someone came into the lounge at that point. The conversation was interrupted, and we never had the opportunity to complete it. Some years later I attended Munn's funeral. The signing of blank detention orders was a supreme abuse of power, and if done inadvertently, the height of negligence. A policeman could simply fill in whatever name he wanted on a signed blank detention order.

The information given by the senior police officers in which Minister Munn signed orders for detention were not based on any written records. Many of the detainees were incarcerated on information "phoned in". The alleged typewritten list which was compiled by the Criminal Investigation Department (CID) in respect of persons considered to be subversive or involved in criminal activities compiled before the State of Emergency was admittedly destroyed in 1977, as Mr. Larry Trout, head of the CID, saw no necessity to keep it. Did such a list exist? Who knows? It was never produced before the Smith Commission.

During the 1976 election campaign, Edward Seaga and his team had been on the road four or five times per week. It was not likely that Michael Manley, as a prime minister in office, would have been able to maintain such a punishing schedule. It seemed that whether there was justification or not, the JLP campaign had to be stopped in its tracks. I therefore came to the conclusion that the purpose of the State of Emergency was to smash the JLP's campaign and prevent the party from winning. My point of view was supported by Professor Carl Stone in his foreword to *The Politics of Power* by Pearnel Charles, published in 1989:

> *The PNP strategy of bringing the coercive arm of the state firmly down on the opposition JLP in the final stages of a national election campaign in 1976 gave that party a major advantage both by temporarily discrediting the JLP in the eyes of the voters and by destabilizing the Opposition's campaign. At the time, opinion polls conducted by me confirmed that over 80% of the electorate was convinced that there must have been some grounds to justify these actions. State control over the main media channels gave the PNP more than ample opportunity to shape public opinion on this sensitive issue. Subsequent events have now confirmed that there was neither adequate evidence nor national considerations to justify what has turned out to be a skilful partisan strategy employed to ensure an election victory.*

I was appointed Attorney General in 1986 and subsequently arranged settlements on behalf of Pat Stephens and George Lazarus

CHAPTER 7: POLITICAL LIFE

who had both been wrongfully incarcerated during the 1976 State of Emergency. However, Pearnel Charles and Olivia "Babsy" Grange were not as fortunate, as there were no documents filed to support their claims for compensation. The fact that I knew they had been detained was not enough to warrant a settlement. As I explained to Pearnel Charles when he sought my assistance, "Ossie Harding knew you were detained, but not the Attorney General of Jamaica."

The State of Emergency of 1976 must surely be one of the lowest points in Jamaica's history, when Jamaicans incarcerated Jamaicans for no other reason than to display raw political power. The stark evidence of raw political power was again displayed on February 2, 1977, when agents of the Ministry of Housing forcibly evicted one thousand occupants from their homes in Wilton Gardens, popularly known as Rema. The tenants and all their belongings were violently removed because, according to the Minister of Housing Anthony Spaulding, they had failed to pay their rent. The tenants were JLP adherents, and PNP supporters were reportedly awaiting their eviction in order to take up immediate residence. It was alleged that the minister was violently partisan and was determined that his supporters should occupy the premises. A commission of enquiry was subsequently ordered by the governor general to investigate the circumstances, causes and consequences of the evictions in Rema. Mr Justice Ronald Small was appointed commissioner.

Witnesses described the evictions as traumatic. Superintendent Roy E. Thompson indicated that articles of furniture were thrown from the upper floors of the highrise buildings, and Major F Reynolds complained about the wanton destruction of property. As one of the attorneys appointed to represent the Wilton Gardens Citizens' Association, I sought to cross-examine Minister Spaulding, but Justice Small would have none of it. After making an impassioned plea to the commissioner to reconsider his position, I was allowed to proceed (see Appendix A). I maintained my composure throughout the cross-examination despite Minister Spaulding's uncouth behaviour from start to finish. His body language was insolent, and he admonished me thus: "Don't you ever try your clever little lawyer-boy tricks with me!" We had known each other from our law school days in London. In fact, despite his unruly attitude during my cross-examination, Spaulding stopped to have a friendly chat with me when we met outside the venue.

Some years after the Rema Enquiry, I would meet Tony Spaulding on two other occasions. Once in 1983, my car was stopped at a roadblock during a political demonstration. The JLP was in power at that time. Spaulding and Valerie Neita Robertson, a lawyer whom I had taught at law school, were at the roadblock. I asked them to let me through, and they did. A few years later I encountered Spaulding outside a townhouse in Barbican. He greeted me, and then pointed to a young woman walking towards us. She was wearing a long skirt similar to those worn by Rastafarian women. Looking admiringly at her, he said: "See that? One hundred percent Socialist." As she got near to us, I extended my hand and said, "Ossie Harding, Labourite." She was speechless. We entered the townhouse where several people were gathered. Spaulding made a disparaging comment about Prime Minister Seaga, and expressed disappointment that his brother Winston Spaulding and I were supporting him. His cronies then ushered Tony Spaulding outside. When he returned, his tone had changed. Maybe they had advised him to watch his words. That was the last time I saw Anthony Spaulding. He died in 1998 at the age of sixty-four, having suffered from Alzheimer's disease during the last ten years of his life.

The evictions in Rema resulted in the uprooting of twenty-six families. Whatever may be the truth about allegations concerning Tony Spaulding, I have come to the conclusion that what took place in Rema was political cleansing. To paraphrase the definition of ethnic cleansing by the 1993 United Nations Commission: It was the planned

CHAPTER 7: POLITICAL LIFE

deliberate removal from a specific area, of persons from a particular political group, by force or intimidation, in order to render that area politically homogeneous. Perhaps Jamaica ought to set up a Truth and Reconciliation Commission as was done in South Africa in 1995 after apartheid was dismantled.

JLP shadow cabinet, 1986: standing – Edmund Bartlett, Derrick Smith, Hugh Dawes, Rudyard Spencer, Audley Shaw, Brascoe Lee, Hector Wynter; seated – Oswald Harding, Enid Bennett, Prime Minister Edward Seaga, Percival Broderick, Anthony Johnson

At cocktail event, with (l-r) Mabel Tenn, Dr Mavis Gilmour and Col. Robert Neish, 1988

CHAPTER 8

Public Life

In George Eaton's Alexander Bustamante and Modern Jamaica, Bustamante is quoted as saying: "Politicians think of votes, statesmen think of the future of their country. The definition of a public-minded man is one who tries to do something for the public" (p. 83). I have never accepted the title or nomenclature of politician nor ever referred to myself as such, but I cannot deny that I am a public man.

Norman Manley is quoted in *The Memoirs of Lady Bustamante* as defining socialism thus in 1940: "Socialism is not a matter of higher wages and better living conditions for workers, though those things are important, but it involves the concept that all the means of production should, in one form or another, come to be publicly owned and publicly controlled" (p. 141). I was never attracted to this philosophy, nor was I interested in a classless society. First of all, I know of no classless society; there has never been one and in my view there never will be one.

What is socialism? Is it a transitional social state between the overthrow of capitalism and the realization of communism? Was socialism/communism undemocratic? If not, why was the ideology in Jamaica called democratic socialism? Whatever the nomenclature, I am wedded to the archaic idea that socialism/communism cannot work; certainly not in Jamaica, knowing the temperament and disposition of the Jamaican people, so why go that way? Michael Manley set up a cooperative on a sugar estate. The members went on strike. Was it that they did not understand the concept of a cooperative, or could its failure be blamed on the way Jamaicans think? This type of cooperative does not work in Jamaica. Even in apartment complexes, strata corporations are difficult to manage.

I have lived long enough to see the Soviet Union disintegrate and the Berlin Wall crumble. The only socialist/communist states that remain are North Korea, North Vietnam and Cuba. China is a special case. It is my considered opinion that the Republic of Cuba would have restructured itself had it not been for the United States' inept policies of embargo against Cuba. With all my love for the Cuban people and the respect I have for Fidel Castro, whom I had the privilege of meeting in Jamaica when he invited me and Edward Seaga to go duck shooting in Cuba, I would not join hands with Michael Manley to walk hand in hand with "Castro to the mountain top", not even around the corner.

On September 20, 2010, the *Gleaner* newspaper reported that in an interview with American journalist Jeffrey Goldberg, Fidel Castro was asked if he thought the Cuban model was still worth exporting. "The Cuban model does not even work for us anymore," was Castro's reply. Later there was some retraction or clarification of the statement, indicating that he did not mean to say that. It might well have been an off-the-cuff remark, but the truth is that the Cuban economy as currently configured has to change, though not necessarily to free-market capitalism.

The significance of Castro's statement was later confirmed with the announcement by the Cuban regime that five hundred thousand persons would be dismissed from Government jobs – an estimated 84

CHAPTER 8: PUBLIC LIFE

percent of the workforce – and that up to one million would ultimately be dismissed. Despite Cuba's success in eradicating illiteracy and improving health care, when communism collapsed in Moscow the Cubans had to confront the deficiencies of their system. I am satisfied that my assessment of socialism for Jamaica was accurate and my conclusions correct.

On the political spectrum I would consider myself a progressive conservative; this is not an oxymoron. John Diefenbaker, prime minister of Canada from 1957 to 1963, led the Progressive Conservative Party. He was opposed to the apartheid system in South Africa and opposed their re-entry to the Commonwealth. He introduced the Bill of Rights in 1960 as a federal bill. He was the first Canadian prime minister to appoint a woman, Ellen Fairclough, to a position in the federal cabinet. These were all enlightened and progressive policies, although Diefenbaker was a conservative. He had defined progressive conservatism as "the ultimate balance of free enterprise, profit making on economic ground on one hand, and social justice and respect for the interest of the common man on the other". (See Senator Hugh Segal's 2000 book *In Defence of Civility: Reflections of a Recovering Politician*, p. xii.)

The Jamaica Labour Party was described as a party with liberal policies and a progressive outlook that would recognize the legitimate claim of both labour and capital. Bustamante placed the working class at the centre of political activity and this became his preoccupation. The fact is that Bustamante saw himself as representing all classes in Jamaica, but with special responsibilities towards the poor and deprived. He was certainly not against free enterprise, but he was undoubtedly a fighter for social justice and for the interest of the common man. That was good enough for me.

In 1977, the Leader of the Opposition, Edward Seaga, summoned me to his office on Knutsford Boulevard in New Kingston and announced, "I am appointing you a senator. Please let them have a copy of your CV." I was appointed a senator, the first of several occasions to come, on December 19, 1977. I took the oath of allegiance on December 30, and was welcomed by Senator Dudley Thompson, QC, Leader of Government Business. He predicted that my contribution would be serious, not a short or passing one, and that I would contribute to history. We developed a mutual respect while in the Senate. When the JLP won the general election in 1980 I was elected President of the Senate and re-elected in 1983. I was appointed Leader of Government Business (Majority Leader) in 1984, and later that year Minister without Portfolio in the Ministry of Foreign Affairs and also Chairman of the National Council on Drug Abuse.

On my appointment to the Senate in 1980 and my election as president, the *Gleaner* editorial on November 26, 1980 stated: "Fortunately the Senate has but three members appointed to the ministerial levels . . . but with Mr. Harding removed from the debating arena by his elevation to the presidency, his debating experience and skill will be sadly missed." In 1986 I was appointed Minister of Justice and Attorney General, Chairman of the Legislation Committee and Chairman of the National Committee for International Year of Peace. I was made a Queen's Counsel (QC) in 1987, the highest rank in the legal profession.

On the occasion of the visit to Jamaica of Queen Elizabeth II on February 14, 1983, I was warmly congratulated by Senator Thompson on my speech of welcome to Her Majesty. Dudley Thompson was a man of razor-sharp wit and a master of repartee. He had gained international acclaim for his participation as a lawyer in the Jomo Kenyatta case and the trial of the Mau Mau leaders in Kenya in 1952. His sterling contributions to the Pan African movement are a matter of record. He served as Jamaica's envoy to Nigeria, Ghana and Namibia in the 1990s.

On January 14, 2010, Ambassador Dudley Thompson delivered a special guest lecture at the Norman Manley Law School entitled "Legal Aspects of Reparations". I was deeply interested in the lecture as I did not know enough about the subject, considering it no more than a request for compensation for the acts of uprooting our ancestors

CHAPTER 8: PUBLIC LIFE

from Africa and condemning them to slavery. I was personally greeted and warmly welcomed by Ambassador Thompson. The lecture was stimulating and dealt with the Pan African movement. Dudley Thompson still exhibited the sharp wit and repartee for which he had become known.

Two weeks before I had knowledge of the proposed lecture, a photographer named Errol Harvey had come to my house one Sunday and delivered a photograph which I had not ordered and which came with no invoice. He simply said that if we used the photograph he was to be given credit. The photograph depicted me greeting Dudley Thompson in the presence of two past custodes of Kingston and St. Andrew, Dr. Aubrey McFarlane and Dr. John Martin. I told Ambassador Thompson about this unusual event and promised to let him have a copy of the photograph. He subsequently came to my law office and I went outside to hand him a copy of the photograph. Although he had to move about with the aid of a walker, he insisted on coming out of his car and stepping into my office. He admired the collection of paintings decorating my office walls. I remembered then that he had studied for a while with the renowned artist Barrington Watson, and that he himself painted. When I handed him a copy of the photograph he looked at it and said only one word: "Serendipity." He celebrated his ninety-third birthday in Jamaica on January 19, 2010, before returning to Florida, USA, where he had migrated several years before. He died in 2012.

In April 1988, at a meeting of the attorneys general of Caricom held in Dominica, I joined forces with Selwyn Richardson, attorney general for Trinidad and Tobago, to lead the way in committing the Caricom countries to support the establishment of a Caribbean Court of Justice. My decision was influenced by the Federal Supreme Court established for the West Indies Federation which, though short-lived, had functioned well in my view. I was also driven by my desire to see the development of a Caribbean jurisprudence.

When the People's National Party returned to power in 1989, the administration seemed in undue haste to establish the CCJ – whether out of some atavistic reversion to Federation, it is hard to say – but instead of negotiating with the Opposition JLP to achieve that end, they thought that with their large majority they could overcome any obstacles.

It also appeared that an atmosphere was created in which most Jamaicans felt that the United Kingdom Privy Council was not in favour of hanging, as demonstrated in their decision in the *Pratt and Morgan* case. This reinforced the view that we had to establish the CCJ as quickly as possible. However, *Pratt and Morgan v. Attorney General of Jamaica (1991) 43 W.I.R* did not declare against capital punishment. The decision of the Privy Council upheld the principle that a delay in excess of five years or more after conviction would constitute cruel and inhumane treatment contrary to the constitution of Jamaica.

In an attempt to circumvent the decision in the case of *Pratt and Morgan*, the Patterson administration withdrew from the Optional Protocol of Civil and Political Rights of the United Nations, as this would offer another avenue of appeal which would further delay the process. In order to engage the Optional Protocol, the applicant would have had to exhaust all domestic remedies. The Government of Jamaica delivered the Instrument of withdrawal from the Optional Protocol to the International Covenant on Civil and Political Rights (ICCPR) in New York to the Secretary General of the United Nations on Thursday, October 23, 1997.

At about the same time, Minister of Foreign Affairs Seymour Mullings circulated a one-page document in Parliament expressing the government's intention to withdraw from the appeal procedure in the Inter American system of the Organization of American States (OAS). Under Article 8 of the Charter, persons who feel that their human rights have been violated may petition the Inter American System. Noteworthy also was that by virtue of Article 131 it does not restrict applications being made to the United Nations as well. Unlike the UN protocol, Jamaica would have had to withdraw from the entire Inter American Charter. This, of course, would make no sense, so no further action was apparently taken in this regard.

CHAPTER 8: PUBLIC LIFE

Although the Government seemed determined to resume hanging, various obstacles stood in their way. After the case of *Neville Lewis v. Attorney General of Jamaica 1994*, the presumption that the sentence of death after five years was unconstitutional, as in *Pratt and Morgan*, was actually treated as a rule. It should be borne in mind, however, that the CCJ is not required to follow the judgements of the United Kingdom Privy Council as precedent, though they may accept these judgements as persuasive.

In 2004, the Privy Council held that the mandatory death penalty as applied in the case of *Lambert Watson v. the Attorney General of Jamaica* was unconstitutional and therefore invalid. Attorney General A J Nicholson stated that the decision of the Privy Council would be followed, but that the government would be giving serious consideration as to whether the law should be amended after the judgement. The administration felt that having the CCJ as the court of last resort would remove obstacles from the state's ability to carry out capital punishment.

In *We Want Justice: Jamaica and the Caribbean Court of Justice*, Delano Franklyn quotes Phillip Paulwell as saying in Parliament on May 13, 2003: "While the old argument for a Caribbean Court of Appeal was hinged on the issue of capital punishment, that is not the case in this new paradigm" (p. 23). In my view, with respect to the establishment of the CCJ the administration had "moved the goal posts" and therefore my enthusiasm for its establishment has waned. It is ironic that the last person to face the gallows met his fate in 1988 under my watch as attorney general. Although I am against capital punishment, the law has to be enforced as long as it remains the law.

On January 21, 2010, I attended a meeting at the Norman Manley Law School dealing with the CCJ. The guest speakers were Professor Simeon McIntosh, formerly dean of the Cave Hill law faculty, and Professor Winston Anderson, a Jamaican resident in Barbados. On the issue of the CCJ, I publicly stated that Jamaica was paying 28 percent of the cost of the court, and although I was informed that seven Jamaicans – including a former judge of the Court of Appeal – had applied, no Jamaican had been appointed to the court. Was it that none of the Jamaican applicants were qualified?

It was announced that on the retirement of Mr. Justice Pollard on June 10, 2010, Professor Winston Anderson, a Jamaican national resident in Barbados, would be appointed judge of the CCJ and would be sworn in on June 15 at King's House. During the week of June 9, I received an invitation from King's House to attend the swearing-in of Mr. Justice Anderson to the CCJ, and later I received a personal phone call from Professor Anderson, the nominee, inviting me to attend. I accepted with great pleasure and offered my congratulations.

At the ceremony many speakers mentioned that this was the first appointment of a Jamaican to the court. Instead of viewing this as a special achievement or honour, however, it had the opposite effect on me of rubbing salt into the wound. The Rt. Honourable Michael de la Bastide, president of the CCJ, reiterated that Professor Anderson had been appointed on his merits and erudition and not because he was a Jamaican. He had been selected from a shortlist of three persons. He went on to state, however, that all in the shortlist of three were Jamaicans. Interesting, I thought, that a Jamaican would inevitably have been appointed.

I am not inclined to believe that my public declaration had anything to do with such an appointment, but I might have been reflecting a Jamaican point of view which echoed elsewhere.

In September 1988, a meeting of the attorneys general of the Caribbean Commonwealth States was scheduled to take place in Trinidad. I said to Selwyn Richardson, the attorney general of Trinidad and Tobago, "Why don't we have the meeting in Tobago? We are always coming to Port of Spain." He took me seriously and organized the meeting in Tobago. It was my first visit to that island. I found Tobago hospitable and the people more like Jamaicans. The first thing I enquired about was whether we could get a goat. I directed the chef in our hotel how to make "goat's head soup". It came out

CHAPTER 8: PUBLIC LIFE

quite well, and when some of the locals heard that it was reported to have aphrodisiac powers, men and women waited in line to have the goat's head soup. The conference went extremely well; but then tragedy struck, as far as the Jamaicans were concerned.

On September 12, 1988, torrential rains accompanied by 115-mph winds struck Jamaica – a direct hit. This was Hurricane Gilbert. It was devastating. I watched the satellite imagery as the hurricane passed over Jamaica. It reminded me of a fried egg – the yolk was the eye of the hurricane. I was addressing the meeting and found that I could hardly speak. My heart was palpitating and my voice became inaudible. The welfare of my wife and younger son consumed my thoughts. Our elder son was at school abroad. Perhaps the household helper might have been at our house.

Do you believe in miracles? It is said that a miracle is an extraordinary and welcome event that cannot be explained by natural or scientific laws. A miracle was about to take place. In Jamaica all communication was cut off – both internally and externally because all the cable and telephone lines were down. The 115-mph winds had seen to that, so this was no surprise. In my hotel room in Trinidad, I kept dialling my house number over and over, almost mechanically, and then the impossible occurred. My wife answered the phone and said they were all right, and then the line went dead. No one else was able to reach Jamaica by telephone.

All the members of our delegation were extremely anxious to get home. Chief Justice Zacca had left Tobago a day earlier but could not get out of Trinidad. No planes were flying to Jamaica. I heard that there were some US cargo planes going to Jamaica from Panama carrying emergency equipment. I thought I would try to get to Panama. BWIA was not stopping in Jamaica. There was no radar and there were no air traffic controllers. I was able to get to Miami, but before I could think of going to Panama an Air Jamaica pilot came from behind the airline counter and said, "I am going home. Who wants to come?" I was the first to accept his offer. The flight had to leave immediately as it could not land after 4:00 p.m.

The fact that there were no air traffic controllers on duty meant that the pilot had to use all the skills at his command to land that plane. It was a heart-stopping experience, and increased my respect for our Jamaican pilots whose reputation is legendary. What is more, he landed the plane without a single bump. On disembarking, we would experience a most unusual occurrence: there was not one immigration or customs officer in sight. We all simply walked through the airport, unimpeded. I had my carry-on luggage and a portable standby unit given to me in Trinidad.

My faithful driver Rueben Kelly was waiting for me outside the airport. I think he simply took a chance to come out there, for there was no certainty that I would be on that plane. Ever since he became my official driver in January 1987, Kelly has impressed me as a very resourceful person. He has exhibited loyalty, trustworthiness and reliability, and is capable of maintaining a punishing work schedule. In the past twenty-four years he has had a spotless driving record. The only faint blot on his copybook occurred one morning when he bumped into a garden fence while reversing in my driveway. Ironic, isn't it?

After my arrival from Trinidad, Kelly and I left the airport and meandered our way home as he circumnavigated the debris like a footballer trying to get around the defence. When we reached Jacks Hill we saw the repair trucks with their cradled baskets containing workmen high up in the air, working feverishly to restore electric lines. I thought to myself: "Jamaica Public Service is really on the ball," but as I got closer and was passing the trucks I saw written on the vehicles: "Florida Light and Power." Prime Minister Edward Seaga had arranged for those vehicles to come in with fuel and workmen. Light and power were restored in a very short time. Priority was given to pumping stations and this allowed water to return in record time. In a speech which I delivered some years later I asserted that this was Edward Seaga's finest hour.

On my return to Trinidad eight years later, in 1995, my friend Selwyn Richardson, the former attorney general, entertained me royally. We

CHAPTER 8: PUBLIC LIFE

went to Maracas Beach where we ate a local delicacy called "shark and bake". He took me to his new home and proudly showed me his mango tree which he claimed bore the sweetest mangoes in Trinidad and which few people owned. The mango was sweet, but it was one of the commonest mangoes back home in Jamaica. It was what we call a hairy mango, for it is loaded with fibres. He took me back to my hotel, and as we drove around Port of Spain we spoke of the new Courts of Justice and the contribution he had made as attorney general.

On my return to Jamaica that weekend I conveyed to Carl Rattray, former attorney general of Jamaica, how grateful Selwyn had been to receive the cases sent by Carl because they had been useful in a court matter. On the Monday morning Carl called me to convey shocking news: Selwyn had been murdered at his home. I wondered whether the killers had been stalking us the whole time I was with him. Who knows? We heard that his killing had something to do with Yasin Abu Bakr and the Jamaat al Muslimeen. His murderers were reportedly killed after they left his house. Abu Bakr and his cronies had attempted to stage a coup d'état against the government of Trinidad and Tobago in July 1990. I know nothing of these speculations. What I do know is that I lost a friend and colleague in a most tragic way.

When the PNP assumed office in 1989 I was appointed Leader of Opposition Business in the Senate (Minority Leader). In the same year I became advisor to the Caribbean Law institute in banking and insurance law. In 1991 I was elected deputy chairman of the JLP and in April 2006 I became treasurer of the party. I had the privilege of addressing the United Nations General Assembly at the thirty-ninth, fortieth and forty-first sessions on behalf of Jamaica.

I had begun my career in Parliament as president of the Senate in 1980; I concluded my term in September 2011. The last meeting of the Senate was held at the Jamaica Conference Centre, Kingston as Gordon House was being refurbished. It was at this meeting that I declared that I would not be returning to the Senate, whatever would be the result of the impending general elections.

I became the longest-serving senator in the history of Jamaica, having served for twenty-five consecutive years from 1977 to 2002. I was reappointed to the Senate on September 24, 2007, and elected president for the second time, the nomination being seconded by the opposition; and then completed twenty-eight years. I was made a member of the Order of Distinction, Commander Class in 1995, and the Order of Jamaica in 2003 – the fourth highest order of the nation.

In December 2011, Prime Minister Andrew Holness, designated me as the head of the delegation and his special representative to the fourth Caricom-Cuba Summit held in Port of Spain, Trinidad and Tobago on December 8, 2011.

In March 1984 Marigold and I were privileged to entertain the Most Reverend Dr. Robert Runcie, Archbishop of Canterbury, when he visited Jamaica along with his Chaplain Reverend Witherton, and his personal assistant Terry Waite. When the archbishop arrived from Belize, he was suffering from a sore throat. Terry Waite, a huge fellow with a beard, immediately asked whether we had a doctor. As a former Foreign Service officer, I had made all the necessary arrangements for a visiting VIP. Dr. Ronald Irvine, a well-known internist and Leader of the Senate, was on standby. Terry Waite immediately enquired about the doctor's bona fides, reminding us of the place of the archbishop in the order of precedence after the queen. On hearing of Dr. Irvine's qualifications, he was satisfied.

They were our house guests for their four-day stay in Jamaica. We found the prelate quite affable, unassuming, engaging and friendly. My wife got along with him especially well. The chaplain was a most modest man. The pillows in his room were on top of a cupboard. The housekeeper had not gone into his room as it was strewn with clerical robes. He had not seen the pillows and did not ask, so he slept the first night without pillows. I later wondered whether his sense of good manners prevented him from enquiring;

CHAPTER 8: PUBLIC LIFE

perhaps he thought we had none and then it would have been embarrassing. He could not have imagined that in these strange lands we did not use pillows! We advised him that he was our guest and could ask for anything he needed, and if we were not available he could ask our housekeeper.

Terry Waite was a big man well over six feet in height. On one occasion he went out to lunch on the wooden deck beside the swimming pool in his stocking feet – no shoes! My younger son, Zachary, was fascinated. Terry Waite became Archbishop Runcie's Assistant for Anglican Commission Affairs. He had been successful in negotiating the release of several hostages in Iran in 1980. Later in 1987 he himself was taken hostage and spent several months in captivity. Sometime in 1991 he wrote a book titled *Travels with a Primate*. I don't suppose his visit to Jamaica would be mentioned in it, as nothing particularly eventful occurred.

On the day of the archbishop's arrival, we decided to prepare an early brunch after he had settled in. Our helper wanted to serve him some good Jamaican stew peas with roly-poly flour dumplings, but we thought that smoked salmon and a light salad would be preferable. We did think, however, that a good brandy (cognac) might help his sore throat. Terry Waite, with great English aplomb, suggested that no doubt His Lordship would prefer to go up to his room, to which the archbishop readily agreed. Our helper, not having seen an archbishop or perhaps an Englishman before, took the tray up to his room. On her return she reported that he took the brandy and just "whips-it-off". When I awoke the following morning and looked outside, I wondered whether I was under house arrest. Both the front and the rear of my premises were littered with uniformed policemen. I suddenly remembered that we had house guests and who they were.

In my capacity as president of the Senate, Ambassador Sotirhos of the US arranged a trip for me to visit Washington and the Parliament in Louisiana, June 8–19, 1980. On my arrival I was assigned an African American guide. He was about six feet tall and had his head shaved. I referred to him as the black Kojak – a black version of Telly Savalas who played a beefy police detective with a penchant for lollipops. My guide was friendly, knew his way around, and had a keen sense of humour. Having noticed that jogging was a favourite pastime during the lunch hour in Washington, I asked him whether he jogged. He replied with a strong African American accent, "Whenever you see a jogger with a smile on his face, I'll take up jogging."

I was accompanied to see Strom Thurmond, the president pro tempore of the US Senate. There were many items of gossip about him. He was nearing seventy-nine when we met: he had married twenty-two-year-old Miss South Carolina in 1968 when he was sixty-six years old and he was reported to have had a hair transplant. It was more important for me to be briefed before our meeting that he was a former governor of South Carolina who had run for president in 1948 as a member of the States' Rights Democratic Party, commonly known as the Dixiecrats. This was a short-lived segregationist party in the Southern United States which originated as a break-away faction of the Democratic Party in 1948, and which sought to protect the Southern way of life under siege from an 'oppressive' federal government. The party opposed racial integration and was determined to retain white supremacy. By 1950, however, nearly all the Dixiecrats had returned to the Democratic Party.

I was told that Strom Thurmond granted only five minutes for courtesy calls. We were in conversation for over twenty minutes. He was particularly interested in the anti-communist position of the JLP. As I was leaving, he asked whether there was anybody in the White House I would like to see, other than the president or vice president, but I told him no. When I arrived at my hotel I got a call repeating the same message; but there was no one there I needed to see. Despite his segregationist views, I learnt afterwards that Strom Thurmond had fathered a daughter with his black maid Carrie Butler.

I led the Jamaican delegation to the Fourteenth Session of the Organization of American States held in Cartagena, Colombia, in

CHAPTER 8: PUBLIC LIFE

December 1985. Baena Soares, a Brazilian diplomat, was the secretary general. Our hosts wanted certain changes to some sections of the charter with respect to the powers of the secretary general. We had no objections to the requested changes, but we argued for a certain quid pro quo: we wanted the admission of Guyana and Belize to the OAS. These countries were barred from membership on the basis of Article 8 which states: "The Permanent Council shall make no recommendation nor shall the General Assembly take any decision with respect to a request for admission on the part of a political entity whose territory became subject in whole or in part to a territorial dispute."

Guyana had a border dispute with Venezuela, and Belize with Guatemala. I met with the leader of the Barbadian delegation and worked out an approach, then we met with the other Caricom countries and developed a unified position. As a result of the initiative taken by Jamaica and Barbados which was supported by the other Caricom states, the Protocol of Cartagena was adopted and signed by the parties on December 5, 1985, and ratified by Jamaica on November 31, 1986. This Protocol allowed the entry of Guyana and Belize to the OAS.

Before the agreement was reached, Colombia seemed to have had serious negotiations with Venezuela – it did not appear to us that there was as much discussion with Guatemala. Guatemala ratified the protocol on April 10, 1991, and Venezuela ratified it on May 20, 1993. The US, Peru, Chile, and Panama signed statements with their ratifications. At about the time of the Colombia meeting, Guyana was in full flight with the Socialist Cooperative Republic. When I reported to Prime Minister Seaga on my return, he asked me why I was sticking out my neck for Guyana and Belize. I said my position was quite simple: I wanted two more votes in the OAS where the Latin American countries had a large majority.

As Minister of Justice in 1986 I felt that there were injustices in the society, either because existing legislation had become outdated and ineffective, or because no laws existed to correct certain wrongs in the modern-day situation. Consequently I undertook a programme of reform and introduced eight bills in this regard. Perhaps I could have been accused of using the law as a method of social reform. The bills are as follows:

Maintenance Orders (facilitates for Enforcement) Act:
This act extended maintenance orders to non-Commonwealth countries.

The Divorce Act:
This act introduced only one ground for divorce, namely that the marriage had broken down irretrievably. The Christian Lawyers Association raised the issue that those whom God had joined together no man should put asunder. I indicated to them that I was not creating divorce but attempting to correct the current situation. I had some concerns about the Roman Catholic Church, knowing their stance on divorce. Once they saw the section on counselling and attempts at reconciliation, I had no difficulty – after all, divorce was already a fait accompli.

The Judicial Proceedings (Regulation of Reports) Bill:
This bill was intended to prohibit the printing or publication of lurid details of certain events which may have occurred during a marriage and might be the basis for the divorce. Certain sections of the press were generally critical of the legislation. Many columns were written by my late friend Carl Wint that the press had a right to know and that we might as well have divorces tried *in camera*. I asked where was the right to know what goes on in people's private bedrooms. Was it in the Common Law or stated in any statute? If not, I would not recognize such a right.

In an article in the *Daily Gleaner* of February 17, 1987, Carl Wint stated inter alia:

CHAPTER 8: PUBLIC LIFE

It was an impressive presentation by the Leader of Government Business, the Minister of Justice Senator Ossie Harding. Backed by history, cemented in law, and rendered in a mood of self-righteousness, he sought a place in the pantheon of social legislations, and the chances are he will get it. They claim that they are not infringing press freedom. That is a lie. Senator Harding lied when he said the Bill did not do that. Once the Bill limits the amount of information the press can carry about divorce cases it is impinging on press freedom.

The Hon. Hector Wynter, a former senator for the JLP and journalist writing on public affairs in the *Gleaner* of March 1, 1987, weighed in on the issue in support of Carl Wint. As the bill had been passed in the Senate, he was appealing to the House. I stood my ground, garnering little or no support from my party members. Of course, it was in the interest of the newspaper to maintain the status quo, because lurid details sell newspapers.

My motivation to introduce the legislation was largely due to a letter I had received from a child psychologist who catalogued some of the mental and emotional damage caused to some children by the publication of sordid details concerning their parents. Whenever I think of this piece of legislation I recall a conversation I had with a retired councillor in a rural district at a branch meeting one night. He said to me, "I am the man who brought light into this district; people may not remember, but I know." Nobody may recall, nobody may know, but I will remember: no lurid details in divorce cases have been published since then. Press freedom was not attacked, and newspapers still sell.

The Inheritance (Family Provisions) Act:
The Courts in Jamaica cannot change "the provisions of a valid will or succession rights where the deceased had not left a will". The intention of the new law was to make a reasonable provision

for the maintenance of the family and dependents of the deceased person to be paid out of the estate.

The Intestate Estates and Property Charges Act:
The intent was to increase the claims of the surviving wife or husband, and to provide for the circumstance where, if a man and woman lived together without making a will, the survivor would be entitled to a share of the deceased's estate.

The Offences Against the Person Act:
 It was felt that the penalties were inadequate for a householder who induced or encouraged unlawful and carnal knowledge of young girls on his premises. The penalties were increased: imprisonment for life when the girl is under the age of twelve and so on. The age of consent was then fourteen years. I thought that this was inconsistent since a girl could not marry without the consent of her parents until she was sixteen years old. I later raised the age of consent to sixteen years. Some persons thought that it should have been raised to eighteen, the age of majority, but I could defend the position I had taken.

The Criminal Records Act:
I had a case of a young man who in his late teens had been convicted of being in possession of or smoking a ganja cigarette (marijuana). He was now thirty-five years old with a common-law wife and four children. He applied to go to work on the overseas employment (farm work) programme. He had committed no offence against the law other than his teenage conviction. He was refused entry. It seemed to me only fair that society should be kinder to those citizens who had led law-abiding lives after committing a minor infraction. In my view they should be able to have a clean record, and I argued that minor offences should be expunged from the records. I felt especially comfortable with this piece of legislation.

CHAPTER 8: PUBLIC LIFE

Writing in the *Gleaner* on law reform and rehabilitation, Arthur Kitchin stated:

It may be instructive to note that since 1980, and at Mr. Harding's urging, nearly 200 new laws and/or amendments to existing laws above have been either introduced in or passed the drafting and printing stages and are now ready to be tabled.

As Minister of Justice I was responsible for the prisons. On the weekend of January 2, 1988, prisoners on death row in the St. Catherine District prison took two warders hostage to press their demands for commutation of their sentences. When I arrived at the prison, there was, as would be expected, an air of tension, if not despair, because the condemned prisoners had nothing to lose, having already been condemned to death. Father Brian Massie SJ, a Canadian Roman Catholic priest, was the chaplain there. The warders in captivity were E.G. Adams and L. Richards. According to reports, at about 10:00 a.m. on Sunday the warders were in the act of performing regular duties when they were "jumped" by the prisoners. When I arrived I asked whether there were any dominoes available. Many of the warders were astounded; this was not a time to play games. It was my signal that we might have been in for a long haul.

As it turned out, the negotiations lasted about eight hours. When I asked the superintendent if he had any whisky, he denied that there was any on the premises as that was not allowed. I had reason to believe otherwise, but the superintendent said he would send off the premises to get some. All this time the priest was observing me. I was simply attempting to create an atmosphere of calm. I asked to see the negotiating team for the prisoners. When they arrived I asked them their Christian names and began to address them accordingly. The idea was to negotiate with them on a personal level and not treat them as objects. These were dangerous men who had nothing to lose. One of the negotiators was called "Lucifer". He never looked you straight in the face, and always kept his head cocked at an odd angle.

During the negotiations for the release of the hostages, my colleague Errol Anderson, Minister of National Security, was in constant touch with me. I was unaware, however, that he had a team of men waiting to storm the prison if necessary – an Entebbe-style rescue mission. In 1976 the Israeli Defence Force had successfully stormed an aircraft at Entebbe Airport in Uganda which had been hijacked by Palestinian terrorists.

I advised the prisoners that their action would not gain any sympathy or support from the public. While the negotiations continued with the able assistance of Superintendent of Police Bertram Millwood, a lawyer whom I had taught in law school, we were able to have the first hostage freed by 8:00 p.m. This now became the most dangerous stage of the operation, for with the last hostage as a pawn, his release would destroy their bargaining power. Minister Anderson and I were in control and had things moving in the right direction when all of a sudden we were made to understand that Prime Minister Seaga was on his way, accompanied by Olivia "Babsy" Grange – Minister of Information, and Tom Tavares-Finson, attorney-at-law. My limited understanding of security operations indicated that the head "honcho" should never be put in this situation. Along with Superintendent Millwood, we were able to have the second hostage freed by ten o'clock the same night, just before the prime minister and his party arrived, so it all ended well. The Entebbe-style rescue was averted.

Afterwards I petitioned the governor general for a temporary stay of execution for the condemned prisoners, which was granted. The *Star* newspaper of January 8, 1988, carried the headline "Harding saves the day for hostage warders". I was recommended by one LeGrange Nelson for the Gleaner Honour award on February 2, 1988. Reverend Brian Massie S.J wrote to me on January 20, 1988, saying inter alia: "The purpose of this letter is to express my gratitude and admiration at your realistically compassionate handling of the recent warder-taking incident at the St. Catherine District Prison."

CHAPTER 8: PUBLIC LIFE

The Bar Association paid tribute to me, as reported in the *Daily Gleaner* of January 3, 1989 (see Appendix D), for "introducing important legislation in Parliament" during the year. According to the *Gleaner*, their annual report for the period July 1987 to August 1988

> *commented on the excellent relationship members have enjoyed with the Minister. The report also noted Senator Harding's interest in restoring and refurbishing courthouses across the island.*
>
> *"The Bar is aware and grateful for its excellent relationship we have enjoyed with the Attorney General... He has been unfailing in his support, and his willingness to discuss our concerns and to liaise with us in regard to proposing legislation is noted in appreciation...*
>
> *"We appreciate his efforts, his frankness and his helpfulness in the interest of justice," the report said.*

The *Sunday Gleaner* of April 3, 2009 stated:

> *Taking a cursory glance through the history of parliamentary debates since the 1970's, Dessler Smith, a 30-year veteran staff member at Gordon House, highlighted some outstanding legislators over the period such as former parliamentarians, such as the late Michael Manley, Dudley Thompson, David Coore, Carl Marshall and President of the Senate Oswald Harding who have all made Smith's list of most eloquent presenters. These are parliamentarians who are beyond the surface; they rise above the rest when it comes to debates.*

I felt well harnessed in the position of attorney-general, but before I could really gallop, the People's National Party returned to power after the general elections held in February 1989. As a result, I was unable to complete many of my objectives.

Receiving the Order of Jamaica from Governor General Sir Howard Cooke, 2003

President of the Senate, 2007

At the awards ceremony, with (l-r) Justice Clarence "Billy" Walker, Justice Lloyd Ellis, 2003

With Archbishop Desmond Tutu and Hugh Shearer on the occasion of Tutu's visit to Jamaica, 1987

With former US president Jimmy Carter, 1982

Being presented to President Nelson Mandela, 1991, with (l-r) Dwight Nelson and Ryan Peralto looking on

CHAPTER 9

Cameos

In preparing the manuscript of my life's story, I had various flashbacks about some notable international figures that I have met, as well as some Jamaican personalities, and thought I might include them.

Delegates at the 1985 Commonwealth Heads of Government Meeting

The Commonwealth Heads of Government meeting which was held in the Bahamas on July 29, 1985 had among its delegates the Commonwealth leaders Rajiv Gandhi, prime minister of India, Margaret Thatcher, prime minister of the United Kingdom, Kenneth Kaunda, prime minister of Zambia, Robert Mugabe, prime minister of Zimbabwe, Brian Mulrooney, prime minister of Canada, and Edward Seaga of Jamaica. I was his alternate. On my right sat Prime Minister Gandhi, as we were placed in alphabetical order. I had the opportunity of speaking with him. I found him a most congenial person, easy to talk to, calm and attentive. I was extremely saddened to learn of his untimely death when he was assassinated by a suicide bomber in 1991.

Margaret Thatcher, I found, was stately and very firm in her statements. She was most courteous to Kenneth Kaunda, but it was noticeable that there was tension between herself and Robert Mugabe of Zimbabwe. He once exclaimed *sotto voce* that "if it were not for my men in the bushes we would still be a colony".

One of the more memorable events I can recall that took place during that conference occurred during a discussion about South Africa. There was talk that the execution of an African freedom fighter was scheduled to take place. The Nigerian delegate, Oebitu Ukive, Chief of General Staff, suggested that the conference should condemn South Africa for this action. The meeting tried to indicate that no execution had yet taken place and that the meeting should try to intervene.

Brian Mulroney, Canadian prime minister, in what then seemed like a little game of one-upmanship, indicated to the meeting the next day that his envoy had contacted the South African government, and the execution had taken place nonetheless. The Nigerian representative began by saying, "As I was saying, we should pass a resolution condemning South Africa." It had been his attempt to suggest that the execution was inevitable.

Margaret Thatcher

Margaret Thatcher made an official visit to Jamaica in July 1987. In preparation for the visit my wife, a horticulturist, was invited to beautify the government's gardens. She began by cutting down several cassia trees, which were extremely old. This caused some public concern; in fact a few people asked outright, "What mad person could be cutting down the trees?" Prime Minister Seaga wanted them replaced with canna lilies, even though he was advised that they would cost a lot to maintain. Nevertheless, that was what he wanted. When Margaret Thatcher visited the cannas were in full bloom, and she commented on how beautiful they were. Interestingly, her visit coincided with the same time that Douglas Vaz, who was then a minister in the Seaga-led JLP administration, was having some issues with the JLP. During the visit there was a quip amongst some persons that "the flowers are blooming but there is no Vaz".

Ronald Reagan

I had occasion to meet the fortieth president of the United States, Ronald Reagan, in 1982 during his official visit to Jamaica. As he made his way through the Norman Manley International Airport on April 7, 1982, then Prime Minister Edward Seaga was to his left and I, who was then President of the Senate, was immediately behind him. Then I suddenly heard a voice from behind me say, "Mr. President, you are too close to the President." I was annoyed that anyone could tell me where to stand in my own country; but the Secret Service agent was of course correct.

George H. Bush

In 1983 when US vice president George H. Bush visited Jamaica, I reminded him that Lindon B. Johnson, who also visited as vice president, went on to become president of the United States, and I predicted that it would be the same for him.

I found him very informal, relaxed and quite easy to talk to. And as I predicted, he did become president of the United States.

Fidel Castro

World-renowned president of the Republic of Cuba, Fidel Castro, made an official visit to Jamaica in the 1980s during the prime ministership of Edward Seaga. Despite Mr. Seaga's well-known objections to the communist regime, it was a very cordial meeting. I had the opportunity to talk with him during their official meeting, and found Fidel Castro to be a very charismatic person. In fact, when he found out that Mr. Seaga had an interest in bird shooting he invited both of us to come duck hunting. I don't believe that the offer was ever taken up. In any event, I was not that interested in bird shooting.

Hugo Chavez

I, along with Edward Seaga, met with the Venezuelan president on his visit to Jamaica in 1999. During his meeting with Mr. Seaga, I recalled a past visit I had made to Venezuela's capital, Caracas. I remembered that in the presidential palace there was a painting of a very large white horse with three men attempting to mount it. There was a native Indian, a black man and a white man, all trying to get on the horse. The inscription in Spanish read, "Here there are no Whites, Indians or Blacks – only Venezuelans." The memory prompted me to raise with him the question of colour in Venezuela. He replied, "Look at me, I am all three." Again, this was a most charismatic person.

Parliamentary Delegation to Moscow

I was a member of the Jamaica Parliamentary delegation to Moscow-Leningrad from August 6 to 11, 1991. Also among the delegation were the then Speaker of the House of Representatives, Headley Cunningham; Clerk to the Parliament, Headley Deans; and Carl Rattray, MP.

On our visit we met a number of high-ranking officials, including Vice President, Mr. Gennadiy Yanayev, who had assumed the position of Acting President. Mr. Gorbachev was unable to meet with us as we were told that he was on vacation in his dacha in Georgia. Georgia was then a part of the Soviet Union.

Mr. Yanayev seemed very nervous, somewhat agitated and was chain-smoking. He asked us about Cuba and suggested that Cuba's future belonged with the Caribbean. After we returned to Jamaica, we subsequently learnt that he had been imprisoned, as there had been an aborted *coup d'état* – no wonder he was so nervous.

CHAPTER 9: CAMEOS

Members of the First Cabinet, April 24, 1962

Edwin L. Allen, Minister of Education

The late Sir Florizel Glaspole, former Governor General of Jamaica, once said to me that Edwin Allen was the greatest Minister of Education that Jamaica had yet seen.

Edwin Allen was from the parish of Clarendon – a short man, who was very rural-looking. Minister Allen made several visits to England during my time in the Foreign Service, and I had several occasions to interact with him. His first visit was in the sixties, and he arrived in London wearing an overcoat, nearly to his ankles, reminiscent of the length worn mostly in Russia. I found it somewhat amusing. After we acquainted ourselves I gently asked him, "Do you like your coats long, Minister?" To which he replied in the affirmative. I knew no other way of raising the subject.

Minister Allen had assisted many nursing students to get to England to study. On his arrival, many of them came to see him at the hotel where he was staying. I do not know what transpired between them, but by the next day I saw him in a spanking new overcoat just knee-high. His nurses apparently had taken control.

He had travelled with about three suitcases, referred to by Jamaicans as "grips" – travelling bags. He had in them an entire wardrobe including a white dinner jacket, and clothes for formal wear. He wanted to ensure that he would be properly attired for any occasion. I advised him that there were local stores that hired formal wear and that it was not necessary to travel with them. He exhibited a sense of humility.

Whenever Edwin Allen arrived in London he would ask me what was the price of ginger. I had no idea and always had to enquire from the officer responsible for trade. Of course, at the time I was unaware that he was from an area in Clarendon that grew ginger for export. I believed that perhaps he himself was a ginger farmer.

He shared many of his ideas about education with me. We spoke, among other things, about the establishment of comprehensive schools; the possibility of making attendance at schools compulsory and the introduction of truant officers. The conversations were stimulating as I had taught at schools in London. He was a dedicated man and one of the earliest teachers to have obtained a BA degree.

On my return to Jamaica I had occasion to visit him in his final days. He was in a public ward at the University Hospital of the West Indies looking quite down and forlorn, this great educator, after whom a school would be named. In my opinion he was the greatest Minister of Education of his day. He died in 1984.

Donald B. Sangster, Minister of Finance

Minister of Finance, Donald B. Sangster, who would later become Prime Minister, would have long talks with me whenever he came to London. He was especially interested in quizzing me as to what I thought of the fusing of the legal profession. He seemed quite open to the idea. I was a barrister and he was a solicitor. The professions were ultimately fused after the Legal Profession Act, of January 1972.

The last occasion on which I saw him was on Duke Street across from the Bustamante Industrial Trade Union (BITU). He was on the opposite side standing with arms akimbo and talking to someone – no security in sight. As I hurriedly tried to pass him, not wanting to interrupt him as he was in conversation, he hailed me from across the street.

Donald Sangster died on April 11, 1967 at the Montreal General Hospital in Canada. It was said that he suffered a brain haemorrhage.

CHAPTER 9: CAMEOS

David "Clem" Tavares

Clem Tavares was a well-built individual of mixed blood. He somewhat resembled a person of East Indian extraction. He took a liking to me, and whenever he came to London the High Commissioner had to release me to accompany him wherever he wanted to go.

On one of his visits to London there was a formal reception hosted by the High Commissioner. As a visiting minister of government, he was placed in the reception line immediately after the High Commissioner. He later asked me whether he had been placed in the correct order at the reception. He said, "In my protocol, first there is God, then the prime minister and then ministers." I explained to him that an ambassador or high commissioner was accredited to the head of state in the country in which he is serving. Clem simply laughed.

One day I was visiting with my cousin in Greenwich Farm which was in his constituency. My cousin was a strong supporter of the People's National Party. I asked him what was happening across the street where there was a small crowd and where a car was parked there. He curtly replied, "Clem Tavares, the JLP minister."

I said, "I must go over and see him." My cousin stayed put with his arms folded.

I went over and joined the line. When I arrived at the window, he said, "How can I help you?"

I replied, "I need a job." He recognized my voice and looked up. He was happy to see me. That was the last time we met.

Ken (K.A.N.) Jones, Minister of Communication and Works

He was one of the twin sons of Mr. Fred M. Jones of Portland. Ken travelled often to England to the Farnborough Airshow. He became quite knowledgeable about airplanes and transportation.

On his last visit to London, we had a pleasant parting drink. Shortly after he arrived in Jamaica, we heard the sad news that he had fallen off the balcony at the Sunset Lodge Hotel in Montego Bay and died.

Roy A. McNeill, Minister of Home Affairs and Local Government

Roy McNeill was a solicitor and had the responsibility for the police force. We had some sessions about the possibility of merging the Special Constabulary Force with the regular Police Force. That never materialized. On his retirement I would undertake some of his personal legal work.

On his ninetieth birthday, he invited his old friend Dr. Badir Shoucair, retired Member of Parliament Ms. Enid Bennett who had been his secretary many years before, and me. I drove both of them to his birthday reception in Negril. His nephew Wykeham McNeill was there. Shortly afterwards on his return to the United States, he passed away.

Hugh Lawson Shearer, Minister without Portfolio

Hugh Shearer of the BITU was perhaps like the son of national hero and former prime minister, Sir Alexander Bustamante and his wife Lady Bustamante. It came as no surprise, therefore, that he would become prime minister after the passing of Donald Sangster.

Hugh Shearer came to my home in Hope Pastures one evening in 1974 and took me to a branch meeting of Dr. Adrian Bonner, MP for Central St. Thomas. At the end of the branch meeting, in semi-darkness in this rural area, Dr. Bonner provided a bottle of wine. Mr. Shearer laughed and told him, "Thanks, but that is for Mr. Harding."

At Dr. Bonner's funeral in 1980, the newly elected Prime Minister Edward Seaga, Hugh Shearer, I and a number of party supporters

CHAPTER 9: CAMEOS

attended the funeral. It was a very small church and the clergy had to squeeze by our benches to get to the pulpit.

The Anglican Bishop of Jamaica Reverend Neville deSouza squeezed by without recognizing any of the Labour Party dignitaries. The Roman Catholic Archbishop, Samuel Carter, recognized the party of officials in his passing by nodding to us and, unlike Bishop deSouza, recognized the prime minister when addressing the church. Perhaps Bishop deSouza did not support the Jamaica Labour Party.

L.G. Newland, Minister of Labour

L.G. "Doc" Newland was the father of the National Insurance Scheme (NIS). It was said that some of his detractors referred to it as 'SIN". He was a very polite, soft-spoken man, and I found him in very lonely circumstances after his retirement.

Robert Lightbourne

Robert Lightbourne was a tall man, with at times very piercing eyes. He was well-spoken, articulate, and very full of ideas. He seemed to have ideas on almost everything.

When travelling he would sometimes call his team at odd hours whenever he had a new idea. He used to read cowboy stories before he went to bed. We both worshipped at St. Margaret Anglican church in Liguanea. We had a joking relationship. In one instance he came to me saying his knees were hurting him badly. I began to wonder whether it was arthritis, but then he said his knees were hurting him from the number of times he went down on them to pray for me. He had a brilliant mind and may be regarded as perhaps the finest Minister of Trade that Jamaica has seen. Robert Lightbourne, along with a Mr. Barclay Baetz, his partner, invented a process for extracting valuable mineral by-products from red mud in 1971. Lightbourne and Baetz filed patents in several countries and applied for and obtained a patent in Jamaica. Lightbourne held this patent in his capacity as a private citizen.

Wilton Hill

When I joined the Jamaica Labour Party in 1974, Wilton Hill, MP had succeeded Clem Tavares, on his death. Wilton Hill had sought my support in his campaign to become a deputy leader.

Wilton Hill was a colourful politician who had attended Kingston College and Gaynstead High School, and was also educated at West Indies Training College in Mandeville.

Wilton Hill was a brilliant attorney and noted criminal lawyer. I thought of him as the Charles Laughton of the Jamaican Bar, having seen the 1967 American film *Witness for the Prosecution*. Wilton Hill died in England in 1987. I attended his funeral at the Seventh Day Adventist Church on North Street, in Kingston.

Another Colourful Political Figure

Harold Brady, Attorney-at-Law

I had taught Harold Brady in law school. Edward Seaga had appointed him Secretary General of the International Democrat Union (IDU), headquartered in London. The IDU was the counter organization to Socialist International. We would often have lunch at the Cumberland Hotel in London, near Hyde Park, where you could consume as much as you wanted, including champagne, but it was expensive.

Prior to his appointment to the IDU, Harold Brady was a recognized actor. He appeared in the popular satirical review of the seventies, *Eight o'Clock Jamaica Time*, which incidentally never started at 8:00

pm. In the play he gave an excellent impression of Rex Nettleford, university academic and founder of the National Dance Theatre Company.

Harold Brady brought back to Jamaica on his return my most treasured Ladi Kwali ceramic pot.

He was later to be embroiled in the Manatt/Dudus Commission of Inquiry where he refused to testify and later had to appear in the Resident Magistrate's Court. He was found guilty and charged five hundred Jamaican dollars or thirty days in jail. He appealed the decision, and in January 2013, he was successful and the appeal was dismissed.

CHAPTER 10

Jamaican Eagle Does "Floy Hoy"

Barbados is a gem in the Caribbean. It is reported to have the highest literacy rate in the English-speaking Caribbean, and is noted for its unique accent among English speakers in the region. At a function once held at McGill University during West Indian Week, one of the professors enquired why the Bajan accent was so different, even among its Eastern Caribbean neighbours. Someone quipped that it sounded like a Nigerian who had been taught English by a Scotsman.

To underline this point, the apocryphal story is told of a Bajan visitor to Jamaica looking up at a turkey buzzard – a scavenger bird known locally as "John Crow" – and reportedly saying, "Jamaican turkey does floy hoy." Well, much like the buzzard, the Jamaican Eagle Financial Network, founded by Dr. Paul Chen-Young, did indeed fly high.

I have no clear recollection of where or how I met Dr. Paul Chen-Young. It was, however, early in his entrepreneurial journey. I recall visiting him at his Haining Road address where he operated Paul Chen-Young and Associates in what was ostensibly an apartment.

In 1975, he started Caribbean Lease Financing Corporation, which was later transformed into Eagle Merchant Bank.

I was invited, along with actuary Daisy Coke, quantity surveyor Brian Goldson, accountant and development banker Barry Johnson, accountant Geoffrey Messado, accountant and credit union officer Stan Moore, economist Michele Chen-Young, and attorney-at-law Maurice Robinson, to form the Eagle Board. This first board of Eagle Merchant Bank was perhaps one of the best boards assembled in any private company at that time. Daisy Coke was the first Jamaican to qualify as an actuary, Brian Goldson was the president of the West Indies Quantity Surveyors Association, and Barry Johnson was a senior member of the Jamaica Development Bank. Formerly of the Ministry of Agriculture and the Jamaica Cement Company, Stan Moore was an officer in the Credit Union League. Geoffrey Messado was a chartered accountant and business executive, Michele Chen-Young an American-trained economist, and Maurice Robinson, a well-known lawyer in a leading law firm.

Dr. Chen-Young wanted to be chairman. Lodrick Atkinson, a stockbroker and a friend of Dr. Chen-Young, suggested that he should not take the chairmanship; accordingly I was made the first chairman of Eagle Merchant Bank in 1982 until I became a member of the cabinet of the government of Jamaica in 1984 and consequently resigned from the board. I suggested that my wife Marigold replace me on the board, clearly to protect our family interest. For reasons best known to Paul Chen-Young, he invited my law partner Alan Deans to replace me. As soon as I demitted political office I resumed my position on the board, replacing Alan Deans. By this time Paul Chen-Young had become executive chairman of the board and all its subsidiaries.

Paul was uncompromising about being in charge. In his book *The Entrepreneurial Journey in Jamaica: When Policies Derail*, he said, "I got an offer from Eddie Lai to run his Corporation. I accepted the offer because of the challenge of being in charge" (p. —). When we formed

CHAPTER 10: JAMAICAN EAGLE DOES "FLOY HOY"

a company to do mortgage insurance, I incorporated it on a fifty-fifty shareholding basis. Paul was unhappy about this, and the ratio had to be changed to 51 percent–49 percent so that he could own the majority share.

It was suggested to Paul Chen-Young that perhaps he ought to have separate chairmen for each of the companies, and he agreed. Trevor Dillon became chairman of the Eagle Commercial Bank and I became chairman of Eagle Permanent Building Society which was established in 1989 and began operations in 1990. It became necessary because of the rapid growth of the Eagle Financial network. I chose the name "Permanent" Building Society knowing the history of building societies, for there was a time when building societies would dissolve when all the members had obtained their mortgages.

Within three years of operation, Eagle Permanent became the fourth largest building society in Jamaica. In 1995 the society recorded a net profit of J$5.6 million, with a total asset net worth of J$201 million for the year ending 1995. The loan portfolio increased to J$889 million. The society was first managed by Herman Ming who came to the job with credit union experience, and Leroy Flowers, who had building society experience. I came to this board with mortgage experience in the life insurance industry.

Tensions later developed with Paul Chen-Young when it appeared to him that he was not in total control of the society, especially after we carried out and maintained the regulations established by the Bank of Jamaica. BOJ wanted a "Chinese wall" to be maintained between the various Eagle companies, and we attempted to deposit some of our assets in other financial institutions outside of the Eagle Financial network.

Eagle went overseas. In 1991 I accompanied Chen-Young to Cayman where we applied for and obtained a licence to operate a branch of the bank in 1992 through the Office of the Royal Bank of Canada. Eagle then acquired First Equity Corporation, a full-service investment banking and security brokerage in 1994. I was a member of that board. In the 1990s Leroy Flowers and myself visited the United Kingdom to promote the Eagle Premium Growth Fund. There was some interest in the product but it certainly did not catch like wildfire. We returned to find out that the product was also not successful in the United States of America. Luckily our local bases were always covered and we managed to easily navigate that turbulence.

The Eagle Merchant Bank did indeed fly high. At the end of operations in 1983 it had assets of $29 million, shareholders' equity of $13 million, and at the end of 1996 the capital base of the Merchant Bank stood at $488 million. The Eagle Unit Trust advertisement stated: "Your investments soar with us." As stated by Mark Ricketts in *The Money Index* of May 12, 1992: "The Eagle soars, the image conveyed by the Group is obviously accurate, given the pace of the growth of the company." But there was a note of caution in the following comment by Elaine Ferguson: "And while no one can deny Eagle's ascendancy, stature and market position, the feeling persists that the group has grown too fast too quickly and that the base is insecure" (p. 23).

I have asked myself many times, why did Eagle, which soared so high, come crashing down? After mulling it over all these years, I came to the conclusion that there were two principal causes: interfering government policies, and Paul Chen-Young's style of management.

I claim no expertise as an economist or even as a student of economics, but from my experience as a board member of several companies and from the analysis of many commentators and my general reading, I share most of the views expressed by Dr. Chen-Young about Eagle's demise. He states in *When Policies Derail*:

> *As an instrument of monetary policy, the Bank of Jamaica relied heavily on the use of liquid reserves from the commercial banks and merchant banks (as a form of 'near banks) to curb the growth in credit and the demand for foreign exchange. The government proceeded to increase the cash reserve ratios for commercial banks and near banks – while attempting*

CHAPTER 10: JAMAICAN EAGLE DOES "FLOY HOY"

> *to control demand for foreign exchange by the aggressive use of liquid assets, the Bank of Jamaica was at the same time increasing money supply at undesirable levels. This created inflation and devaluation, thereby voiding the likely benefits from its liquid assets too . . .*
>
> *The fundamental mistake was to continue the high interest rate policy, on the assumption that this was necessary to stem potential outflows and to make it expensive to convert Jamaican currency by aggressive increases in liquidity reserves of the banks. (pp. 54–55)*

My layman's analogy is: when the swimming pool is overrun with algae, a sudden shock with acid will clear it up. But to continue this treatment over a prolonged period would be a mistake, because it would become ineffective – as ineffective as maintaining a high interest rate policy.

Dr. Chen-Young owned some sixty percent of the shares in the Eagle Financial Network. He therefore could not be outvoted, nor was there any attempt to do so. Although there were sometimes consultations and some advice was taken and followed, to a large extent the financial network was run like his private fiefdom. Sometimes decisions were taken unknown to members of the board and then ratification sought. The executive chairman always had to be in control; that is how I saw it, and I am prepared to be contradicted or proven wrong.

Paul Chen-Young in his book *When Policies Derail* indicates a penchant for aphorisms which he calls philosophic maxims. Here is one of his most impressive aphorisms, which I believe to be original: "There is nothing in Jamaica which is a secret" (p. 10). As to internal matters in the operation of the Eagle companies, I would apply that aphorism and would conclude with the famous words uttered by Great Britain's first prime minister, Robert Walpole: "Let sleeping dogs lie." This quotation appears on page 11 of *When Policies Derail*.

It was suggested on page 94 that Crown Eagle Life Insurance caused the Eagle Group to fail. Before the insurance company was acquired, however, actuarial work had been done by Coke and Associates and the reports showed that the capital requirements were well within the capacity of the Merchant Bank to make the investment and that it could be a small viable entity. An examination of the books of Crown Eagle at the time of the government takeover will show that the insurance operations of Crown Eagle broke even. Therefore any collapse of the Eagle Financial network could not be attributed to the insurance company and its operations.

It was further suggested that "unlike the other types of businesses, the more business a life insurance company generates, the less profitable it is in the initial years". But this was well known to us. Daisy Coke, the deputy chairman, was an actuary, and I had experience in the life insurance industry. It is what is sometimes referred to as "new business strain", i.e., when the cost of putting the business on the books costs more than the premium received, but this alters in subsequent years on each policy. Future income will repay this initial outlay.

The real question to be addressed was this: Why was Crown Eagle made the holding company of the Eagle Group, a function which was transferred from the Eagle Merchant Bank, which was referred to as the flagship company of the Eagle Group on page 87 of *When Policies Derail*? Dr. Chen-Young must have had a compelling reason.

Dr. Chen Young brought an action against the Government in March 1997. On page 93 of *When Policies Derail* he stated that directors Coke, Harding and Milling became state witnesses against him, but this was an unfortunate and mistaken view. We were required by the Government to give evidence, and in my case I will exhibit correspondence between the Ministry of Finance and myself (See Appendix B). Further, on the unfortunate advice of his lawyers, Chen-Young joined the directors as co-defendants, thus making us jointly liable should the government succeed in the case against him and the Eagle Group. That was certainly no way to keep friends and win allies, especially when decisions were often taken outside of the board by Dr Chen-Young. The directors had to employ lawyers at their

CHAPTER 10: JAMAICAN EAGLE DOES "FLOY HOY"

expense to defend their position, but subsequently that adversarial approach was discontinued.

I was the second largest shareholder, with about 20 percent of the Eagle Group. Someone at the time of the government takeover estimated my shareholdings to have been worth at that time about J$200 million. I cannot speak for the principal shareholder, but all the other shareholders lost their investment when Eagle collapsed. We were proud, however, that no depositor lost any investment. When the government acquired the Eagle Financial network, both Daisy Coke and myself were restored to the new board of the insurance company, which in my mind vindicated both of us, indicating that we were not responsible for any excesses or imprudent management of the company.

In his foreword to *When Policies Derail*, Edward Seaga states: "The fundamental assumption that bears no argument is that confidence is the glue that holds together the elements of financial undertakings, *except gambling* which is based primarily on risk" (my emphasis). The unanswered question is, when does a risk-taker become a gambler? With respect to Chen-Young, Seaga continues: "Perhaps he should have guided his institutions to make more prudent provisions instead of riding the tide of dangerous monetary policies which excessively increased money supply to explosive levels."

In *The Money Index* of May 12, 1992 Chen-Young refers to "a horticultural venture they went into without sufficient expertise and consequently lost money" (p. 30). Chen-Young had entered into an agreement with some overseas Chinese to develop horticultural products for export. Perhaps this showed that Eagle was flying so high that sometimes it overshot the runway. Surely this was not what Rockefeller meant when he said to Edward Seaga, "May your spirit soar like an Eagle," which was the inspiration for Chen-Young to name his company Eagle. Eagle will not rise again like the phoenix, but it did "floy hoy", and what a ride!

CHAPTER 11

Academia

When I got into the honours programme in anthropology at McGill University, I was granted a teaching assistantship, and began to lecture to first-year students in anthropology. As a consequence, my teaching career actually began when I was only nineteen years old. I learnt that one of my students referred to me as "Ossie pooh-pooh", because I seemed to be critical of most theories which I "pooh-poohed". During those early days, I came under the influence of Professor Philippe Garrique. He was thoughtful, encouraging and very supportive. During my undergraduate days, he first whetted my appetite for knowledge and research, which has lasted me a lifetime. He was French-speaking, but he was not a French Canadian – I believe he was from Belgium. He later left McGill and went to the University of Montreal. Through Professor George Eaton, a longstanding friend, I was able to contact him in his retirement and sent him a copy of the acknowledgement and appreciation of his support in my thesis in which he was mentioned.

One unhappy incident during my early teaching stint occurred when I had to fail a Jamaican student at McGill because he came nowhere near the passing grade. Apparently he was deeply wounded, because many years later when he was working in real estate development in Jamaica, he met my son Zachary and enquired if I was his father. When Zachary said yes, my embittered past student immediately launched into the story, complaining that I had failed him in a course at university.

I applied for a scholarship to Northwestern University in Evanston, Illinois, but I did not receive the grant that I wanted, and Professor Herskovits, the well-known anthropologist I would be working with, would be off for a year doing research somewhere in Asia. I decided that if I had to pay my way, then I would do law as a profession. This changed my line of academic pursuits, and I went to the London School of Economics to study law, and then to the Inner Temple to qualify as a barrister. A few years after returning to Jamaica I was invited to teach at the Norman Manley Law School, where I taught from 1975 to 1980 – the first five years of that institution. I became president of the Senate in 1980, and while marking law school scripts on a flight to Washington I knew the time had come to give up teaching. I was appointed to the emeritus status of honorary tutor on leaving the law school.

By 1993, my sons had completed their studies abroad and had returned to Jamaica. I was happy to be relieved of the burden of meeting school expenses in foreign exchange. I had also just completed the election campaign for Central Manchester. Although I made a good showing, the history of the constituency indicated that a JLP candidate would probably not be successful. I decided that it would not be profitable to continue my representation in the constituency for the next five years while waiting to contest the seat again. It would be time-consuming and expensive, with little guarantee of my ultimate success.

After due consideration, I made up my mind to return to academia and pursue a doctorate in philosophy. When I made the announcement to my family, Marigold seemed confused and could not understand

CHAPTER 11: ACADEMIA

why I would want to undertake such a venture – I had graduated from two universities, I was now a practising lawyer – what would these studies do to enhance my career? Well, it was just something that I wanted to do and felt that at this point in my life I had the freedom to do it. My sons were very supportive and urged me on: "Dad, if that is what you want to do, go for it!"

One of the Sunday newspapers had advertised the courses available at UWI, and I noted that the MPhil and PhD degrees in philosophy were being offered. When I approached the university, however, I was told that the information was incorrect. I returned with another copy of the Sunday paper which had repeated the advertisement about the courses being offered. Finally, I was sent to a Dr. John Williams, an Australian lecturer who apparently was the philosophy lecturer. We had a satisfactory interview and I decided to apply for the September term.

I was required by the university to have two sponsors. I approached Professor Edward Baugh of the English Department who was the Public Orator at UWI and was well known to my wife through some relatives they had in common. I also approached Professor Errol Miller of the Department of Education, who had been appointed an independent senator by Prime Minister Edward Seaga during the one-party parliament after the PNP had boycotted the general elections of 1983. I then followed up the application and discovered that they could not find Professor Miller's recommendation. He was kind enough to resubmit it.

Registration for higher degrees candidates for 1993/94 took place from September 23 to October 1. I applied for the part-time MPhil programme in philosophy. I had registered as a part-time MPhil student for 1992–93 to take a qualifying course in that year. However, there was no one to teach the course. Apparently the Australian lecturer had not returned. I was forcibly granted retroactive leave of absence from the programme. I then requested that the fees already paid be applied towards the fees for 1993–94. I was advised by the

Campus Committee on Graduate Studies that I should withdraw temporarily from the MPhil programme and register as a specially admitted student, to take a number of undergraduate philosophy courses in the 1994/95 session, and then reapply to enter the MPhil programme the following year. However, I would not be able to use such courses for credit at a later date.

On July 5, 1994 I wrote to Dr. Pauline Christie, dean of the Faculty of Arts and General Studies, expressing my disappointment with the recommendation of the chairman of the Campus Committee on Graduate Studies, who had expressed the view that the additional courses would not be granted credit in the MPhil programme. Finally, it was recommended that the course in Recent Western Philosophy would be more appropriate. Having obtained a B+ in the course, I was now eligible to register for the MPhil programme. With the weakness of human nature, I wondered whether someone in the system wanted to frustrate me. I would rather like to think, however, that I simply got caught in the cobweb of institutional bureaucracy. During this frustrating period Dr. Christie was very helpful and I thank her for her many courtesies.

I took courses from both Dr. John Bewaji and Dr. Earl McKenzie. The courses were all taken while I was in the Senate and occupied with my law practice. I thought that all that was required to remain in the course was to pass the exams. I was not told, nor was I aware of the regulations which required at least a B average. I wrote exams in May and heard nothing from the university up to September. Perhaps if I were a regular undergraduate I would have seen the results posted?

One day I was on the UWI campus, where I had presented a Ma Lou yabba pot to the Archaeology Department. I visited Dr. McKenzie and told him how much I had enjoyed his course, then asked him whether I had passed the exams as I had heard nothing from the university. He said I had, but he could not tell me the results. It was not clear whether he was unable to tell me the results because he did

CHAPTER 11: ACADEMIA

not have the marks or whether he was not permitted. He referred me to the Registrar. When I got there, Miss Edris Hill of the Registry said, "Senator, I was just going to write to you." I had passed the exams with B+ averages, which meant that I could remain in the programme. In April 1997, I formally applied to the head of my department, Professor Hubert Devonish, to upgrade the required status to PhD, under the procedure guide for MPhil. In May 1997 I was advised that my supervisor would be Dr. Bewaji, who would be in contact with me regarding my thesis proposal and seminar, and also that my upgrade seminar date was approved for September 1997.

Earlier that same year I had occasion to visit Washington, DC where I had lunch with Dr. Richard Bernal, Jamaica's ambassador to the United States. He was also an academic. It was a most profitable encounter. The ambassador briefed me on what happens in some university graduate schools. He warned me about professional jealousies and rivalries, and urged me to try to get a supervisor whose ideas were not in conflict with my thesis proposals.

I had taken courses with both Dr. Bewaji and Dr. McKenzie. Dr. McKenzie had studied art at the Alberta College of Art and creative writing at Columbia University, before gaining his doctorate in philosophy. A published poet and painter, he taught philosophy of art and philosophy of literature. He once suggested that perhaps I could write my PhD dissertation on Caribbean aesthetics, but I had no interest in doing research in that area. It appeared to me at that time to be somewhat nebulous and indeterminate. That could have contributed to my lack of interest. I found Dr. McKenzie to be very caring, considerate and kind to the students and very committed to his vocation, which was teaching. Each time I submitted a chapter of my thesis to my supervisor Dr. Bewaji, I would pass a copy to Dr. McKenzie. However, he neither made comments nor offered any suggestions.

Dr. Bewaji was a thorough academic philosopher. All his undergraduate and postgraduate studies were in philosophy. He had an eye for details and showed a very clinical approach. I had studied philosophy of mind with him, and that was the area of research I had chosen to explore. I was fortunate to have had him as my supervisor. The guidance of Ambassador Bernal served me in good stead.

As my supervisor, Dr. Bewaji advised me as to the format of my proposal and the arrangement for my upgrade seminar. Since I had not been to an upgrade seminar before, I visited Professor Baugh, who had been one of my sponsors, and asked whether I should attempt a powerpoint presentation. He advised me that that would not be necessary. I had circulated my outline proposal, including a short bibliography or reference. For the upgrading seminar, Dr. Victor Chang, deputy dean of the Faculty of Humanities and Education, presided in the absence of the dean. Present were Dr. McKenzie; Reverend Austin Milner, dean of studies of Saint Michael's Seminary – an Englishman who I presume was a priest and supposedly learned in philosophy; Dr. Gagindra Persaud, a psychologist; Professor Hubert Devonish, head of the Language, Linguistics and Philosophy Department (who kept coming in and out as he was in negotiation with WIGUT – the staff union); my son Zachary; several students; and my supervisor Dr. Bewaji.

During my presentation Reverend Milner kept huffing and puffing while making notes on his copy of my written submission. He did not seem to follow the presentation. Had I not been a mature student I would have been disconcerted by his attitude and posturing. Dr. McKenzie said he did not see the names of any philosophers in the bibliography or reference. This was not correct; perhaps he was not familiar with those listed. Dr. Persaud asked many questions. My son later asked me if we were quarrelling. Not at all, I told him. It was a jousting match which I found stimulating; Dr. Persaud was simply attempting to display his knowledge of philosophy.
The students were particularly enthusiastic about my presentation. They were fascinated by my views on out-of-body experiences.

I was subsequently advised that the upgrade had been turned down. I imagine Milner and McKenzie voted against it. I found this

CHAPTER 11: ACADEMIA

rather strange since I had submitted copies of my drafts to Dr. McKenzie all along as the ideas developed, but he never made any comments to me about the work I was submitting nor offered any advice. Now what did this mean? Did it mean that my submission was not good enough for the upgrade to PhD or that it was not even up to MPhil standard? What would be next? Should I resubmit it? I had no idea.

Afterwards there were rumours that the department had sent the submission to another campus where it was approved (I would later learn that this was untrue, and that it was approved by Professor Ronald Young in the Graduate Studies section). I really did not know what transpired. I knew that Dr. Bewaji was furious; he said that they were either ignorant or did not know the "cutting edge of philosophy". I also heard that Dr. McKenzie had said that the study of near-death or out-of-body experience was not philosophy. A view reportedly expressed, however, was that the book on philosophy of mind which we were using, written by Professor George Graham, included a chapter on near-death experience. If it were not philosophy, why would it be included in a book on philosophy of mind? Of course I cannot authenticate or verify any of these rumours. The worrying situation was: where would we go from here?

Dr. Bewaji seemed to have intervened and raised the matter that my subject was not in the specialization of the two other assessors, and sought permission to seek overseas evaluation. I could not verify the rumours that Dr. Bewaji had intervened. However, I later found out that he had written to the head of the department as follows:

Mr. O. G. Harding's Upgrade Seminar Presentation titled "Near Death Experience (NDE) and the Nature of the Mind – A Holographic Approach"

a) *Mr. Harding has demonstrated that the topic is an important one, which creates an issue in the area of philosophy known as Metaphysics – specifically, the Philosophy of Mind.*

b) *He has presented an initial working thesis statement (hypothesis) which can be argued to generate new insight. He has clearly stated the objectives of the work, and scope of the research, with a properly formulated understanding of the issues, locating the research within the emerging intersecting area of neuroscience and philosophy.*

c) *Mr. Harding has demonstrated clear familiarity with the literature, mastery of the various positions regarding such matters as end-of-life, near-death, out-of-body issues and philosophical problems attendant on them.*

d) *In my judgment, this is a research that not only contributes to scholarship in a significant way, but it charts new directions for scholarship, and deserves encouragement.*

Bearing in mind that there is limitation on staff competent in Philosophy, and especially capable of working with the student to carry out this very commendable, ground-breaking research at the Mona Campus of the University of the West Indies, and indeed in the University of the West Indies family as a whole, I will recommend that external assistance be sought to evaluate the work that the student is proposing to carry out, to determine the validity of his thesis, research agenda and potential to contribute to knowledge and scholarship.

We did not have any particular person in mind that we could contact. I suggested Professor George Graham, the author of the textbook *Philosophy of Mind* which was the principal book used in the course. Professor George Graham was chair and professor of philosophy and professor of psychology at the University of Alabama at Birmingham, and author and co-author of several books and publications. We then thought that we would approach Professor Graham as an external examiner. He in turn suggested Dr. Robert Almeder of Georgia State or Dr. Stephen Braude, University of Maryland.

In the end, Professor George Graham became co-supervisor with

CHAPTER 11: ACADEMIA

Dr. Bewaji, and Robert Almeder became the external examiner – Dr. Almeder had published over seventy philosophical essays in academic journals and published or co-published twenty books and was the editor of *The American Philosophical Quarterly*. It was fortunate that I had not chosen Dr. Braude, for it turned out that his views were antithetical to my own. In fact, in my thesis I severely attacked his views, and I remembered once again Ambassador Bernal's advice.

On Saturday, February 26, 2000, I successfully defended my thesis – "Near Death Experience: a Holographic Explanation". Present at the defence were Professor Robert Almeder, external examiner; Dr. Anthony B. Bogues of Brown University and UWI (second examiner); and Dr. John Ayotunde Bewaji (supervisor). In attendance were Mr. Joe Pereira, dean of the faculty; Dr. Kathryn Shields-Brodber of the department; my old college friend Stanley Moore; Guy McIntosh of the Frame Centre Gallery; my son Zachary Harding; my wife Marigold; Professor Hubert Devonish; Dr. Persaud; and a number of students.

The degree of Doctor of Philosophy in Philosophy was awarded to me on May 3, 2000. I received a letter from Professor Kenneth O. Hall, Pro Vice chancellor, Principal of Mona Campus dated May 25, 2000 which reads in part:

Dear Senator Harding:

Please accept my sincere congratulations for your recent outstanding achievement in attaining a Doctor of Philosophy degree from the University of the West Indies (UWI). I note that this is perhaps the first time that a sitting member of our Jamaican Parliament has earned a PhD. It is also very noteworthy that you have earned the distinction of the first to be awarded this degree in Philosophy from UWI.

Congratulations to you once again for your achievement, and I am very proud that you said publicly that you are pleased to be a graduate of our own University. We are also delighted to have you as one of our exceptional graduates.

GRANDSON OF ESSIE: A JAMAICAN AUTOBIOGRAPHY

On the publication of my thesis in August 2002 by LMH Publishing Ltd., Professor George Graham had this to say:

Dr. Harding's objectives in this book are clearly and judiciously stated. His methods judiciously combine conceptual analysis with relevant empirical data and he has achieved his stated objectives. His contribution to the literature is original insofar as it intensively locates debate over possibility of near death experiences in the context of a type of metaphysical theory known as 'holographic theory'. To my knowledge, no one has attempted this relocation before at the level of imaginative integration which Dr. Harding achieves. His interpretation of empirical data is essentially sound and plausible, and he has presented his material in a clear and effective manner. Dr. Harding's book tries to tackle a very difficult topic, and he does so with humility and imagination, a combination of features all too rare in works of this type. It is a must-read for all scholars and persons interested in issues of body-mind problem, near-death experience, out-of-body experience and holography.

Professor George Graham, AC Reid Professor,

Wake Forest University, North Carolina.

I was first appointed part-time senior lecturer in the Department of Language, Linguistics and Philosophy at UWI effective January 1, 2000. Although I had received my doctorate in May 2000, I had completed and submitted my thesis in August 1999. I therefore like to tell my students that I completed my doctorate in the last century. At the UWI, I taught philosophy of mind, philosophy of art, philosophy of religion, philosophy of law and a postgraduate course in metaphysics. I also supervised a number of tutorials. My lecture classes often numbered between 100 and 130 students, and there seemed to have been a heightened interest in philosophy. Dr. Bewaji was able to attract some overseas lecturers on contract and the department began to grow.

CHAPTER 11: ACADEMIA

Having completed my doctorate in philosophy of mind, I wanted to study more about the brain. I joined a neuroanatomy class conducted by the well-known psychiatrist, Professor Freddie Hickling. In the class were some three or four graduate doctors who were going to specialize in psychiatry and one PhD psychology student. The anatomy of the brain was fascinating. As an academic philosopher, I always enquired where the mind was located – my colleagues responded with some derision and mockery about philosophy, all in good fun. I asserted that Descartes had said that the soul was in the pineal gland. In class I was called upon to dissect a brain. At first I was a bit squeamish, but I soon overcame that, and having dissected the brain discovered that the pineal gland was about the size of a pea.

A rumour began to circulate that I was seeing psychiatrist Freddie Hickling and that I was visiting Ward 21, the psychiatric ward. There was a common entrance to Dr. Hickling's office and to Ward 21. I had a good laugh, for all of the observations were correct, but my reasons for visiting Dr. Hickling were not for medical treatment. However, I suppose that people who talk about out-of-body experiences might be regarded as being mad.

I was appointed honorary research fellow in the graduate school on December 10, 2002, and I continued to teach. I was promoted to senior lecturer in July 2007, with Professor Errol Morrison being dean of the graduate school. On October 20, 2009, Dr. McKenzie personally invited me to an exhibition of his paintings and a reading of his poetry at the Philip Sherlock Centre for the Creative Arts. It was an enjoyable evening and I was happy to attend.

On Professor Morrison's appointment as president of the University of Technology (UTech), I wrote to him in August 2007 suggesting that he establish a Faculty of Law, Economics and Philosophy, as UTech needed to have studies in the humanities. I was appointed adjunct professor in August 2007 and became a member of a transitional committee with the Institute of Law and Economics. It was agreed that the core course for the LLB programme would be finalized by September 2008. With the establishment of the Faculty of Law at

UTech, I was re-appointed adjunct professor of law and philosophy in the faculty on August 1, 2008. I was intent on ensuring that the faculty maintain a level of high standards, and agreed to write the syllabuses of the entire LLB programme, but the enormity of the task was more than I had realized. At the time of writing I have completed the syllabuses for nineteen courses.

In September 2009 I began teaching jurisprudence. The classes numbered about sixty students – some full-time and others part-time. The part-time students were mostly working persons. Under my guidance the part-time students had a successful public lecture on human trafficking in April 2010, the first faculty lecture. It is my view that the faculty should establish a law journal and plans are now afoot to realize this objective. The way forward – to teach, to write, to find a way to share and to give back: that should be our legacy.

On September 2, 2010, my special contract as adjunct professor was extended to November 30, 2010, pending my application as Professor of Law and Philosophy. On September 30, 2010, UTech offered me a contract as Professor of Law and Philosophy in the Faculty of Law after the submission of my personal dossier including my publications, teaching experience and positions held. This was forwarded to a promotion committee which approved the submission and forwarded it to the University of Technology Council where it was also approved.

In a letter addressed to the dean of the Faculty of Law dated December 7, 2010, a law student expressed his discontent with the administrative direction of the faculty: "For two years, we suffered from the ineffectiveness and unprofessional attitude of the administration, as it disregards the contractual obligations owed to their students." However, he made the following comments about me: "For six consecutive semesters, save for the astute leadership provided by Prof. the Hon. Oswald Harding – and believe me he stands out above them all – we are yet to receive any form of feedback on our assignments." In January 2011 I was promoted to acting dean of the Faculty of Law.

The law faculty now has about five hundred students enrolled.

CHAPTER 12

At Home

After we returned from Mexico in 1968, my wife and I were assigned a government house at 23 Garden Boulevard in Mona Heights, St Andrew. This community was the first housing scheme to be built in Jamaica, and was located on prime real estate in close proximity to UWI. The neighbours to our left were Mr. and Mrs. Gerald Eaton, their daughter Flo Forrester and their son Ken. A most congenial family, they were the parents, sister and brother of Professor George Eaton, my longstanding friend from McGill University. We bought a Volkswagen Beetle from another neighbour who happened to be the daughter of Keble Munn, a PNP member of parliament who would serve as Minister of Agriculture then Minister of National Security from 1972 to 1980 in the Michael Manley administration.

The VW was a very popular car in Jamaica back then. It was compact and sturdy, and traversed flooded roads with the greatest of ease. I can't recall my VW ever breaking down. The headlights could have been a bit brighter, but that was a minor complaint. The strong chrome bumpers warded off dents to the front and rear ends, unlike the situation with modern cars where the slightest contact with another vehicle often warrants a visit to the body shop. That plucky little car was our sole means of transport – for work, shopping, drop-offs, pick-ups, jaunts to the country – everything. We christened her Betsy and she performed like a champion for the three years that we owned her.

Marigold, who was a trained medical technologist, did not return to her profession. She had worked for several years at Nuttall Hospital Laboratory after being a laboratory technician at Goldstein Medical Centre, New York and had been in charge of the medical laboratory at Andrews Memorial Hospital for seven years when we met. On our return from Mexico, she became an employee of Leslie Moodie and Sons, a pharmacy on Church Street in downtown Kingston, as a representative supplying doctors with medical supplies. With this job she was assigned a car, a little Ford Anglia. This was a welcome relief to our tight transport situation.

Immediately across from our home was the Mona Primary School. On one occasion we were invited to attend a school function where the guest speaker was Dr. Mavis Gilmour. I was seeing her in person for the first time. She was slender, elegant and articulate, and wore her hair severely pulled back in a bun. She struck me as a woman of great determination, unswerving and relentless in whatever goal she was pursuing. She spoke so effusively about Prime Minister Michael Manley that I was convinced he must have been a demigod. She served as Parliamentary Secretary in the Ministry of Health from 1972 to 1974 in the Manley regime. However, she left the PNP abruptly in 1974 and joined forces with Robert Lightbourne, a former JLP Minister of Trade and Industry, to launch a new political movement – the United Party; but this movement lasted no more than a few months. Sometime later I was attending a meeting at the JLP headquarters on Belmont Road in Kingston when, to my surprise, I saw Mavis Gilmour seated at one end of the conference table. She joined the JLP, became Member of Parliament for the constituency of West Rural St Andrew, and served as Minister of Education in the

CHAPTER 12: AT HOME

administration of Edward Seaga from 1980 to 1986. Marigold, as a horticulturalist, assisted her in beautifying the ministry.

Having resigned from the government service, I had to vacate the Mona house which had been assigned to another civil servant. However, before we could move out, he had his furniture delivered and stacked on the front verandah! One of my friends in the Jaycees movement, Roy Barnarsee, was leaving his rented premises at 11 Keble Crescent, Hope Pastures. It was a house owned by A.G.R. Byfield, a PNP Member of Parliament, and the rent was twenty-nine pounds a month. Had it cost one more pound we could not have afforded it. It was a three-bedroom house typical of those in the Hope Pastures housing scheme. Our first son, Jeremy, was born while we were living there. It was comfortable and the neighbours were friendly and welcoming. Immediately across from us lived Dennis Ziadie and his family. Dennis had played football for Jamaica and was coach of the national team. He would die tragically in a motor vehicle accident while attending the 1986 World Cup series in Mexico. Jackie Bell, another coach from Jamaica who was travelling with him, met the same fate.

Immediately to our left was a banker who was raising his two daughters without a mother. In the mornings we could hear his young daughters complaining about how he was combing their hair. Nearby was Dr. Venice Bernard-Wright and her husband Norman Wright, attorney-at-law. Sonny and Joyce DaCosta lived further around the circle. Other neighbours were Pat and Hester Rousseau; Bunny and Pam East and their three sons – David, Paul and Gregory; Mrs. Germain and her grandson Paul; Martin and Pam Mordecai; Jackie and Beverley Minott; Dr. Wilson Williams and Beryl Williams. It was a most agreeable neighbourhood. Sonny DaCosta died suddenly in 2010 without any warning or known illness.

One quiet evening as Marigold and I sat talking in the living room, we suddenly gasped in wonderment as Jeremy took his first unsteady steps and started toddling across the room, looking proud of himself and slightly bemused at the same time. It was a magical moment. He could not believe what he had just done, so he took off in the opposite direction! We watched him with a mixture of love and vague apprehension, our hearts bursting with pride. Our baby was growing up! We had allowed his hair to grow somewhat, but when it was time to have it trimmed I took him to a barber shop at Matilda's Corner. He sat in my lap facing the barber. As the barber approached with his scissors clipping away, Jeremy was terrified. I held him close to me and for a moment I felt his fear, though I knew there was no danger. I then experienced what it was like for a father to be bonded to his child.

Marigold and I decided that it was time for us to have a home of our own. We started house hunting. We went to look at a house for sale around the loop of the circle of Keble Crescent, but it had uncovered air conditioning vents running throughout. I was furious at how the owner had spoiled the house. Marigold chided me and said, "You don't have to buy that house. Anyway, that was the owner's choice." On the way back I stopped at Pat Rousseau's house at 6 Keble Crescent and asked if it was true that he was selling it. Located diagonally across from where we lived, the house was indeed for sale. We agreed on the terms, and I was to send him a "binder" the next day.

When I told Marigold that we had bought the house and how much it cost, she asked, "Where are we going to get the money?" As luck would have it, I had bought a house in the Hughenden housing scheme to accommodate my father if he ever returned to Jamaica and preferred to live on his own. Marigold's father had attempted to discourage me in his strong Chinese accent when he said the houses were like "matchboxes". As it turned out, Dad passed away while we were still at 11 Keble Crescent, so the sale of the Hughenden house provided my downpayment. When I sent Pat Rousseau a cheque for five hundred pounds the next day, he called and asked if I was serious. I indicated it was a "binder". As lawyers we eliminated fees between us, and I took over the mortgage.

CHAPTER 12: AT HOME

Our move to 6 Keble Crescent was a back-breaking exercise. The proximity of the houses had led us to believe that it would have been relatively easy to move furniture across the road without professional help. How wrong we were! The task was unbearably difficult. Even with friends and family lending a hand, we suffered severe stress, sore backs and extremely weary arms. Marigold and I needed massages and bed rest before we could even think of straightening out our new residence. I can smile now at how naive we were, but it was a very painful experience.

Immediately behind 6 Keble Crescent lived our friends the Minotts, but they later relocated to Mandeville. The premises were next occupied by Dr. Archie Hudson-Phillips and his wife Angela, who had been my batchmate in the law faculty at the University of London. They were wonderful neighbours, but they had a crazy dog named Rock who displayed all the symptoms of schizophrenia. Archie was the only person who could go near him. On one occasion Rock escaped and came over to our premises. No one could venture outside until Archie came for him.

These premises were somewhat larger and had more yard space for Marigold to plant her flowers. We had a healthy-looking polypodium, popularly called a Trinidad fern, which was suspended from a trellis. It must have been in the right spot getting the right amount of sunlight, because it grew to an enormous size. Someone suggested that it should be exhibited in the horticultural show and I encouraged Marigold to enter it. When they saw the fern, members of the horticultural society advised her to apply for membership, otherwise she would not be awarded a cup even if she won. Her polypodium did win the cup in that class. Thus began her odyssey in the horticultural world which led to her fame as a floral artist and designer.

On five separate occasions Marigold won the Banksian medal at the annual horticultural show, which was held in those days at the National Arena in Kingston. This was an award granted by the Royal Horticultural Society (RHS) of Great Britain to a member of the

Jamaica Horticultural Society for obtaining the most points in the annual show. The award was named in memory of Sir Joseph Banks who founded the RHS with John Wedgwood in 1804. Whenever Marigold entered the show, several truckloads of plants were delivered from our house. I think she must have had exhibits in every class. More trucks were used in participating in these annual shows than were required when we moved house!

While we were living at 6 Keble Crescent, our second son Zachary was born. It was a pleasant August night and I was fast asleep. Suddenly I felt a sharp elbow digging into my ribs and heard Marigold's voice: "It's time to go." Off we drove to Nuttall Memorial Hospital, leaving Jeremy with a cousin on my father's side, Dr. Gloria Robinson. She was called "Sister" because she had been a nun in the religious order of the Franciscan Missionary Sisters, popularly known as the Blue Sisters. When we arrived at the hospital, our neighbours the Ziadies were there on a mission similar to ours. I said to Dennis jokingly, "Why didn't you tell me? We could have come in one car!" That night their daughter Kim was born. But it must have been the season for babies: our neighbour Pam Mordecai had her child around that time, and so did Dr. Franklin Johnston's wife, all residents of Keble Crescent. Someone quipped that there must have been something in the water. It was a regular birthing festival. That night at the hospital we also ran into Marigold's cousin Monica Chen who gave birth to her son Craig.

In 1976, Zachary was just over two years old. On the night the JLP lost the general election, there he stood wearing my green campaign shirt which fell below his knees, both hands held high in the air giving the "V" sign adopted by the JLP. He must have wondered why no one was shouting "High up", the party slogan that had been on the lips of all JLP supporters during the pre-election campaign.

When Zachary turned three years old, it was time for him to begin kindergarten and join his brother at Priory. I took him to school on his first day. His initial excitement turned to consternation when

CHAPTER 12: AT HOME

he realized I was leaving him in these strange surroundings. I tried to say goodbye, but he wouldn't let me go. "Don't worry, Zach, don't worry," I said in my most soothing voice as I patted his head. "Mommy will soon be back for you." I knew that the little ones spent no more than two hours a day in school. But despite my best efforts, Zachary would not be placated. He was terrified, probably thinking that I was abandoning him, perhaps giving him away. A wave of tenderness welled up inside me. I literally had to tear myself away from him as he whimpered and clung to me. Frankly, he was not the only one to suffer an emotional ordeal that day, as I was poignantly aware of the tug at my heartstrings each time I played that scene over and over again in my mind. At the kindergarten Zachary got his mat where he would lie down at rest time each day, and soon he began to enjoy playing games and interacting with the other children.

Priory was an interesting school, founded by Henry Fowler, a Jamaican who had studied at Oxford University but who never lost his Oxonian affectations. The school was seen by the public as an elite institution. The classrooms were made deliberately small so that they could accommodate no more than fifteen or sixteen students. Mrs. Narinesingh headed the kindergarten, Mrs. Jean Bertram the junior school, and Mrs. Marie Gregory the senior school. It was undoubtedly one of the best preparatory schools available in Kingston. Priory hosted some thirty-four nationalities, and English was taught as a second language. There was no American school in Jamaica at that time, and the children of foreign diplomats formed a large part of the student body. Mr. Bert Fox of the American Overseas Schools had a link with Priory and made regular visits to the school.

Natasha Manley, daughter of then prime minister Michael Manley and his wife Beverley, attended Priory accompanied by her mother's security officer, Rosie MacDonald (now Barker). Among the children of diplomats attending the school was Victor, the son of Cuban ambassador Ulises Estrada. This was at the height of Michael Manley's flirtation with Cuban politics. Estrada's little son was obstreperous and disruptive. My son Zachary was put in charge of him; it reminded me of the lead horse which leads out the unruly horse about to enter a race.

Estrada is best remembered for commandeering our national television station and telling the Jamaican people that it was only a matter of time before the Communist revolution would succeed in Jamaica. No foreign representative in this country had ever behaved in this imperious manner, and none has done so since. Estrada was an African Cuban with a completely shaven head. I resented his lack of respect for our political system and vowed that I would never speak to him. He was the only diplomat that I ever avoided socially. At a function at the Police Officers' Club, when he approached me in the buffet line, I moved to another food station. After the change of administration, we were to see each other again in Angola. I was now a minister of government attending a non-aligned conference. He kept looking at me, but it seemed that he could not recall who I was until he saw my official car arrive flying the Jamaican flag. On another occasion while visiting Cuba I saw him at a conference. He was then working for *Granma*, the official newspaper. I ensured that we never met. The Cuban people have always been our friends, but Estrada's brand of diplomacy did not enhance the relationship.

In 1974 I became chairman of the Priory School Board (see Appendix C). Members included Peter Moss-Solomon, who was a product of Priory, Mike Fennell, Dr. Val Cotterell, my wife Marigold, and the headmaster, Patrick Bourke, who was the stepson of Henry Fowler. Priory produced many notable students and was quite innovative in some ways. As the economy of the country worsened, however, it became more difficult to maintain a private school. Although we resisted it for some time, Priory eventually became a government-assisted institution. The entry requirements had to be widened and consequently the character of the institution changed.

With her passion for cultivating plants and flowers, Marigold wanted a larger garden space to indulge in her horticultural pursuits.

CHAPTER 12: AT HOME

I told her I would agree to move from Keble Crescent, but I didn't want any place too high in the surrounding hills of St. Andrew. She found a house just about a mile up from Barbican Square, an ideal location not far from the city and within easy reach of the Liguanea shopping area.

The premises were located at 9 Hyperion Avenue in Jacks Hill. It was a two-storey house, sometimes referred to as a split-level. I went around to the backyard. It was spacious enough, there was a vinyl-lined swimming pool, colourful awnings, and the property was well fruited. After a cursory look I admitted that the place was lovely, but I told Marigold that we could not afford that architect-designed house. It would cost twice as much as our Hope Pastures house.

John Russell, the businessman who owned it, said it would be ideal for a young family and strongly advised us to buy it. I calculated that the net proceeds from the sale of our house would cover no more than one-third of the cost. Grandma Essie always said, "Never hang your hat where you can't reach it." In this regard I was inclined to agree with her. One week later I went to John Russell's business place to tell him that although we loved the house, we could not afford it. On arrival I noticed that the store windows were all taped up with newspaper and that goods were being emptied from the store. I asked for Mr. Russell, only to be told that he had left the island. I never saw him again. A few days later I received an envelope which contained, to my great surprise, the title to the premises and a signed blank transfer. I thought this man must be mad to sign away his house without any deposit being paid.

I took possession of the property, and then discovered that the house was highly mortgaged and with at least two caveats lodged against it. Perhaps Russell had done this to obtain as much money as he could before leaving Jamaica. It was rumoured that the manager of the bank which had the mortgage was interested in acquiring the premises. We hurriedly completed the sale of our house which enabled us to pay off the mortgage so that no legal action could be brought against the Hyperion property, but there were still the caveats to be discharged. At a social function not long afterwards, I was approached by a former bank manager who asked me why I had not paid off the loan secured by the caveats. I advised her that I had not borrowed any money from her bank, and had no personal liability. Of course the property could not be transferred with the caveats. In due time we paid off the loan secured by the caveats and transferred the property into our names.

Nine Hyperion Avenue became Hardingham, the home of the Hardings. Marigold now set about her gardens and trees and made the grounds the envy of our friends. It turned out that the architect who had designed the house was Herbie Bradford from the well-known firm of Rotowski and Bradford. He assisted us with whatever modifications we desired. Although the awnings were colourful and attractive, we knew they would require occasional replacement due to weathering. A more permanent cover was therefore installed. The vinyl lining of the pool made the water feel soft, but as shrinkage would lead to its eventual replacement, we had the pool reconstructed with a steel base. Beyond the swimming pool we built a sun deck designed by Herbie Bradford, but weathering and lack of use led us to replace it with a large gazebo which created an outdoor sitting and dining area. The carpeted floors in the house were replaced by wooden floors. The garage was extended; unused open spaces were covered, increasing the usable space in the house. We enjoyed our dogs, especially the Akitas, that we used to show at the Kennel Club. Hardingham became our home, wonderfully decorated by Marigold: our collection of paintings adorning the walls, some of the ceramic collection exquisitely exhibited, always with her breathtaking orchids and floral arrangements on display.

When they left Priory, my sons attended Campion College, a school founded by the Roman Catholic church and staffed mainly by priests. The volume of lay staff grew over the years as the priests left one by one. After my sons graduated, I was invited to sit on the

CHAPTER 12: AT HOME

school board where I served for seven years. We sent Jeremy and Zachary to Ashbury College in Ottawa, Canada, after they left Campion. We had a policy for their education: firstly, that they would both attend the same schools in order to share common experiences and not complain of favouritism; secondly, we would not send them to school abroad until they had completed their education in Jamaica and had come to understand who they were and where they were from. On returning to Jamaica, they experienced none of the problems I had encountered so many years before with reintegrating into the society. They found their old friends again and easily re-established their former relationships.

Jeremy enrolled at McGill University in 1988 to study chemical engineering, but decided after a while to return to his first love – music. He had studied at the Jamaica School of Music and had reached grade 8 in the Royal College of Music examinations. He decided on the Trebas Institute of Music and I endorsed his choice, but I pointed out to his mother that this school was more expensive than McGill. After two years he graduated from Trebas as a producer and studio engineer. On his return to Jamaica we built him a small studio where he began his career. Some journalists expressed the view that we were disappointed in him, because record producers in the island were mostly associated with "ghetto youth". But if we were disappointed in Jeremy, why did we have a studio built for him? In addition, a few narrow-minded commentators dismissed Jeremy and Sean Paul Henriques, a middle-class dancehall artiste he produced, as "uptown yout'", implying that those pursuits were the sole preserve of the economically deprived. Jeremy has been a success and Sean Paul has become an international dancehall celebrity. Jeremy was in the maths club at both Campion and Ashbury. He is bright, focused, hard-working and talented. We are proud of him and have always been supportive of his career. He is married to Nina Chang and has a son, Chase, and a daughter, Layla.

Zachary, whom I sometimes teasingly call my baby son, has always had an outgoing and engaging personality. I recall him saying to his mother as a small boy, "If I see a pretty girl wearing a pretty dress, can I go up to her and say, `You are wearing a pretty dress'?" When I want to tease his mother I remind her that he said "daddy" before he said "mommy". Zachary started to study law at the UWI and told me after a few months that this was not for him. His mother felt that I gave in too soon to his wishes because it was difficult to get into the law faculty. I should have put my foot down, she said. I felt differently. Perhaps initially he thought he wanted to be a lawyer because his father was one, but when he found out otherwise, he had no obligation to continue. His career has taken him through public relations, advertising, tourism, sales and marketing. He has done extremely well in marketing. Some newspaper columnists refer to him as the "marketing guru". He is now venturing into his own +enterprise and I am sure that he will be a success. He is married to Tamara Morin and they have two daughters, Tori and Zara.

In January 1994, Valerie Falconer joined our household as a live-in helper. She is a capable, articulate worker whose skills have improved over the years after my wife arranged her participation in various domestic and catering courses. Valerie is now an excellent cook. When my granddaughter Tori was a toddler she called her "Volo" as she found "Valerie" difficult to pronounce. Needless to say, "Volo" has become Valerie's pet name. Several members of her family have worked for us in various capacities – as handymen, office cleaners and the like. Some of them have worked at my son Jeremy's house as well. Valerie not only cooks exquisite meals but has become our treasured housekeeper and a companion to Marigold, whom she calls "Madam". She looks about our laundry and ensures that we are always smartly attired whenever we are leaving the house. She has become our general factotum and part of our extended family. We are as devoted to her as she is to us.

Marigold and her team won a silver medal in 1997 and the silver gilt award at the Chelsea Flower Show in London in 2000 and 2001. She was also awarded the Grenfell medal by the Royal Horticultural Society in 1997. Marigold was the first Caribbean flower show judge

CHAPTER 12: AT HOME

to be invited to judge at the Floralies of Ghent in Belgium and the Shengyang Horticultural Exposition in China in August 2006. I accompanied her on both occasions in China. She designed and executed floral exhibitions at the National Cathedral in Washington, DC for three consecutive years – 2007, 2008 and 2009. She was a guest demonstrator at the National Capital Area Garden Club held in upstate New York in 2009, on which occasion I accompanied her. Marigold was co-chair of Cariflora in 2002 at King's House, residence of the Governor General of Jamaica. She developed a passion for painting flowers, and had a successful solo exhibition at Bolivar Gallery in Kingston in March 2005. On September 2, 2010, Marigold was installed as Custos of St Andrew and in the following month was awarded the Order of Distinction, Commander Class – the fifth highest national honour. She retired from the position of Custos in 2015.

At the end of April 2012, Jamaica was the honoured country at the Annual Flower Mart Show at the National Cathedral, Washington, DC. This coincided with Jamaica's Fiftieth Anniversary of Independence celebration. As part of the celebrations, the KC Boys Choir participated.

It all started when I said to Marigold that if the Flower Mart was held at the Cathedral then there ought to be a choir. I jokingly said, 'but there is only one choir in Jamaica – the Kingston College Boys Choir'. She spoke to my friend Dr. Robert Wan who chairs the choir committee. Thus their visit was arranged for Washington. The Kingston College Old Boys provided the airfares, looked after the accommodations, and gave each boy some pocket money. The choir did Jamaica proud – their performance was outstanding. I was proud to have joined Marigold and Dr. Robert "Bobby" Wan in Washington for this event, and to have helped in bringing forty-two boys and their choirmaster to Washington.

Our lives continue to be enriched as we share memorable occasions with our friends and acquaintances. We accommodated the Most Reverend Dr. Robert Runcie, the former Archbishop of Canterbury, when he visited Jamaica in 1984. We have hosted fundraising events for various colleagues, and celebrations marked the occasion when I was awarded the Order of Jamaica in 2003. The farewell dinner for Anthony Johnson on his appointment as Jamaica's ambassador to Washington in 2008 was held at Hardingham. In attendance were Brenda LaGrange Johnson, then US ambassador to Jamaica, and Professor Gordon Shirley, Jamaica's former ambassador to the United States. In 2009 we hosted the farewell reception for Lola and George Ramocan, Jamaica's consul general to Toronto. We have also entertained members of the Chaîne des Rôtisseurs International Gourmet Club, and guests have included the head of the European Delegation to Jamaica, Ambassador Marco Mazzocchi Alemanni, and former prime ministers Edward Seaga and P.J. Patterson.

Hardingham has also been the venue for several weddings. Zachary and Tamara's wedding reception was held there, with Reverend Ian McPherson officiating. So too were the nuptials of Denise Brown and Reverend Serrano Kitson, as well as her sister Heather Brown and Dr. Emerson Henry. Both brides were the daughters of my McGill friend L.P. Brown and his wife Merle.

From the top balcony looking westward, we can see the undulating mountain range in the distance, dotted with houses on the hillside. Southwestward in an arc we see the outline of the seashore interrupted by the jutting cranes of the Port Authority. To the left we have a clear view of aeroplanes taking off and landing at the Norman Manley International Airport. But most spectacular is the kaleidoscope created by the setting sun, with hues of gold and orange sometimes filtering through the magenta, purple, and dark grey clouds. Below us stretch acres of green trees, shrubs and verdant vegetation, while flocks of birds fly past, chirping their night calls. A sky painted with vivid streaks of colour. This is Hardingham at sunset. Soon it will be dark, and only the dots of light from houses scattered on the mountainside will be visible. The night toads will begin their whistling as the scent of night jasmine wafts through the air. This is Hardingham at evening time.

CHAPTER 12: AT HOME

The following lines from "September Song" I find most appropriate.

Oh it's a long, long while from May to December,
But the days grow short when you reach September . . .
Oh the days dwindle down to a precious few, September, November,
And these few precious days I'll spend with you . . .

— Lyrics by Maxwell Anderson & Kurt Weill

It may be our September song, and the days grow short in the autumn of our lives. But Grandma Essie, your prayers were not in vain. Marigold and I have enjoyed our lives together. We have been blessed with the gift of our beloved sons Jeremy and Zachary, and our grandchildren Tori, Zara, Chase and Layla, along with their mothers Tamara and Nina. We continue to pray that your soul finds its eternal resting place.

Always, your grandson Ossie.

Top: Marigold and I at Hardingham

Bottom: Jeremy (left) and Zachary Harding at Hardingham, New Year's party, 1988

APPENDIX A:

Rema Commission of Enquiry, 1977

A Commission of Enquiry was set up to investigate the events which took place at Rema on February 2, 1977, in connection with the removal of occupants from premises owned by the Ministry of Housing. The Commissioner Mr. Justice Ronald Small denied attorney-at-law Mr. Oswald Harding's request to be allowed to cross-examine Minister of Housing Anthony Spaulding. Below is the text of Mr. Harding's plea for the Commissioner to reconsider his position:

Commissioner: "Mr Harding . . . I have refrained from asking, inviting Mr. McLean to ask the witness any question. Having done so, are you prepared to take the same course, are you prepared to abide . . ."
(Mr. Harding stands)
"Well, he didn't stand."

Mr. Harding: "I think I might operate better on my feet, Mr. Commissioner."

Commissioner:	"I prefer you to sit down."
Mr. Harding:	"As you wish, sir."
Commissioner:	"Yes, what do you have to say?"
Mr. Harding:	"I am not content with that, sir. I came here to represent the people of Rema. This witness has been allowed a great deal of latitude. He has slandered many public figures, and I am being asked at this time not to ask this gentleman any questions. I could not be content with that at all, sir, I am not happy about that, and I think if I am not allowed to ask this witness any questions, the public will view this Commission as a waste of time, a waste of taxpayers' money, because again it will show the complete bias that has taken place in this society. The witness is a colleague of mine; I do not wish any protection from this Commission. This is a witness that I have asked to come here, sir, it's one of the few witnesses that has given us certain information sir, and I am being asked if I am content not to ask the Minister any questions. I am certainly most unhappy about that, and I will always respect the ruling of this Commission, indeed I must in my profession, but I assure you, and I wish you would reconsider that matter now sir, if you would wish, sir, because there are a number of matters that must be asked, that have to be asked. There are inferences, allegations about other political persons in this country; we have been plagued with platitudes,

APPENDIX A: REMA COMMISSION OF ENQUIRY, 1977

of quotations from Shakespeare, and this is one way that somebody can come out here smelling like roses. There are many, many questions, Mr. Commissioner, indeed questions concerning policy of the Ministry, and that is what I want to ask about, and the allocation of houses, the fact that there were empty houses in Rema, I need to test the witness on those particular points, sir, and I am very distressed, and I would certainly ask that you would reconsider that point, because I think it has reached a stage in this Commission, that if this witness cannot be cross-examined, that whatever comes out of this Commission will have no value as far as the people of Jamaica are concerned, sir, and I am very distressed, very upset about it, and I can't express it any more forcefully, but within the confines of decency of this Commission, I must urge you sir, to reconsider that position, because other than that, I am afraid that I have wasted my time and the people whom I represent, again I have failed them."

"The question I ask is, I cannot understand the reason why when this witness comes here, is there any special privilege? All otherwitnesses have been cross-examined. Sir, is there some immunity to this particular witness? Indeed, he has called for other public figures to come here. I am totally confused and I do not understand this proceeding. Mr. Commissioner, I have been here, and I have been very patient. I did not interrupt the witness when he made a lot of allegations that were not substantiated. I sat here and saw a statement put in issue. I was not given the courtesy of being referred to the statement. I do not know if what is in the statement is inaccurate or a lie. I sit here and I hear the security forces being called liars in this Enquiry, which in my opinion is deliberate, and I am not allowed to ask any questions as to how these conclusions were reached. I know my learned friend, if he was sitting here, would understand the position, that this is not personal, but professionally I am obliged to do that. I must urge you to reconsider the position, sir."

Commissioner: "You are finished?"

Author's note:

I did not understand why the Commissioner did not want the Minister to be cross-examined by Mr. McLean or myself. My vehemence was cultivated. I was not that overwhelmed, but as a technique it worked.

APPENDIX B:

Letter from Minister of Finance concerning Suit against Paul Chen-Young, 1999

OFFICE OF THE MINISTER OF FINANCE AND
PLANNING
30 NATIONAL HEROES CIRCLE,
P.O. BOX 512,
KINGSTON,
JAMAICA

June 7, 1999

TELEPHONE 922-8600-16

Senator Oswald Harding
(Attorney-at-Law)
1 Melmac Avenue
Kingston 5

Dear Senator Harding:

Suit Against Dr Paul Chen-Young

The relevant officers of FINSAC have briefed me concerning the suit filed against Dr Paul Chen-Young, Ms Dorit Hutson and two companies controlled by Dr Chen-Young, Ajax Investment Ltd and Domville Ltd. I believe you are aware of these suits as I am told that you have been interviewed by Myers, Fletcher and Gordon who are acting for Eagle Merchant Bank and Crown Eagle Life in the matter. However, the officers of FINSAC and the legal team have informed me that you have so far declined to sign your statement on the grounds that you do not wish to be involved in the trial. The legal team has advised that if you refuse to testify, the case of Eagle Merchant Bank/Crown Eagle Life will be seriously weakened.

I write to you in order to ascertain whether the report which has come to me is indeed accurate. If it is, I would appreciate hearing from you the precise reason for your taking such a stance. I should indicate that I would be extremely disappointed if this were indeed a correct representation of your position as the decisions to maintain you as an appointee to the Eagle Board and not to join you as a co-defendant in the suit against Dr Chen-Young, were taken as I am convinced that you were not party to the improper actions which are attributed to him.

I look forward to hearing from you as quickly as possible.

Yours sincerely,

Omar Davies
Minister

APPENDIX C:

Citation Presented to Senator Oswald Gaskell Harding, Attorney-at-Law

Your association with the Priory School began with the arrival of your son, Jeremy, as a student of the Kindergarten/Junior Department. Your younger son, Zachary, soon joined the student body too, and thus started a long and fruitful era in our school's history.

You became a member of the Priory School Trust Council in January of 1974 and in December of that year you became the Chairman of the Council.

It was through your instrumentality and the assistance you so ably secured from the United States Agency for International Development that the school was placed in a viable position and was able to start a Capital Development Fund.

Your sense of history was clearly demonstrated following the devastation of Hurricane Gilbert on 12th September, 1988, when you were the prime mover for the restoration of the Priory House to its former glory, culminating in the grand opening on 16th March 1990.

GRANDSON OF ESSIE: A JAMAICAN AUTOBIOGRAPHY

Your concern for the beautification of the environment and the aesthetic appearance of the Priory will always be remembered by the school community. The Priory community was always a matter of deep concern to you and you were at pains to meet with and share your own and the school's philosophy with the administration, the parents, the academic staff, as well as with the student body.

In the management of the school's affairs you always had your watchword at the forefront: "To exist is to struggle, to survive is to conquer". The school is fortunate to have had at the time in its history the services of a Chairman who was not deterred by the difficulties created by a lack of capital but rather you accepted the challenge, worked hard at it, and finally came up with a solution, a memorable achievement. As Chairman of the board for over 17 years, you gave unstintingly of your time and energy for the advancement of our institution.

We owe you a debt of gratitude and we take this opportunity to salute you and to honour and thank you for your contribution to the advance of the Priory school and to education in Jamaica.

May God bless you and your family in all your future endeavours and may these be as successful as your association with the Priory.

Jean Bertram *Claudette Carter* *Marguerite Narinesingh*
June 26, 1992

APPENDIX D:

Jamaica Gleaner article:
"Jamaica's Articulate Politicians Hailed"

Jamaica's articulate politicians hailed
Published: Sunday | April 19, 2009

Ross and Thompson

TAKING A cursory glance through the history of parliamentary debates since the 1970s, Dessler Smith, a 30-year veteran staff member at Gordon House, highlighted some outstanding legislators over the period.

It is instructive to point out that the Standing Orders, or rules of Parliament, prohibit the verbatim reading of a speech during a debate.

In this regard, many current legislators would fall short of the mark if the Speaker of the House or president of the Senate insisted that the 'letter of the law' should be upheld.

Former parliamentarians, such as the late Michael Manley, Dudley Thompson, David Coore, Carl Marshall and President of the Senate Oswald Harding have all made Smith's list of most eloquent presenters.

"Michael, O my God, he was a world-renown speaker!" said the Hansard editor who described those he selected as a cut above the rest.

"These are parliamentarians who are beyond the surface; they rise above the rest when it comes to debates."

Acceptable standards

Clarke and Coore

Jamaica Gleaner News - Jamaica's articulate politicians hailed - Lead Stories - Sunday | April 19, 2009

"They made simple notations, a few lines, and then you find pages upon pages reeling off, as it were from rote, and then they could take it back and summarise backwards."

Carl Marshall, who was appointed Speaker of the House in 1993, received high marks for how he presided over the business of Parliament during his tenure.

According to Smith, Marshall was "a very scholarly, articulate, forthright and classy type of individual".

Another notable member of the House during the late 1980s, Headley Cunningham performed his duties as Speaker with distinction. Smith describes him as a standard-bearer of class. "Anywhere you put him he stands tall."

Harding and Manley

Smith also remembers the late Alva Ross for his firm hand in conducting parliamentary affairs. "Brassy and outgoing, and he was always hoping and trusting. That was his little catch phrase, 'hoping and trusting'."

Claude Clarke, former St Andrew West Rural MP of the late 1980s, was distinguished for his forthrightness and non-partisan approach to national issues.

Smith adds: "He was a principled and very decent politician."

He mentioned outstanding senators, such as Fred Hamaty, Douglas Orane and the late Alfred Rattray, who brought a nationalistic fervour to bear on their parliamentary contributions.

- Edmond Campbell

Daily Gleaner clipping:
"Lawyers Praise Harding"

THE DAILY GLEANER, TUESDAY, JANUARY 3, 1989

Lawyers praise Harding

THE Bar Association of Jamaica has paid tribute to Minister of Justice and Attorney General, Senator the Hon. Oswald Harding for among other things, introducing important legislation in Parliament during this year.

In its annual report, covering the period July 1987 to August 1988, the association also commented on the excellent relationship members have enjoyed with the Minister.

The reported also noted Senator Harding's interest in restoring and refurbishing courthouses across the island.

"The Bar is aware of and grateful for the excellent relationship we have enjoyed with the Attorney General during the period under review. He has been unfailing in his support, and his willingness to discuss our concerns and to liaise with us in regard to proposed legislation is noted with appreciation", the report read in part.

The association said the Minister had during the year introduced "important — if sometimes controversial — legislation" and that he had displayed particular zeal in regard to the Courthouse Restoration Programme.

"We appreciate his efforts, his frankness and his helpfulness in the interest of justice," the report said.

BIBLIOGRAPHY

Bustamante, Gladys Maud. *The Memoirs of Lady Bustamante*, Kingston Publishers, 1997.

Charles, Pearnel. *The Politics of Power*, Kingston Publishers, 1989.

Chen-Young, Paul. *The Entrepreneurial Journey in Jamaica: When Policies Derail*, Hats off Books, 2004.

Eaton, George E. *Alexander Bustamante and Modern Jamaica*, LMH Publishing, 1995.

Franklyn, Delano. *We Want Justice: Jamaica and the Caribbean Court of Justice*, Ian Randle Publishers, 2005.

Johnson, Anthony S. *The Brave May Fall but Never Yield: History of Kingston College 1925–2006*, Iskamol, 2008.

Segal, Hugh. *In Defence of Civility: Reflections of a Recovering Politician*, Stoddart, 2000.

www.ingramcontent.com/pod-product-compliance
Lightning Source LLC
Chambersburg PA
CBHW031311150426
43191CB00005B/176